100 Bible Films

BFI Screen Guides

Matthew Page

This book is dedicated to:

my Granny who unearthed my passion for discussing films;
my Granddad for a mind that loves order, numbers and lists;
my other Granddad for sharing his love of the Bible;
and my Grandma who treated everyone like they really mattered.

THE BRITISH FILM INSTITUTE
Bloomsbury Publishing Plc
50 Bedford Square, London, WC1B 3DP, UK
1385 Broadway, New York, NY 10018, USA
29 Earlsfort Terrace, Dublin 2, Ireland

BLOOMSBURY is a trademark of Bloomsbury Publishing Plc

First published in Great Britain 2022 by Bloomsbury
on behalf of the
British Film Institute
21 Stephen Street, London W1T 1LN
www.bfi.org.uk

The BFI is the lead organisation for film in the UK and the distributor of Lottery
funds for film. Our mission is to ensure that film is central to our cultural life, in
particular by supporting and nurturing the next generation of filmmakers and
audiences. We serve a public role which covers the cultural, creative and economic
aspects of film in the UK.

Cover image: *Noah*, 2014, Directed by Darren Aronofsky; Russell Crowe.
(MMXIV Paramount Pictures Corporation/Regency Engtertainment/DR/Collection
Christophel/ArenaPAL)

Series design: Louise Dugdale

A catalogue record for this book is available from the British Library.

A catalog record for this book is available from the Library of Congress.

ISBN: HB: 978-1-8390-2353-8
       PB: 978-1-8390-2352-1
       ePDF: 978-1-8390-2355-2
       eBook: 978-1-8390-2354-5

Series: BFI Screen Guides

Project managment, typesetting and layout by ketchup/Tom Cabot
Printed and bound in India

To find out more about our authors and books visit www.bloomsbury.com and sign
up for our newsletters.

Contents

Acknowledgements

I would like to thank the dedicated and supportive team at BFI/Bloomsbury Publishing: Camilla Erskine for commissioning the book; Anna Coatman for taking it through to completion; Veidehi Hans for ongoing, regular support; Tom Cabot, Sophie Contento and Louise Dugdale for images, layout and design; Yoshimi Takaaki for proof-reading; and Bryony Dixon and Espen Bale at the BFI National Archive.

Particular thanks are due to Mark Goodacre, Fran Fuentes, Stuart Jesson, Joanna Page and Chris Thornhill whose advice, input and friendship here and elsewhere has been invaluable. I am indebted to the editors of the previous work I have had published on this subject whose patience, commitment and encouragement helped me develop along this path: Lee Jackson, Bruce Stanley, Heather Fenton, Brent Plate, Rhonda Burnette-Bletsch, Richard Walsh and Wickham Clayton. Thank you also to, Tag Gallagher, James Mackay, Bruce Marchiano, Nader Talebzadeh, Dave Cowan, Biko Nyongesa and Alexandra Sophia Handal for supplying images.

I am extremely grateful for the online community at artsandfaith.com. My friends and those who deserve my thanks are too numerous to mention individually, but Peter Chattaway and Steven Greydanus are particularly worthy of note as fellow enthusiasts for this subject, good friends, sources of wisdom and their encyclopaedic knowledge.

I want to thank the many friends who have attended film nights I've hosted, or trekked with me to see obscure films at local cinemas. I also appreciate the role of the different faith communities that encouraged me and enabled me to get better acquainted with the Bible: St Barnabas (Leeds), Open Heaven (Loughborough) and All Saints (Loughborough). In addition I am grateful for the numerous people who have contacted me via my blog or via social media, shared their own insights or pointed me towards films that were new to me, particularly Thomas Langkau, Richard Campbell and David Wilson.

Most importantly I'd like to thank my wife Mel for years of encouragement, advice, patience and great ideas (some of which probably appear here uncredited) and my children who have sat through more Bible films than any teenager ought to have endured. Finally to Mum and Dad for hours wading through English homework, teaching me about the Bible and for their ongoing love, support and advice.

Introduction

In the middle of October 1888, Louis Le Prince carried his camera into a Leeds back garden and the movies were born. In the 135 years or so that have followed, the love of motion pictures has spread across the globe. The sheer volume of films produced across fourteen decades and six continents is so vast that it is impossible for any of us to have an intimate knowledge covering the entire field. Instead, we seek ways of grouping films together to help us understand the stories cinema tells and the impact it has on our world. We adopt methods to condense the world of film, gathering by genres, countries of origin, ideology, significant eras or specific filmmakers. The path I explore here uses a different method: telling the story of film via screen adaptations of our most widely-known literary/historical /religious text, the Bible.[1]

Whether you see the Bible as a force for good, or a source of evil (or even a bit of both), few would deny the impact it has had on our world. Stories covering a thousand years of the history of Abraham's descendants have become almost universal. They have shaped our world and become our stories. Little wonder that from the earliest days, some of our most revered filmmakers have turned to it for their inspiration – Martin Scorsese, Jean Luc Godard, Roberto Rossellini, Alice Guy, Luis Buñuel, The Coen Brothers, Derek Jarman and Carl Dreyer. Adding the various biblical films involving Orson Welles; unrealized works by Ingmar Bergman, and Robert Bresson; and Lotte Reiniger's lost *The Star of Bethlehem* (1921) generates an illustrious list. The Bible is so pervasive that filmmakers from all kinds of backgrounds, politics and ideologies have adapted its stories, delighting some, infuriating others, undertaking complex negotiations between art, commerce, entertainment and religion. This book is an attempt to capture the diverse array of films and television based on the biblical narratives, covering a wide variety of genres and styles, crossing national borders, cultural backgrounds and religious perspectives.

A Brief History of the Bible on Film

Ever since Le Prince's invention of moving pictures, filmmakers have found the Bible an irresistible theme, adopting a wide variety of approaches to its stories. The very earliest films about Jesus, going back to the 1890s were simple passion plays. Most films at this stage were not narrative drama, but filmmakers documenting the world around them. The line between documentary-like recordings of passion plays and

---

1 Throughout this work I will use the terms 'history', 'historical' etc. in the sense of 'pertaining to the past', rather than the narrower understanding of 'verifiable events which occurred in the past'.

specifically-created dramatic reconstructions became clearer around the start of the twentieth century.[2] Subject matter also began expanding to include other Bible characters such as Samson and Daniel. These earliest tableau films were often sold in individual sections so establishing which were released as independent movies in their own right is difficult. The length, scale and volume of these films grew gradually such that more biblical films were released in the years from 1909 to 1911 than at any other time, with most films coming from Europe. By 1913 and the release of the Italian adaptation *Quo Vadis?* the era of the biblical epic had begun. *An Unsullied Shield* (1913) inspired several films which intercut storylines from different historical eras, an approach used variously from Dreyer's *Blade Af Satans Bog* (1920) to Curtiz's 1928 *Noah's Ark*, as films made in the USA began to dominate following the onset of World War I. Despite the sudden growth in talking pictures at the end of the 1920s, and the USA's newly-introduced Hays Production Code imposing considerable restrictions on films portraying religious figures, biblical movies continued to be produced, including epics, independent films and some church-funded productions.

Following World War II, a desire to bolster 'American values', producers trying to outshine the new technology (television) and audiences' need for escapism, resulted in the rebirth of the biblical epic. The genre dominated the box office for well over a decade, until expensive failures in the 1960s made producers more cautious. Television stations across the globe began producing and broadcasting biblical productions around this time. These tended to be reasonably conservative in nature, as were a growing number of church-funded films such as *Jesus* (1979). Meanwhile, 1970s cinema began to explore more radical interpretations with titles such as *Jesus Christ Superstar* (1973) and *Monty Python's Life of Brian* (1979). This trend continued in the 1980s perhaps most infamously with Martin Scorsese's 1988 *The Last Temptation of Christ*. Many such films were heavily criticized by the growing Christian right in the USA and Europe. The 1990s were relatively quiet until the end of the decade when the new millennium inspired a tranche of new Jesus films.

At the start of the new century many commentators assumed that, aside from documentaries, biblical films were unlikely to prove popular. All that changed with Mel Gibson's *The Passion of the Christ* (2004) whose unexpected success at the box office launched a volley of new biblical films including blockbusters such as *Noah* (2014) and multi-series crowd-funded television like *The Chosen* (2020–). Improvements in digital cameras and the resultant improved access to them meant that new independent and experimental works grew exponentially. Moreover, the improvements in distribution technology via the internet also made biblical adaptations outside of the western world more accessible. Faith-friendly films and church productions increased significantly during this period, indeed one of the challenges in writing this book was knowing where to draw the line between blockbusters at one end of the scale and short amateur films on YouTube at the other. The result has been a growth in films from outside of Europe and North America. Output from across the spectrum will likely continue in the years ahead.

---

2   For more on this see the discussion of *La Vie et la passion de Jésus-Christ* (1898)

Diversity in Approaches

The history of cinema and the Bible encompasses silent film, classic era, international movies and independent cinema. It brings us into contact with less fashionable film-making cultures and their aesthetics, which do not necessarily correspond to those popular in western multiplexes or art-house cinemas.[3] It's not only about blockbusters, but about films on tiny budgets far from self-perpetuating 'greatest films' lists. Bible films form a thin but consistent seam that runs throughout film history, taking in its major movements: a distilled-down essence of the story of the movies.

There are numerous ways that filmmakers adapt, appropriate and reference the text. In many cases, such as *Magnolia* (1999), it might simply be a passing visual, aural or textual allusion, either directly or indirectly. The Bible can also be a signifier of Christian belief, as in *The Apostle* (1997), or as a talisman with a power beyond its physical components. Other movies, such as 'Christ figure' films like *Shane* (1953) and *Cool Hand Luke* (1967), have appropriated biblical stories, an approach Julie Sanders describes as a 'more sustained imaginative … reworking of the source text'.[4] Fuller adaptations range from modernized versions of the story, through to word-for-word recreations of the text.

Much of the previous literature about the Bible and cinema has essentially posed the question 'How can exploring the Bible and film inform our understanding of the Bible?' My own concern is to look at the question from the other side of the spectrum: How can Bible films inform our understanding of cinema? The unique contribution of biblical films in this respect flows from the fixed nature of the text on the one hand, and its adoption into diverse cultures around the globe on the other. As a result there are numerous filmmakers who consider these to be interesting or profound stories in which they are already invested. This provides an anchor from which to observe the changes and varying approaches which different eras and cultures bring. It retains a fixed point of comparison from which to experience the story of film. As a result, this book will primarily focus on films where at least a significant section of the film adapts one or more stories from the Bible.

The Bible's impact on cultures across the world, to varying degrees, requires engagement with an array of different movements, histories, outlooks and ideas. Having been written predominantly in Asia, over the centuries it spread across Europe and North Africa. Centuries of colonialist activities carried it across the globe and it often remains a cultural force in those countries.

Biblical films provide an advantage precisely because they cross so many boundaries, and because they have been around from the very beginning of film history, and remain popular today. While certain movies based on the Bible have given their name to a particular genre, (the biblical epic) many approach the subject in entirely different ways. The range of films gathered together here encompasses many of these different perspectives in a way that is quite different from some of the other approaches to cinema listed above. Filmmakers as diverse as gay atheist Marxist Pier Paolo Pasolini and conservative Iranian Muslim Nader

---

3   See the discussion around the screening of popular Ghanaian movies at film festivals primed to expect '*Heritage Africa* or high-profile francophone movies' in Birgit Meyer, *Sensational Movies: Video, Vision and Christianity in Ghana*, (Oakland, California: University of California Press, 2015) p. 292.

4   Julie Sanders, *Adaptation and Appropriation: The New Critical Idiom*, 2nd ed. (Oxford , New York: Routledge, 2016) p. 37.

Talebzadeh are juxtaposed as unlikely bedfellows. An examination of tribal tensions in Genesis from Mali can sit alongside a Welsh-Russian 3D-animated film about Jesus.

It is easy to assume that the story of the Bible on film has an unusually narrow focus, amounting to little more than a handful of Cecil B. DeMille epics and his imitators. In fact, nothing could be further from the truth. The earliest film based on the Bible, the *Höritz Passion Play* was filmed in the Czech Republic back in 1897.[5] Since then over 800 such films have been made across six continents and covering an array of genres: musicals, comedies, sci-fi, horror, epics and the avant-garde. Filmmakers from all kinds of religious perspectives (or none at all) have used it to explore ideas they are interested in or to champion the causes that matter to them.

The Selection

The focus of this book, therefore, is on dramatic films based on characters / narratives from the Bible. Excluding Christ figure films, movies with religious themes, 'spiritually significant' cinema, miracle movies, biopics about Christians, and documentaries, over 800 such films have been produced.

With an average of six Bible films being created per year, the challenge of writing a book like this is of what to *exclude*. Jason Wood, author of the *100 American Independent Films* entry in this series, finds that selecting a hundred films 'seems to suggest, tantalizingly, the comprehensive nature of this project whilst actually undermining that comprehensiveness'.[6] It seems inevitable that the next few years will be spent trying to explain the reasons why I left out *Black Jesus* (1968), or omitted *Jesus Christ, Vampire Hunter* (2001).

Only films that still exist have been selected, even if some are yet to be liberated from the archives. For this reason, those first passion plays, films such as 1918's *Salomé* starring Theda Bara, the Egyptian film *The Life and Passion of the Christ* (1938),[7] and the pornography film *Him* (1974), have all been excluded.[8] Similarly, I have only discussed films which I have been able to see.[9] Unfortunately, it remains difficult to access biblical films from outside Europe and North America, raising questions about perceived audience demand. Not dissimilarly, significantly fewer women have directed biblical films which may suggest either a lack of opportunity, or that perhaps the subject is less interesting or valuable to female directors.

The danger is that any list of films considered worthy of discussion becomes self-perpetuating. Therefore, I have sought to diversify the canon of Bible films typically examined so that voices aside from those of

---

5   At the time *Höritz* was in Austria.

6   Jason Wood *100 American Independent Films* (London: Palgrave/BFI Publishing, 2013), Introduction: [ebook available via app].

7   'The Egyptians were the first to produce a film about the Passion of Christ, 1938'. (26 March, 2015). Available from: <www.masrawy.com/News/news-ayamzaman/details/2015/3/25/487083> (accessed 13 December 2021)

8   *Him* has been discussed both in Harry and Michael Medved, *The Golden Turkey Awards* (London: Angus & Robertson, 1980), pp. 122–3; and subsequently in Richard C. Campbell and Michael R. Pitts, *The Bible on Film: A Checklist, 1897–1980* (Metuchen, NJ, and London: Scarecrow Press, 1981), p. 173. Despite some speculation that *Him* was a 'fake', Richard Campbell confirmed to me in private correspondence that the film was genuine.

9   A list of where the 100 films can be viewed is at <https://biblefilms.blogspot.com/2020/12/see100biblefilms.html>

straight, white, European/North American men are included. As such, I have prioritized films which occupy largely uncharted territory over those that exist in a similar cinematic space to other entries. While the majority of the films included are still from the USA or Western Europe, I have chosen works of filmmakers from a range of countries and backgrounds. Naturally films from across cinema's 120-year history are featured. Nineteen of the films featured here are from the silent era and I've sought to ensure that even relatively quiet eras are covered, in order to discuss the full history of biblical films.

Some Bible films are so highly regarded in their own right as to demand inclusion. Pasolini's *Il vangelo secondo Matteo* (1964) is considered by many critics to be one of the finest films ever made. *Ben-Hur* (1959) still jointly holds the record for the highest number of Oscar wins. *Life of Brian* regularly tops popular lists of the funniest films of all time.[10] In contrast, other films have been selected regardless of their perceived quality because either they have something significant to say about cinema and the Bible, or by virtue of them being widely discussed either within academic circles or by those relating to religious audiences.

Bible films made by the celebrated directors listed on page 1 have a similarly strong case for inclusion. The subject was one for them to adopt, adapt, interpret, uphold or rally against, so in many cases these filmmakers worked outside the boundaries of the biblical epic. It seemed important, therefore, to incorporate a variety of different genres and styles, such as musicals (*Jesus Christ Superstar*), comedies (*Life of Brian*), neo-realism (*Il vangelo secondo Matteo*), sci-fi (*Assassin 33AD*, 2020), surrealism (*La Voie Lactée*, 1969), materialism (*Moses und Aron*, 1975) and the avant-garde (*Lot in Sodom,* 1933). Furthermore, films from other, wide-ranging, movements in cinema have also been included: silent film; queer cinema[11] (*Salomé*, 1922); and animation (*The Miracle Maker*, 2000); as well as those such as *The Green Pastures* (1936) which defy simple classification. This is not to dismiss the biblical epic. One cannot write a book like this and not admire DeMille in full flow. It is simply to say that if epics are not your aesthetic preference, then you are in good company: some of the cinema's most celebrated artists have rejected those same aesthetics.

In addition to prioritizing this array of historic, geographic and generic contexts, I have also selected a range of philosophical and theological perspectives. Christians do not have a monopoly on interest in Jesus, even less so the array of characters from the Hebrew Bible (a preferred term for the Old Testament), indeed, these stories fascinate a broad sweep of people, from devout Christians, through to their fiercest opponents. There are films here from Catholics, Protestants, Jews, Muslims and others besides. Martin Scorsese is not alone in making a biblical movie to 'get to know Jesus better'.[12] For some, filming the Bible was part of spreading, or opposing, particular messages.[13] Others the appeal was exploring their cultural heritage.

---

10   See for example '*Life of Brian* tops comedy poll', BBC News website. Available online: <http://news.bbc.co.uk/1/hi/entertainment/948331.stm> (accessed 22 June 2021).

11   While not all those of gender and sexual minorities are happy with the use of the word 'queer'. Nevertheless, 'Queer Cinema' has become the dominant term used to label the movement by GSM filmmakers and critics.

12   Quote from David Thomson and Ian Christie, *Scorsese on Scorsese* (London: Faber and Faber, 1996), p. 120.

13   Effectively, the filmmakers have a specific audience in mind at the pre-production stage.

Regular worshippers, wrestling agnostics and wryly-provocative atheists have all brought their artistic sensibilities in tackling the material.

Finally, I wanted to ensure the major stories from the Bible were included at least once. Certain narratives prove popular again and again. Aside from the events around the life of Jesus, the stories of Moses, David, Samson, Noah, Lot and Salome seem enduringly popular. Other stories have been chosen less consistently, but are important to include nonetheless. Tales about women, for example, are rare enough in the Bible itself, but have also tended to be adapted less than stories about men. Thus women have been doubly marginalized. Even the 1950s trend to include female characters in film titles (1949's *Samson and Delilah*, 1951's *David and Bathsheba* and 1959's *Solomon and Sheba*), did not result in better developed female roles. Given such poor representation, I have prioritized those rare films with better developed female heroes. For those who are particularly interested in the range of biblical narratives, Appendix 1 details six different series which have covered multiple biblical stories.

The final selection, then, includes films from at least twenty countries,[14] fourteen decades and covers the stories of 32 sets of characters.[15] In terms of films from the USA the focus has been on those that have been most discussed academically or have had the greatest cultural impact in Europe and North America, though I have included a few smaller independent films to reflect different faith perspectives.

Questions of Race

If the range of films made is broad in terms of history, theology and genre there are other areas where diversity is sadly lacking. Opportunities for women and people of colour to direct biblical movies are still very rare. Gendered and sexual minorities are under-represented and when they are seen on-screen, homophobia and/or transphobia are often evident. Moreover, ableist attitudes often occur in films where healings are an integral part of the story.

However, the most obvious area where Bible films have lacked social inclusivity is in casting. While it should go without saying that these stories largely took place in the Middle East, all too often the Bible is perceived as a white text when it is anything but. Jesus was Jewish. Moses was an African. St Paul was Asian. Yet as the historic centres of Christianity moved from Jewish Jerusalem, African Egypt and Asian Damascus towards European Rome, so interpretations of the text began to privilege white-skinned Europeans over other races. Texts such as Genesis 9.25 were used to argue that white-skinned Europeans were superior to other races and to justify the Atlantic slave trade. This, combined with the Christian tendency to portray God in our own image, resulted in cultural and artistic depictions of Jesus, and other key biblical characters, as white.

By the time cinema was invented, slavery had been made illegal in most nations. Yet extreme discriminatory practices, such as Jim Crow laws and racial segregation in the United States, and the expansion of

---

14 Some of the films in this book were financed from multiple countries. The twenty countries mentioned here have funded at least a third share of one or more films.

15 It is difficult to devise a measure here for biblical coverage. I have adopted 'sets of characters' here which counts 'Adam and Eve' as one set, but overlapping characters such as David and Solomon as two sets.

European colonialism, continued unabated in the 1890s and well into the Twentieth Century. The earliest biblical films were low budget affairs originating in Europe and the USA. Combining Euro-centric ideology with European artistic tradition and the practicalities of casting from among predominantly white populations meant that almost all of the actors in early silent biblical films were white. Historical accuracy and racial integrity were not priorities for the earliest movies and even though the makers of films such as *From the Manger to the Cross* (1912) trumpeted historical verisimilitude, this only really extended to issues such as locations, sets and faithfulness to the text.

In the later silent era, films began to be made by Black and Asian directors such as Oscar Micheaux, Dhundiraj Govind Phalke, and Eloyce Gist, including films with religious themes. The resulting popularity of films featuring African-American actors led to white filmmakers casting Black actors in *The Green Pastures*, including Rex Ingram as one of the first such onscreen portrayals of God. This phase was short lived and biblical adaptations reverted to using largely white actors. The 1950s saw the biblical epic become the dominant genre in cinema, yet despite the progress of the civil rights movement, filmmakers gave the lead roles to blond-haired, blue-eyed actors such as Charlton Heston and Max von Sydow, rather than casting actors whose complexions were more typical of the Holy Land. The 1970s saw films such as *Jesus Christ, Superstar* and *Karunamâyadu* (Man of Mercy, 1978) begin to turn the tide, notably 1976's *The Passover Plot* starring a Jewish actor (Zalman King) as Jesus. In general, however, filmmakers continued to cast white, often blond, actors in western-made Bible movies without too much criticism until around the start of the new millennium.

More recently the tide has turned. Audiences seek more authenticity from historical films and biblical adaptations choosing white actors have been criticized. Christian Bale's casting as Moses in *Exodus: Gods and Kings* was accused of 'whitewashing'.[16] In the midst of 2020's #BlackLivesMatter protests the Archbishop of Canterbury Justin Welby discussed the need to reassess white statues of Jesus,[17] while other writers have called the casting of white actors as Jesus a 'falsehood, a symbol created by the effect of white-supremacist fiction'.[18]

Some 21st century filmmakers have chosen actors from more diverse backgrounds for leading roles. 2006 saw Māori actor Keisha Castle-Hughes play the Virgin Mary in *The Nativity Story*, and Black actors Jean Claude LaMarre and Andile Kosi were cast as Jesus in *Color of the Cross* and *Jezile* respectively. 2015's *Killing Jesus* chose UAE born actor Haaz Sleimann as Jesus, perhaps the first western-produced Jesus film to use an actor from the region. Two years later *The Shack* gave the role to Israeli actor Aviv Alush.

---

16 Joel Baden and Candida Moss, 'Does the new *Exodus* movie whitewash the Bible?', *CNN* Entertainment, 11 December 2014. Available online: <https://edition.cnn.com/2014/12/10/showbiz/exodus-whitewash-bible/index.html> (accessed 22 June 2021).

17 Interviewed on *Today*, BBC Radio 4, 26 June 2020.

18 Chine McDonald, *God Is Not a White Man: And Other Revelations* (London: Hodder & Stoughton, 2021), Kindle Location: 378.

While this is certainly a welcome trend, its universal application to individual films is less straightforward. Doubtless any film promoting itself as being historically authentic ought to cast actors whose heritage derives from the region. However, historical authenticity is only one possible criterion to determine a film's visual appearance. In the case of the Abrahamic faiths, the concept of humanity 'made in God's image' (Genesis 1.27) is important. Similarly, Christianity's doctrine of the incarnation teaches that God became human so his people could better relate to him. More precisely he became Jewish to minister to the Jews. Some would argue, therefore, it is not always inappropriate for a white actor to represent Jesus to a white audience, though few single race audiences exist today. That said, the very specificity of Jesus being sent as a first century Jewish, Middle Eastern man is a strong argument for casting as closely as possible to this reality.

Alternatively, movies should continue to vary the race, gender, sexuality, age and physicality of actors playing this incarnate god, in order that the cinematic Christ relates to all. Some recent historical films such as Armando Ianucci's *David Copperfield* (2019) have rightly been lauded for reversing historical prejudices by casting Black and Asian actors as where the default assumption has been that their characters would have been white. Most people recognize that these are actors, acting a role. While the artistic freedom for individual projects to fulfil their creative vision is important, hopefully the global widening of audiences will drive a far greater diversity of actors being chosen in biblical films. Audiences are right to demand, particularly from those films trumpeting their supposed historical authenticity, that these roles typically go to those who more closely resemble Jewish people during the biblical era.

Antisemitism

Another important race issue related to biblical films is antisemitism. Many Christians are shocked to discover the ways texts about the 'Prince of Peace' have historically been distorted to smear Jewish people as 'Christ-killers' and to justify and inspire horrific acts of violence. Yet dramatic adaptations of the Gospels have been particularly damaging in this respect. Passion plays from the medieval age onwards frequently inspired violent reprisals. The plays caricatured Jewish people, creating, perpetuating and intensifying antisemitic stereotypes. Perhaps the most dominant element of antisemitism has been the blaming of Jews for Jesus' death. While this sounds far-fetched, it is precisely what has happened repeatedly throughout Christian history.[19]

Many of these stereotypes continued into European Jesus films prior to the start of World War II. They were also leveraged in Nazi Germany. Stereotypes and 'othering' develop into indifference, resentment or violent retribution. For those who survived the Holocaust, the Jewish stereotypes in some Jesus films, including some more recent films, are horrendously familiar. Creative appropriations of the story have so often reinforced these ideas that many of us do not realize the antisemitism that is accepted at face value.

---

19 Recently stereotypes depicting Jewish people influenced by the devil or being his children, have resurfaced amongst #QAnon conspiracy theorists.

Such misinformation, in Jesus films and elsewhere, needs to be constantly challenged. Crucifixion was a Roman act. Josephus recalls a time Rome crucified 2000 Jews as revenge.[20] If Rome's dominance is understated in the Gospels, it is because their original audience instinctively felt the fear of crucifixion in the pits of their stomachs. Pontius Pilate was no exception. In addition to ordering Jesus' execution, Luke's Gospel records him slaughtering Galileans as they worshipped (13.1). Philo describes him as 'merciless', noting his 'cruelty' and murder 'of people untried and uncondemned'.[21] He was recalled to Rome after a vicious massacre in Samaria.[22] Yet too many Jesus films alleviate his responsibility for Jesus' death portraying him as thoughtful, noble and civilized, in contrast to the Jewish High Priest Caiaphas who is often shown as greedy, avaricious, or rubbing his hands. What else, aside from antisemitism, could explain why Pilate is consistently made attractive and Caiaphas ugly? Similarly, films depicting a mass of Jewish peasants or their leaders frightening Pilate into executing Jesus are not only historically implausible but guilty of recycling these same dangerous stereotypes.

Moreover none of this is what the text says. The New Testament suggests only a tiny proportion of Jewish people had any part in Jesus' death. John 18 records just the presence of Caiaphas, Annas and a few guards. Mark's Gospel has 'a crowd' come to persuade Pilate to free Barabbas as per the custom. For them, Jesus was just collateral damage. Better he died than Barabbas.[23] The Gospels give no indication about the size of the crowd at Jesus' sentencing. Jesus films love to portray a huge courtyard, packed out with an angry mob, but the space could easily have been significantly smaller, and much less densely populated and be 'crowded'.

Even those who were present did not represent all Jews. The Jews of Jesus' day neither thought nor acted as one. Chief priests, Pharisees, Sadducees, teachers of the law, scribes, Essenes, zealots and even early Christians were co-existing Judaisms. They disagreed but few wanted their countrymen executed by the Romans.

The Gospels also suggest only a tiny proportion of Jewish people had any part in Jesus' death. Indeed the majority may never have heard Jesus' name. There were perhaps 300,000 in Jerusalem the week Jesus died.[24] Even the feeding of the 5000 (Matthew 14.21) suggests a comparatively small number of followers. Most Jews were either unaware of him, or unconvinced, like Gamaliel (Acts 5), who was neither for nor against Jesus. Yet such neutral Jewish characters remain largely absent from Jesus films. It is possible to make Jesus' ministry seem more appealing compared to that of his opponents, without portraying unpersuaded characters as motivated by stubbornness, stupidity, greed or prejudice.

---

20   Josephus, *The Jewish War* 2.5.2.

21   Philo, *Legatio ad Gaium* 301–302.

22   Josephus, *Antiquities of the Jews* 18.85–87.

23   One line from the Gospels, Matthew 27.25 'His blood be on us and our children' is still included in some Jesus films, despite its despicable repeated use in antisemitism as key justification for the belief that all Jews are supposedly Christ killers.

24   Jerusalem in the week leading up to Passover was a very busy place. Josephus, prone to wildly exaggerate, suggests the figure is around three 3 million (*The Jewish War* 6.9.3. c.f. 2.14.3). Writing more recently, E.P. Sanders offers his calculation that 'the Temple area could accommodate about 300,000 to 400,000 pilgrims' *The Historical Figure of Jesus* (London: Penguin Allen, 1991), p. 249 and *Judaism: Practice and Belief, 63 BCE–66 CE* (London and Philadelphia: SCM Press, 1992), pp. 125–8.

Adaptation: Moving Beyond 'Faithfulness to the Text'

The 100 films featured in this book are all essentially works of adaptation. While filmmakers have adapted sources as diverse as board games in *Clue!* (1985), toys in *The Lego Movie* (2014), or text icons in *The Emoji Movie* (2017), most adaptations are based on history, plays or works of literature. As a result, much discussion about film adaptations has descended into debates about whether such works are faithful to their sources or historically accurate. For many Christians, fidelity to the Bible is the primary consideration, or at least a criterion which a 'good' adaptation cannot compromise. However, this tendency is problematic for a number of reasons.

To start with, such an approach overlooks how literature, history, spiritual texts and cinema are all very different forms 'with different expressive and representational possibilities'.[25] While the comparison between these forms is a little more *understandable* than those between architecture and ballet, they are little more *useful*. Generally it turns out that those who claim the book is always better than the film, just do not appreciate cinema that much. The two are fundamentally different forms with their own strengths, values and conventions. Films do not exist primarily to be moving illustrations when we are too lazy to read. Historical movies are more than just a re-enactment of the past.

Secondly, this approach ignores some of the nuances such criteria create. For example, by remaining faithful to the play, Laurence Olivier's *Richard III* (1955) is at odds with historical likelihood; his *Henry V* (1944) preserves Shakespeare's text, but not its spirit, 'softening Shakespeare's brutally uncompromising exploration of kingship'.[26] Such nuances are complicated further in the case of the Bible where the boundaries between history and myth are already much debated and the Bible's literary genres are often obscure to modern screenwriters and audiences. Even within tight denominational boundaries there are frequently many different interpretations of a given passage. This is particularly tricky with the Gospels where there are four different accounts to contend with. Moreover, many biblical films are themselves adaptations of existing adaptations, such as novels, paintings, operas and plays. Some could even be described as remakes of existing films.

A third problem is that textual fidelity is often in tension with the filmmakers' need to create something that is dramatically engaging, artistically interesting, or financially viable at least. Filmmakers adapt these stories for a wide variety of reasons from Mel Gibson's evident pride at his film's 'power to evangelize',[27] to Denys Arcand's desire 'to reinterpret one of the basic myths of Western culture'.[28] Adaptations appeal to some film producers because they come with a ready-made audience who already consider the story to be interesting, profound, moving or otherwise important. Other filmmakers have found a story meaningful and want to explore it in their art. Some wish to persuade others of its importance. However, the Bible does not readily translate into a screenplay. Three of the entries in this book have attempted word-for-word adaptations, and, as a result, viewers

---

25 Thomas Leitch, *Film Adaptation and its Discontents: From 'Gone With the Wind' to 'The Passion of the Christ'* (Baltimore: The John Hopkins University Press, 2007), p. 5.

26 Daniel Rosenthal, *100 Shakespeare Films: BFI Screen Guides* (London: BFI Publishing, 2007), p. 63.

27 Kamon Simpson, 'Mel Gibson Brings Movie to City's Church Leaders', *Colorado Springs Gazette*, 28 June 2003.

28 Ron Burnett, 'Denys Arcand – Jesus of Montreal: A Discussion', *Melbourne Sunday Herald,* 29 June 1990. Available online: <http://rburnett.squarespace.com/denys-arcand-jesus-of-montreal/> (accessed 22 June 2021).

frequently dismiss them as dull. Conversely, others have created a better story, but been criticized for taking too many liberties with the text. As stories transform from one artistic form to another, changes are inevitable, indeed 'restructuring stories to be more compelling and more easily understood is part of a screenwriter's job'.[29]

Finally, while some theologians, church leaders, biblical historians, rank-and-file Christians and cultural guardians may desire biblical fidelity (even assuming they could agree what that entailed), in reality, few of those to attempt it have been successful. Biblical texts' *type* of literature and the purpose for which they are written do not provide the same kind of narrative intentions, or character depth, as modern novels, the writings of Jane Austen or even Shakespeare's plays. To adapt these works into feature films the filmmakers have to add material to provide psychological insights into what characters may have been thinking or feeling, or to add background material to provide more context. This is particularly true of the biblical narratives which are shorter than most novels and take less time to read than the duration of a feature film. The stories of Noah and Samson, two of the most frequently adapted, are just four chapters each, with little other relevant material available, likewise Salome. Those adapting novels of historical stories usually have to cut lots of material; here the challenge is often to pad out brief plotlines to create more fully-realized characters and scenarios.

Adaptation: Image, Sound, Emotion and Meaning

If adaptations should be judged on more than fidelity to their source text(s), how else, should they be assessed? One frequent criterion is whether a film captures the spirit of a narrative. Do characters think and act like the period in question? Many historical films fail on this criterion: typically they reflect the values of their own period far more than period in which the story is set. This is further complicated with biblical texts where the era the story was written in is often significantly later than the time in which the events occurred.

Much as theologians and historians may despair at filmmakers mangling precious texts, movie adaptations prompt their audiences to interact with the texts. Data from Wikipedia demonstrates that traffic to their pages about historical characters soars whenever a film is released about them. Similarly, data from Bible Gateway suggests that biblical films drive people to read the original texts.[30] While some are upset by 'fake news' adaptations of the Bible, they provide opportunities for historians, church leaders and theologians to engage with a wider audience through the media and offer useful correctives. The movies generate interest in these stories and inspire people to look more closely at the original material. 'Filmmakers allow us to think about the past in a different way'.[31] Biblical films can enable people to think about texts in new and exciting ways, helping to highlight bias, blind-spots or prior misconceptions by forcing the viewer to see the events through someone else's eyes. For example, the endings of the different Jesus films each emphasize different

---

29 Alex von Tunzelmann, *Reel History: The World According to the Movies* (London: Atlantic Books, 2015), p. 4.

30 The site found that visits to the Noah story at their site increased by 223% over the opening weekend for Aronofsky's *Noah* (2014). See Andy Rau, '*Noah* Generates a Flood of Bible Readers Over the Weekend', *Bible Gateway*, 2 April 2014. Available online: <www.biblegateway.com/blog/2014/04/noah-generates-a-flood-of-bible-readers-over-the-weekend/> (accessed 22 June 2021).

31 Hannah Greig, 'Film', *Making History* [podcast], BBC, 28 January 2020.

stages on the emotional rollercoaster of that first Easter weekend. Some films convey the despair of Good Friday, others the joy of Easter Sunday.

Crucially, films should also be judged on their artistic merits. Much of this is to do with aesthetics: beautiful imagery, compositions that convey meaning, editing that juxtaposes different moments, expressive camerawork, emotionally impacting sound and music. Not that all art, including cinematic art, need be aesthetically pleasing, or satisfy all of the above elements, but just as it seems churlish to criticize the historical likelihood of the table arrangement in Leonardo's 'The Last Supper', so we should not forget that film is primarily a visual and aural medium. No matter how much a film sticks to the text, all movies involve interpretation to produce the film's aesthetics. The importance of the visuals also stretches in an historical direction as well. Film is an influential medium which has both informed and misled us regarding, the look of a period, the costumes and props, while also reproducing archaeological finds for a mass audience.[32]

Lastly, there are considerations of entertainment. While many would argue debasing the scriptures purely for something as trivial as entertainment fails to recognize their importance or value, inevitably some of the audience for biblical films will be there for recreational purposes. Mel Gibson's *The Passion of the Christ* (2004) was not only a hit with religious audiences, but also with fans of horror movies, including film critic Mark Kermode who called it 'a quintessential horror film'.[33] Even laying such cases aside, it is important to consider if the film's story is told well.

For some, films have the means to move us in ways which the biblical material cannot, particularly when readers are over-familiar with the text. Whilst a film's adherence to the 'original' remains important for many, a more enriching engagement with these adaptations encompasses the visual and aural aspects of film-making and judges them on their own terms, rather than simply the script. Are they artistically successful, entertaining or profound?

Intertextuality

Adaptation is itself a subset of Intertextuality – the dialogue between different 'texts', where information from one informs or evokes meaning in another. These texts can include film, music, novels and other works of art. This can be anything from Matthew's Gospel citing the prophecies of Isaiah, to filmmakers from John Huston to Martin Scorsese seeking to imitate religious paintings in their movies. Rather than adapting the Bible directly, numerous biblical films, such as *Ben-Hur* (1959) have used intermediaries such as novels or plays as their source material. Some biblical movies have hired historical consultants and looked to reproduce historical artefacts, or include insights from non-biblical historians such as Josephus or Philo. *The Prince of Egypt* (1998) incorporates stunning hieroglyphics. Nicholas Ray's 1961 *King of Kings* reproduced shots from DeMille's *The King of Kings* (1927). Gibson worked visual references from horror films and action movies into the imagery for *The Passion of*

---

32 For more on costumes in biblical films see Katie Turner, *Costuming Christ: Dressing & Re-dressing First-Century 'Jews' and 'Christians' in Passion Dramas* (London: T&T Clark, forthcoming).

33 Mark Kermode, 'Drenched in the blood of Christ', *The Observer*, 29 Feb 2020. Available online: <www.theguardian.com/film/2004/feb/29/melgibson.markkermode> (accessed 22 June 2021).

the Christ. 'Every film adaptation that seeks to adapt the Gospels inevitably depends on countless other texts as well in order to authenticate its background, soften its potentially partisan challenges, provide an entertaining narrative, and reassure its target audience ...that their piety is not misplaced'.[34]

Seen from this angle we can more fully appreciate the wider range of influences at play in biblical films. In addition to the text itself they may reference paintings, music, popular scholarship, religious symbols, particular compositions or camerawork, theological positions or an actor's back catalogue, or provide external knowledge of the period's history. Furthermore, commercially successful films have often generated related products and souvenirs, from the branded razors and alarm clocks produced alongside 1925's *Ben-Hur*, to Aronofsky's coffee-table-friendly graphic novel that accompanied *Noah*. As Adele Reinhartz summarizes 'the cinema's use of ancient sources as well as medieval and modern artistic, theological, and other reflections demonstrates that film is an active participant in a long and highly developed tradition of interpretation of sacred stories'.[35] Indeed, so enmeshed are we in a web of intertextuality that it is difficult for filmmakers to avoid the echoes of the past that might affect how their work is received.

Filmmakers, Readers and Viewers

In a post-secular world where religion continues to be influential, it remains important to critique the Bible and explore how it is presented in popular and accessible media such as the cinema. Books about film tend to be tied together by genre or country of origin rather than source, yet, what is remarkable about the films in this book, is how little links them together aside from their subject matter. It is not even the retelling of the same story, but of a series of different, yet related stories: stories that have profoundly shaped the western world, and numerous places beyond. That legacy is complicated, with parts which shame us as well as parts we look to uphold, but our values, language and culture have all been shaped by these narratives. What brings these films together is their exploration of what it means to be human, its possibilities, its dangers, its glories and its absurdities. In many ways, then, the story of cinema and the Bible is not just a story about directors, writers, actors, producers and composers, it's also about us:[36] It is the story of humanity explored through film, a story that is not only worth telling and investigating, but also of celebrating, in all of its diverse glory.

---

34 Thomas Leitch, *Film Adaptation*, p. 58.

35 Adele Reinhartz, *Bible and Cinema: An Introduction*, (London and New York: Routledge, 2013), p. 4.

36 A hundred years later, the earliest biblical films not only portray history, they are history, showing us how our forebears thought about these stories.

La Vie et la passion de Jésus-Christ (*The Life and Passion of Jesus Christ*)
France, 1898 – 11 mins
Georges Hatot and Louis Lumière

DIRECTORS Louis Lumière, Georges Hatot
SCREENPLAY Unknown
CINEMATOGRAPHY Alexandre Promio
PRODUCTION COMPANY La Société Lumière
MAIN CAST Gaston Bretteau

In 1895 Louis Lumière, and his brother Auguste 'invented' cinema by becoming the first to display moving pictures to a paying audience. For a while, the Lumières specialized in actualités, but soon diversified to comedies and the occasional reconstruction of historical events. Georges Hatot, a key collaborator on their early documentary footage, soon began to specialize in reconstructions of famous deaths including those of religious martyrs as in *Exécution de Jeanne d'Arc* (1897).[1]

1897 saw the advent of the first biblical films. Albert 'Léar' Kirchner's *La Passion du Christ* and *The Höritz Passion Play* by Mark Klaw and Abraham Erlanger are sadly lost, as is Siegmund Lubin's *The Passion*

Crucifixion scene from *La vie et la passion de Jésus-Christ* (1898).

Play (1898).[2] Similarly, only a fragment survives of the 1898 silent *The Passion Play of Oberammergau*, (supposedly shot on a New York rooftop rather than in Bavaria). At a time when most moving pictures were little more than brief slices of ordinary life, these films blur the line between documentary footage of plays about Jesus and dramatic reconstructions specifically for cinema.

Hatot and Louis Lumière's *La vie et la passion de Jésus-Christ* falls into the latter bracket, though it retains a documentary feel. Inspired by the competition it was shot in France and is now seemingly the earliest remaining Bible film. No audience is present, but the camera nevertheless seems like it is placed to the side of one. The sets were wheeled round from the nearby theatre, *Fantaisies Nouvelles*, and a fake tree visible in the Garden of Gethsemane pops up in other Hatot films.[3] During the crucifixion scene the shadow of the cross falls not across the ground, but against the back wall.

While the film's title refers to Jesus' life and passion, very little of his ministry is actually shown. It starts with the magi and the shepherds worshipping baby Jesus in a manger, and is followed by the flight to Egypt, where Mary, Joseph and Jesus stop to rest between the paws of a sphinx – a scene reproduced before the Great Sphinx of Giza in *From the Manger to the Cross* fourteen years later. Only a solitary miracle – the raising of the Widow of Nain's son – is shown before Jesus' passion. It's handled in low key fashion. The adult son is brought out to Jesus on a stretcher. Jesus simply raises his arm and the man sits up, his shroud falling away as he does so. Yet Hatot has Jesus miraculously materialize during the Last Supper, using the stop-trick technique that he, and rivals such as Georges Méliès, were pioneering.

Hatot moved to Gaumont shortly afterwards, along with Gaston Breteau (who plays Jesus here). There the pair filmed another Jesus biopic *La Vie du Christ* (1898) and *Les Métamorphoses de Satan* (1898) which used stop-trick to make Mephistoles, Satan and others repeatedly disappear and re-appear. The success of *Life and Passion* encouraged others to produce religious films. In particular, Georges Méliès experimented further with stop-trick in the comic *La Tentation de Saint-Antoine* (The Temptation of St. Anthony, 1898) and double exposure in the more reverent *Le Christ marchant sur les flots* (Christ Walking on the Water, 1899).

Notes

1 Luke McKernan, 'Georges Hatot', Who's Who of Victorian Cinema 2013. Available online: <www.victorian-cinema.net/hatot> (accessed 19 Dec. 2021).

2 Alain Boillat and Valentine Robert, 'La Vie et Passion de Notre Seigneur Jésus-Christ (1902–05)', in David J. Shepherd (ed.), The Silents of Jesus in the Cinema (1897–1927) (New York and London: Routledge, 2016), p. 27.

3 Roland-François Lack, 'Hatot-Breteau: two Lumière filmmakers in Paris c.1897', The Cine-Tourist Undated. Available online: <www.thecinetourist.net/hatot-breteau-1897.html/> (accessed 19 Dec. 2021).

Martyrs Chrétiens (Christian Martyrs)
France, 1905 – 7 mins
Lucien Nonguet

DIRECTOR Lucien Nonguet

PRODUCER Charles Pathé

SCREENPLAY Unknown

PRODUCTION COMPANY
Pathé-Frères

MAIN CAST Unknown

Martyrs chrétiens is a three-part film which bridges from shots of Christians in the Coliseum, to the Fall of Babylon by way of *Daniel dans la fosse aux lions* (Daniel in the Lion's Den), also released as a stand-alone film.[1] The first scene takes place in the Roman arena where a lion tamer performs stunts prior to the execution of two Christians. They bow before the emperor before they are strung up on crosses, conveniently obscuring their bodies from view. In a gruesome finale, having switched bodies during a noticeable cut, the lions tear flesh from the crosses.

This forms a gripping context for the Daniel story, which itself is only a single scene and formed so as to appear like a single shot, though it is clearly several more. Daniel is led out and tied to a post, whilst Darius looks down from the very top of the shot, gesturing mournfully towards his condemned advisor. A gate opens and a pair of lions prowl out, one even approaching, then sniffing, Daniel. The previous scene now supplies a degree of tension, and whereas there it was an obvious switch, here Daniel is unmistakably living flesh and blood. Fortunately, an angel materializes via a primitive double exposure, and Daniel's chains fall to the ground, much to the relief of his anxiously-watching monarch. Leaving the den as he entered, Daniel pauses to give a lion a friendly pat 'as if it were a dog'.[2]

The sight of a man seemingly at the mercy of lions was a far cheaper way for audiences to experience the thrills of lion tamer circus skills, but as such provides one of the earliest examples of 'the spectacular' in biblical films, which has remained a feature of biblical epics ever since.

The final film in the sequence is *Le festin de Balthazar* (*Belshazzar's Feast*) and of the three it is undoubtedly the most interesting and technically accomplished. At a time when montage and inter-cutting were still a thing of the future, an imposing matte shot enables both the film's villain, a bevy of extras and God's mysterious hand to appear in the same shot. The composition is rather awkward with the giant hand and the words it writes dominating the left of the screen while Belshazzar's courtiers are squashed to the right. A *chez lounge* highlights Belshazzar among the crowd of courtesans, dancers and drinking buddies, but its reconstruction of someone watching a projected moving image on a screen forms an early image of cinema itself.

Matte shots (including this one which utilizes a close-up) were in use, as were colour tints, switching here in the middle of the scene, for dramatic effect.[3] The "sky" turns from serene blue to a foreboding red to coincide with the hand's ominous appearance. And then, of course, there is the arrival of the Median army who burst into that same shot centre screen via a pair of large doors. Before Daniel is even called to interpret the message the Medes are upon Belshazzar and Babylon has fallen. Regardless, it remains the most daring and memorable of film based on the Book of Daniel.

Balthazar watches the moving image in *Martyrs Chrétiens* (1905).

Notes

1   Richard C. and Michael R. Pitts Campbell, The Bible on Film: A Checklist, 1897–1980 (Metuchen, NJ, and London: Scarecrow Press, 1981), pp. 1–2.

2   Richard Abel, The Cine Goes to Town: French Cinema 1896–1914 (Berkeley: University of California Press, 1994), p. 163.

3   For more on tinting see Paolo Cherci Usai 'The Color of Nitrate: Some Factual Observations on Tinting and Toning Manuals for Silent Films', in Richard Abel (ed.), *Silent Film* (London: Athlone, 1996), pp. 21–30

La Vie du Christ (*The Birth, the Life and the Death of Christ*)
France, 1906 – 33 mins
Alice Guy

DIRECTOR Alice Guy
PRODUCER Léon Gaumont
SCREENPLAY Alice Guy
CINEMATOGRAPHY
Anatole Thiberville
PRODUCTION COMPANY
Gaumont
MAIN CAST Unknown

Alice Guy was cinema's first woman director and producer, having a hand in a thousand films following *La Fée aux choux* (*The Cabbage Fairy*, 1896).[1] Having revolutionized the infant industry in her native France, she moved to the USA and set up a studio, but not before creating her film on the life of Jesus, *La naissance, la vie et la mort du Christ*.

The film was born partly out of friendly rivalry with Ferdinand Zecca (one of many filmmakers she nurtured). They could not be more different, at least within the limitations of the tableau approach that typified cinema's first fifteen years. Guy's actors perform more naturally than Zecca's over-the-top casts. Cinema was

The middle shot from Guy continuity sequence in *La vie du Christ* (1906).

just a cottage industry using amateurs and theatre rejects, so these more subtle and realistic performances showcase Guy's directorial talent and groundbreaking spirit.

'Mademoiselle Alice' also favoured simpler aesthetics in contrast to Zecca's flashy, theatrical style, aided by shooting on location rather than in a studio.[2] That said, she was not averse to using camera trickery. Five times Guy uses double exposures to produce angelic visitations, such as when they guard the sleeping baby Jesus while Mary pops inside. Her simplistic angel costumes outshine Zecca's more elaborate designs.

Guy's thirst for innovation can be seen in the way she uses the camera, most importantly her transformation of the *tableau vivants* into the kind of long takes later favoured by André Bazin.[3] The meteoric rise of continuity editing in the 1910s over-shadowed the development of the long take. Here Guy pioneers long takes as a creative choice, particularly the scene of Peter's denial (echoing Tissot's compositions). Jesus' appearances though two gaps in the wall only work on screen – not in a theatre – where the composition draws attention to a specific location.

Similarly remarkable is a three-shot sequence 'Jesus Before Pontius Pilate' which develops continuity editing. Jesus is led down steps to the rear of the first shot only to be picked up in the second (below left), a reverse shot taken from a floor down. A fade into a third shot, combined with a slightly repositioned camera, indicating the passage of time.

Another of Guy's innovations is her use of panning shots, most notably from looking down at the crowd accompanying Jesus as they snake up the path to Golgotha. Once Jesus shuffles past the camera, it pans left and upwards to view the rest of the procession from the rear, Guy deliberately choosing to keep all of the action within a single take. In the same sequence an unnamed woman looks on as Veronica wipes Jesus' face. Guy cuts to a mid-shot of the saint displaying the imprint of Jesus' face on her cloth, perhaps cinema's first point-of-view shot, and notable that this first 'representative' of the audience is female.[4]

This female focus continues throughout, emphasizing the birth scenes in the Nativity; Mary's role, including the angelic respite care; the only scenes shown from Jesus' ministry are those about women; 'The scene in which Peter denies Jesus focuses on the women around the disciple as much as on him';[5] Jesus' fall on the Via Dolorosa features women coming to his aid; and the women witnessing Jesus' resurrection.

It's disappointing that it was over a century before a major film surpassed Guy's vision of a Jesus who saw women as central to his plans. But then, few have seen the world in such a remarkable way as Alice Guy.

Notes

1   At the time of making this film she was simply known as Alice Guy. Later, during her marriage to Herbert Blaché, she became known as Alice Blaché and then Alice Guy Blaché following their divorce.

2   For a longer comparison see Dwight H. Friesen, 'La Vie et Passion de Notre Seigneur Jésus-Christ (Pathé-Frères, 1907): The Preservation and Transformation of Zecca's Passion', in David J. Shepherd (ed.) , *The Silents of Jesus in the Cinema (1897–1927)* (New York and London: Routedge, 2016), pp. 87–94.

3   I am indebted to David Bordwell for highlighting the significance of the subtle variations in static shots in the 1910s, see 'Anybody but Griffith', *David Bordwell's Website on Cinema* 2017. Available online: <www.davidbordwell.net/blog/2017/02/27/anybody-but-griffith/> (accessed 19 Dec. 2021).

4   David J. Shepherd, 'La naissance, la vie et la mort du Christ (Gaumont, 1906): The Gospel According to Alice Guy', in David J. Shepherd (ed.) , *The Silents of Jesus in the Cinema (1897–1927)* (New York and London: Routledge, 2016), p. 73.

5   Richard Abel, *The Cine Goes to Town: French Cinema 1896–1914* (Berkeley: University of California Press, 1994), p. 166.

La Vie et passion de Notre Seigneur Jésus-Christ
(*The Life and Passion of Jesus Christ*)

France, 1907 – 45 mins

Ferdinand Zecca

DIRECTOR Ferdinand Zecca
PRODUCER Charles Pathé
CINEMATOGRAPHY
Segundo de Chómon
PRODUCTION COMPANY
Pathé-Frères
MAIN CAST Unknown

Perhaps the best known Jesus film from the early silent era, Pathé's *The Life and Passion of Jesus Christ* was more of an evolving project, running from its first release in 1899 to its fourth major reworking 1914. Pathé's *Life and Passion* is a notable example of an industry that was more fluid than today, with distributors and exhibitors selecting the parts of a given film they wished to screen from catalogues. While these films show a remarkable consistency, technology and technique developed so significantly across these fifteen-years that an initially ground-breaking project ultimately became staid and outdated.

The ascension from *La Vie et Passion de Notre Seigneur Jésus-Christ* (1907).

Little is known about the 1899 version, except that its sixteen *tableaux* (scenes) suggest it was perhaps the longest film then in circulation. Three years later Lucien Nonguet and Ferdinand Zecca began reshooting episodes from the first film adding additional material such that by 1905 the production had doubled in length. Two years later Zecca created a third, 39-scene, version, which is best-known today thanks to a 2003 DVD release.[1]

We can see how the success of Alice Guy's 1906 Jesus film spurred him on. Zecca's remake responded to his friend and rival's innovations, moving more of the production outside and including two close-ups. Pathé's impressive set designs and construction were becoming a major selling point,[2] and were enhanced by Pathè's development of the stencil colouring process, eye-catching black and red intertitles and use of colour filters.

Pathé's developing house style was largely based on a fixed, squarely positioned camera, with occasional pans to allow audiences to admire the set-makers' handiwork. Some mistakenly claim that such static shots were because filmmakers had yet to learn how to position their camera, but the wealth of early documentary footage proves this untrue. The straight-on, static, camera was an active choice – whether aesthetic or pragmatic – which may have mirrored the theatre going-experience, but also allowed the viewer to direct their gaze wherever they wished. 'Continuity editing' may soon have become dominant, but some filmmakers have always preferred the audience to direct their own gaze.

Whilst Zecca was not particularly innovative, he recognized good ideas and incorporated them into his own film-making. Much of *Life and Passion*'s effects derived from Georges Méliès, attracting those seeking spectacle, entertainment and magic alongside the devout. The results include a semi-transparent Jesus walking on water, the hand-drawn dove validating his baptism and angelic appearances throughout. Elsewhere the film incorporates theatrical techniques occasionally in tandem with camera tricks. Most memorably, the final scene features Jesus ascending into Heaven on a hand-drawn cloud before a dissolve reveals God amid an angelic host. While these effects appear primitive to us, they demonstrate how realism was not necessarily the most important aspect of early cinema, particularly in a religious context where 'an icon's lack of naturalism is integral to its transcendent meaning'.[3]

The fourth and final entry in this series came in 1913–14 this time under the auspices of Maurice André Maître. As before, Maître increased the number of tableaux, expanded the cast and improved the sets, typically incorporating Zecca's exact compositions. But Pathé were trapped. While the grammar of film was changing, departing 'too radically from the visual canon it had helped to create' risked undermining its 'own hold on the market'.[4] Sadly the 'old-fashioned' look dated quicker than anticipated as World War I resulted in European filmmakers being overtaken by the burgeoning USA film industry. Nevertheless, the Pathé passion plays continued to be recycled into the 1920s even touring with sound effects during the 1930s.

Notes

1   Whilst the liner notes claim it is the 1902–05 version the evidence suggests it is the later 1907 edition See Dwight H. Friesen, '*La Vie et Passion de Notre Seigneur Jésus-Christ* (Pathé-Frères, 1907): The Preservation and Transformation of Zecca's Passion', in David J. Shepherd (ed.), *The Silents of Jesus in the Cinema (1897–1927)* (New York and London: Routledge, 2016), p. 79.

2   Alan L. Williams, *Republic of Images: A History of French Filmmaking* (London: Harvard University Press, 1992), p. 56.

3   Steven D. Greydanus, 'The Life and Passion of Jesus Christ (1905)', *Decent Films* 2003. Available online at: <http://decentfilms.com/reviews/lifeandpassionofjesus> (accessed 19 Dec. 2021).

4   Jo-Ann Brant, 'La Vie et Passion de Notre Seigneur Jésus-Christ (Pathé-Frères, 1913/14): Pathé's Inclination to Tell and Maître's Instinct to Show', in David J. Shepherd (ed.), *The Silents of Jesus in the Cinema (1897–1927)* (New York and London: Routledge, 2016), p. 162

Jephthah's Daughter: A Biblical Tragedy
USA, 1909 – 6 mins
J. Stuart Blackton

DIRECTOR J. Stuart Blackton
SCREENPLAY Madison C. Peters
PRODUCTION COMPANY
Vitagraph Company of America
MAIN CAST Annette Kellerman

Jephthah's Daughter is one of the few films to tackle the notoriously difficult tale from Judges 11, a disturbing narrative marked by its utterly incomprehensible behaviour. Jephthah, paradoxically both a social outcast and his people's leader, rashly promises that, should he win an upcoming battle, he will sacrifice whatever first leaves his house to greet him.

Jephthah's readiness to commit human sacrifice in exchange for winning a battle is a salient reminder of how mired in the cultic religions of her neighbours Israel was at this point. History is full of military leaders who have risked 'friendly' human lives in the pursuit of military goals, yet the story of Jephthah's daughter is among the most shocking. Both the original text and Blackton's adaptation open up a Girardian reading by giving the victim a voice. Moreover, the film can be read as an early feminist film that goes beyond the text in its positive depiction of a female victim of male violence.

The film is just one of many shorts that USA company Vitagraph made as part of a campaign to try to lend the new cinematic medium greater respectability.[1] Alongside a string of biblical films,[2] they produced a series covering George Washington and numerous Shakespearean adaptations. Blackton himself is remembered as 'the father of American animation', but his historical films were marked by a commitment to 'period detail' and for humanizing his characters,[3] very evident here. Jephthah's mistreatment of his daughter starts long before his infamous promise, in an early scene where he returns home only to depart immediately with the very people who had previously shunned him – the Gileadites – leaving her heartbroken and alone.

The cinematic grammar that forms the template for the movie-battle scenes of today was still unfolding, yet Blackton's chaotically difficult-to-follow battle scene provides a certain realism. Jephthah's victorious army processes home only to be brought up short by his daughter's sudden, jarring appearance. Jephthah returns home to explain his rash promise to his wife whilst his daughter heads to the hills for a two-month stay of execution. There's a brief clip of her and her friends innocently playing badminton before their final farewells, ominously cut short by her closing a curtain, obscuring both them, and her, from the audience's view.

Yet it's the sacrifice scene that creates the greatest impression. There's a sacrificial altar table and a crowd. Jephthah looks downcast. His wife hugs their daughter. The daughter does not seem overly upset, reflecting her apparent unwillingness in the text to contest her father's misguided idealism. Jephthah himself stabs her then lights the fire. In a dramatic final shot, the daughter reappears as a ghostly apparition standing bolt upright. The scene draws on scenes of Jesus' resurrection/ascension from earlier Jesus films, the daughter clearly vindicated, as her body obscures Jephthah from view. Just as the original text ends describing only the daughter's commemoration, not her father's, so her cinematic brilliance, casts him into the darkness.

Jephthah sacrificing his daughter in *Jephthah's Daughter: A Biblical Tragedy* (1909).

Notes

1   William Uricchio and Roberta E. Pearson, *Reframing Culture: The Case of the Vitagraph Quality Films* (Princeton: Princeton University Press, 1993), pp. 55–64.

2   David J. Shepherd, *The Bible on Silent Film: Spectacle, Story and Scripture in the Early Cinema* (Cambridge: Cambridge University Press, 2013), pp. 61–94.

3   Uricchio and Pearson. *Reframing Culture*, pp. 116.

L'Exode (*The Exodus*)
France, 1910 – 13 mins
Louis Feuillade

DIRECTOR Louis Feuillade
PRODUCER Léon Gaumont
CINEMATOGRAPHY
Albert Sorgius
PRODUCTION COMPANY
Gaumont
MAIN CAST Renée Carl,
Nadette Darson, Alice Tissot

Gaumont handed Louis Feuillade his chance to direct following Alice Guy's departure for the USA. Having rallied against cinema's over-dependency on theatre he directed the first 'Jesus Cameo' film, *L'aveugle de Jérusalem* (1909) and two films about biblical heroines – *Judith et Holophernes* (1909) and *Esther* (1910) before producing *Les sept péchés capitaux* (1910) – a series of seven biblical stories each illustrating deadly sin.

While Feuillade is best remembered today for other cinematic series, namely *Fantômas* (1913–14) and *Les Vampires* (1915–16), *L'Exode* is a thought-provoking and challenging work. It opens with Moses and Israel's

Pharaoh shields his son from Moses in *L'Exode (1910)*.

elders deciding to instruct the Israelites to daub their door posts with blood, so the Angel of Death will pass-over their houses. A long take pans gracefully from one door to the next, focussing on doors at different depths, knitting together individual households thematically through its pioneering 'exploitation of the deep space'.[1] It's unflinchingly graphic, with lambs' throats slit and their blood drained off to be sprinkled on Israelite doorposts.

The focus shifts to inside Moses' house as his family gather to share the Passover *Seder* with their servants. The room is simple, with a long unadorned table in the middle, but sunlight streams in through an upper window. Feuillade lingers on this stunning shot long enough for the audience to enjoy its 'Rembrandt lighting'.[2] But here, the film moves jarringly from Moses and the Israelites, to the Egyptians. Pharaoh's son is introduced sympathetically, a normal child who is easy to warm to, but the introduction is overshadowed by our knowledge of his fate. Unusually, we see Pharaoh's tenderness towards him as he begins to display signs of illness. We witness the concern of his carers.

A swift cut reveals a similar situation. A miller and his wife anxiously observe their daughter's deteriorating health. He gently places her on a chair and continues his work. The previous scene and our knowledge of the outcome heightens the tension as the miller slowly grinds the huge millstone through another revolution. First he has his back to her, then the stone itself obstructs his view. By the time he finally returns full circle, the child has died.

Many argue that Pharaoh was responsible for what unfolds, but the miller, whose back-breaking work is almost indistinguishable from that of the Hebrew slaves, is entirely innocent. As the camera first cuts to the scene he seems insignificant – as if another, important, character is about to enter and make an announcement. Only gradually does it dawn on us that this *is* the scene we are waiting for, and that his little girl is doomed.

As if the emotional impact of these two scenes was not great enough, the next is almost unparalleled. Two parents mourn their lost child in a courtyard. Soon they are joined by another grieving couple, and then two more, and so on until the frame is crammed with Egyptian parents lamenting their lost children. It's the kind of scene that is utterly absent from most other adaptations of this story, and indeed the Bible itself, creating sympathy for the Egyptians, and causing us to re-visit this story from the point of view of those on the losing side.

Given these scenes, it's unsurprising that rather than departing joyously with gifts from the Egyptians, the Israelites do not leave, so much as get booted out. *L'Exode* is not so much about the birth of one nation as the deaths in another. The comfort of seeing Moses and the Israelites leave Egypt, is for different reasons than we initially expected.

Notes

1   David J. Shepherd, *The Bible on Silent Film: Spectacle, Story and Scripture in the Early Cinema* (Cambridge: Cambridge University Press, 2013), p. 110

2   Luke McKernan, 'Bible Stories', *The Bioscope* 23 June 2009. Available online: <https://thebioscope.net/2009/06/23/bible-stories/> (accessed 19 Dec. 2021).

Jaël et Sisera (*Jael and Sisera*)
France, 1911 – 10 mins
Henri Andréani

DIRECTOR Henri Andréani
PRODUCER Charles Pathé
MAIN CAST Unknown
PRODUCTION COMPANY
Pathé-Frères

Pathé-Frères went from selling knock-off versions of Edison's kinetoscope to becoming the biggest name in early cinema.[1] Having enjoyed major success with their Jesus films, they began the new decade with a series of sixteen films covering the breadth of the Hebrew Bible, turning to a relative newcomer, Henri Andréani, to direct.

Given Andréani's eye for the visceral (nearly all of his biblical films revolve around a key act of violence) it was inevitable he would end up adapting the Book of Judges. Given its content, it seems amazing that the only time any part of the story of Deborah (Judges 4–5) has received a significant silver screen outing is in Andréani's *Jael et Sisera* 1911 and even then Deborah's role is cut with the kind of ruthless efficiency that typifies the original story.

Andréani had perhaps been inspired by *Giuditta e Oloferne* (1908) and *Judith et Holophernes* (1909), both of which featured the biblical heroine Judith cunningly slaying Israel's enemies. Andréani's work championed biblical heroines more than any other filmmaker: in 1913 he directed *La Reine de Saba* (The Queen of Sheba), *Rebecca*, *La fille de Jephté* (Jephthah's Daughter) and *Esther*. It was an intense five-year period which witnessed the creation of almost ninety biblical movies worldwide.

Here the action starts outside Jael's tent. A group of Israelites are chained up, but as her husband Heber is friends with Canaanite general Sisera, she is able to liberate her countrymen while Sisera's back is turned. They return to Barak so the Israelite army can march out again to attack Sisera's troops.

Andréani's use of locations here, is particularly notable, as is the panning within the shots and the cuts between them. In one shot, the Israelites pursue Sisera's men up a hill. In the next they overcome them on a beach. Sisera's men scramble upon a rock, desperate to avoid a watery grave (recalling Francis Danby's 1840 painting 'The Deluge'). Somehow Sisera survives and escapes back to Jael's tent where, fatefully, he begs her to shelter him.

Whilst the film's climatic moment is bloodless, it's nevertheless surprisingly brutal. Jael's repeated hammering of a tent peg into her sleeping guest's skull is shockingly violent. Barak arrives moments later, kneels beside his foe's lifeless body and kisses the hem of his heroine's robe in tribute. Such moments were not uncommon in Andréani's work: David parading around at the end of *David et Goliath* (1910) carrying the giant's head on a stick; the cramped compositions of *Cain et Abel* (1911) closing with a lengthy shot of Cain dragging himself through the mud of a rocky passageway.

Sadly Andréani's desire for increased spectacle, melodrama and running time ultimately led to a split with Pathé, which was to the detriment of both.[2] Andréani left to form Andréani Films in 1913 but made only a handful of features before his death in 1928. Meanwhile, Pathé decentralized, just as the Great War was decimating Europe and its film industry.[3] The release of Italian feature-length films such as *L'inferno* (1911), *Quo Vadis?* (1913) and *Cabiria* (1914) meant that in just a few years short films such as *Jaël et Sisera* seemed like ancient history. The era of biblical epics was almost underway.

Jael, equipped with tent peg and hammer from *Jaël et Sisera* (1911).

Notes

1   Richard Abel, *The Cine Goes to Town: French Cinema 1896–1914* (Berkeley: University of California Press, 1994), p. 14.

2   David J. Shepherd, *The Bible on Silent Film: Spectacle, Story and Scripture in the Early Cinema* (Cambridge: Cambridge University Press, 2013), p. 153.

3   Abel, *Cine Goes to Town*, p. 158.

From the Manger to the Cross
USA, 1912 – 70 mins
Sidney Olcott

DIRECTOR Sidney Olcott
PRODUCERS Brian Hession,
Frank Marion
SCREENPLAY Gene Gauntier
CINEMATOGRAPHY
George K. Hollister
PRODUCTION COMPANY
Kalem Company
MAIN CAST Robert Henderson
Bland, Percy Dyer, Gene
Gauntier, Alice Hollister, George
Kellog, Samuel Morgan, Robert
G. Vignola

From the Manger to the Cross was the first feature-length film about Jesus and probably the earliest Bible film to shoot on location. Kalem's leading director Sidney Olcott and writer Gene Gauntier, had recently lost a landmark legal case over their unauthorized adaptation of *Ben-Hur* in 1907. Having enjoyed success filming in Ireland, the pair were shooting dramatic and documentary films in the Middle East when Gauntier (suffering from sunstroke) was inspired to create a Jesus film shot at the original locations. Olcott secured further funding, flew to London and immediately cast the inexperienced Robert Henderson Bland: he was the only actor Olcott considered for the part.[1]

In addition to providing a greater sense of authenticity, the locations improved the film's appeal. 110 years ago film was still in its infancy so the opportunity to see moving images of the wonders of the world would have been a significant draw. For some audience members the moment when Mary and Joseph pause during escape to Egypt would have been the first time they saw footage of the Sphinx.

Henderson Bland, who admitted to feeling 'astounded and appalled' when first asked to accept the part,[2] captures both Jesus' humanity and his divinity. Having intended to 'bring out the force of his personality' and 'his keen intellectuality',[3] he was also able to be compassionate and caring, yet his clearing of the temple is one of the most passionate and forceful depictions. The film also captures Jesus' spirituality nicely, in a brief, blue-tinted shot of him praying while Jerusalem waits patiently in the background.

Though the film largely consists of medium shots, there are a few exceptions, including some more visually-pleasing compositions and ideas. Early on, the boy Jesus carries a plank of wood for his father, casting the silhouette of a cross onto the ground. The film emphasizes Jesus' actions more than his words. There are ten or more healings in the film, along with several supernatural dreams, though any angels are kept off screen, in stark contrast to earlier films.

Despite its calm spirituality the film proved highly controversial. Henderson Bland claimed that 'criticism, like an avalanche … poured down upon it from every quarter of the globe'.[4] For some, the medium was considered so depraved no cinematic life of Jesus could be appropriate. Others objected to its omission of the resurrection.

Yet on its release, the film was well received, indeed various Christian groups rejoiced over such an evangelistic opportunity. Given the positive reception, it's hardly surprising that the film achieved a number of subsequent re-releases: some of them with tacked on 'resurrection scenes' under the alternative title *Jesus of Nazareth*, others at the start of the sound era with added sound effects.

Eventually however, the film was overshadowed by DeMille's *The King of Kings*, which outguns this film for spectacle, but fails to capture Olcott's authenticity and serene spirituality. DeMille's Jesus is heralded by overbearing fanfare: *From the Manger* speaks eloquently enough for itself. Indeed some of its images are at their most poignant with no sound at all.

Still for *From the Manger to the Cross* (1912).

Notes

1   Robert Henderson Bland, *From Manger to Cross: The Story of the World-Famous Film of the Life of Jesus* (London: Hodder and Stoughton, 1922), p 33.

2   Henderson Bland, *From the Manger*, p. 30

3   Henderson Bland, *From the Manger*, p. 32

4   Robert Henderson Bland, *Actor–Soldier–Poet* (London: Heath Cranton, 1939), p. 70.

Judith of Bethulia
USA, 1974 – 61 mins
D.W. Griffith

DIRECTOR D. W. Griffith
SCREENPLAY Thomas Bailey
Aldrich, D. W.Griffith, Grace
Pierce, Frank E. Woods
CINEMATOGRAPHY
G. W. Bitzer
EDITOR James Smith
PRODUCTION COMPANY
Biograph
MAIN CAST Robert Harron,
Mae Marsh, Blanche Sweet,
Henry B. Walthall

In the early days of cinema, Judith was the ultimate biblical heroine. Her story may come from a 'deutero-canonical' book excluded from many Bibles, but by the time D.W. Griffith began filming in 1913 there had already been three other adaptations including *Judith et Holophernes* by Pathé's Louis Feuillade.[1]

Griffith is primarily remembered for his three hour, racist, film *Birth of a Nation* in 1915. His *Judith of Bethulia* released the year before (starring Blanche Sweet), was the first time he had produced a feature-length movie and many of the techniques which brought Griffith acclaim are visible here, in their infancy.[2] The greater variety of shots, for example is particularly well utilized in the battle scene, from relative close-ups to long shots with a considerable depth of field. These still seem somewhat disorganized – differentiating which side is which is difficult at times – particularly in comparison with his later big action scenes. The sets are also a significant improvement on previous Judith adaptations, even if they pale in comparison to Giovanni Pastrone's *Cabiria* released that same year, or Griffith's own *Intolerance* two years later.

Griffiths also demonstrates his talent for projecting personal melodrama against a backdrop of major historical events, which is particularly evident in his more famous films. Here Judith's heroics are juxtaposed with the story of Nathan and Naomi a young Bethulian couple.[3] She is captured by the Assyrians just before Judith's mission. He slips into the Assyrian camp to rescue her just as panic starts spreading following the commander's assassination.

This juxtaposition contrasts with the relationship between Judith and Holofernes, emphasizing both Judith's strength of character and their romantic attachment.[4] He is instantly 'ravished with her'. She 'wrestles with her heart' because, despite his crimes against her people and his obvious penchant for semi-clad servant girls, she finds him 'noble'. Later intertitles reveal how his thoughts were 'only for Judith' and how 'she faltered for the love of Holofernes. Griffiths uses an iris shot to visually reinforce Holofernes' lack of interest in his surroundings, quite literally relegating them to the shadows.

The tension peaks when Judith gets her shot at assassination. Holofernes falls asleep and Judith raises a sword above his neck, but hesitates, caught amidst duty to her people and 'vacillation, introspection, amorous melting, lustful desire, self-accusation, guilty horror and renewed resolution'.[5] As she stares into the distance and the film cuts to the well of Bethulia now littered with the bodies of her compatriots, the combination of shots somehow suggesting her knowledge of it. Inspired, she kills the Assyrian leader, though the decisive blow is left off camera as if a testimony to her love for him, further reinforced by her taking her lover's head with her as she flees. Judith's story may no longer directly appeal to filmmakers but her legacy lives on in modern productions featuring beautiful assassins and complex emotions, such as *Kill Bill* (2003–4) and *Killing Eve* (from 2018).

Henry B. Walthall and Blanche Sweet in a still from *Judith of Bethulia* (1914).

Notes

1   For details of other adaptations of Judith see Matthew Page, 'Judith Films', *Bible Films Blog* 17 February 2013. Available online: <https://biblefilms.blogspot.com/2013/02/judith-films.html> (accessed 19 Dec. 2021).

2   Sweet recalls Griffith was inspired by Italian religious epic *Quo Vadis?* (1913) see Kevin Brownlow, *The Parade's Gone By* (London: Columbus Books, 1989), p. 92.

3   The names here suggests Griffith's indebtedness to Thomas Bailey Aldrich's 1904 play *Judith of Bethulia*, see David J. Shepherd, *The Bible on Silent Film: Spectacle, Story and Scripture in the Early Cinema* (Cambridge: Cambridge University Press, 2013), p163.

4   Jeffrey Richards, *Hollywood's Ancient Worlds* (London: Continuum UK, 2008), p. 27.

5   Judith Buchanan, 'Judith's Vampish Virtue and its Double Market Appeal' in Pantelis Michelakis and Maria Wyke (ed.) *The Ancient World in Silent Cinema* (Cambridge: Cambridge University Press, 2013), p. 220.

Intolerance: Love's Struggle Throughout the Ages
USA, 1916 – 198 mins
D.W. Griffith

DIRECTOR D. W. Griffith

PRODUCER D. W. Griffith

SCREENPLAY Hettie Grey
Baker, Tod Browning,
D.W.Griffith, Anita Loos, Mary
H. O'Connor, Walt Whitman

CINEMATOGRAPHY
G. W. Bitzer

EDITORS D. W. Griffith,
James Smith, Rose Smith

MUSIC Joseph Carl Breil,
Felix Günther

PRODUCTION COMPANY
Biograph

MAIN CAST Lillian Gish, Robert
Harron, Mae Marsh, F. A. Turner

When D.W. Griffith's *Birth of a Nation* was criticized for its racism in 1915, Griffith went on the offensive, responding with *Intolerance*.[1] It's a technique that has become all-too-familiar in recent years with those accused of racism launching counter-offensives claiming their critics are 'intolerant' and blocking free speech. Griffith's three-hour epic featured four parallel stories, each representing scenarios he considered similarly intolerant. As Paul McEwan argues 'it was in no way an apology' for *Birth of a Nation*, 'Griffith made clear in

Jesus in the Judean Story in *Intolerance* (1916).

numerous public statements that he had nothing to apologize for … and that *Intolerance* was intended as a commentary on those who had been intolerant of him'.[2] Fearing parallels from Ancient Babylon and the St Bartholomew's Day massacre lacked sufficient potency, Griffith co-opted Jesus to his cause. Of the film's four segments, the 'Judean Story' comprises barely 10 minutes, cut down after Jewish groups objected to Griffith's racist portrayal of them. Even despite such cuts, the final film still betrays its antisemitism: it's plainly the practising Jews in this sequence who are the 'intolerant' ones, to such an extent that they are prepared to kill Jesus for disagreeing with them.

It is 'certain hypocrites amongst the Pharisees' who feature first in 'The Judean Story'. Griffith presents a literalized version of Jesus' 'Parable of Pharisee and the Tax Collector' (Luke 18). Next it's the wedding at Cana, corresponding to the negative portrayal of the leaders of the temperance movement featured in 'The Modern Story'. As with Olcott's *From the Manger to the Cross* (1912) a cross-shaped shadow falls, only here it across Jesus as he performs the miracle, foreshadowing his demise. Shortly afterwards Jesus is called 'gluttonous and a winebibber' (Matt 11.19), before saving the woman accused of adultery (John 8). The last incident from Jesus' ministry sees him welcoming 'the little children' – a phrase from Mark 10, but utterly in keeping with Griffith's affectionate sobriquets for other characters like 'The Dear One' and 'The Little Colonel', which even his contemporaries judged overly sentimental. Three brief, final, moments featuring Jesus' road to the cross and his crucifixion

provide extra emotional power as the movie's three other plots reach similarly emotional climaxes.

Cinematically, it's The Babylonian Story which most impresses, with its epic scope and spectacular sets though, as Martin Scorsese and others have observed, this and many of *Intolerance*'s other 'innovations' should instead be credited to Giovanni Pastrone's 1914 epic *Cabiria*.[3] Indeed this is true for many of the cinematic 'firsts' claimed by Griffith apologists: *Birth of a Nation* was not the first feature film, blockbuster or Hollywood feature, nor was *Intolerance* the first epic, or the first film weaving together differing time periods.[4] He certainly highlighted the cinematic potential of techniques such as parallel editing, cross cutting and the close-up, but neither film was the first to use them. His claims to the contrary mainly demonstrate his formidable talent as master of his own publicity.

As with the bizarre appearance of Jesus at the end of *Birth of a Nation*, the problem with *Intolerance* is that, Griffith simply uses Jesus as 'a means to hallow some characters, (and) to demonize others'.[5] Having been challenged over the racism of *Birth of a Nation*, *Intolerance*'s message amounts to little more than equating those challenging him to those who killed Jesus.

There are things to admire in *Intolerance*, in particular the sophistication with which Griffith draws the four stories together to form such an emotionally powerful climax. But his co-opting of Jesus to denigrate those who criticized Griffith's own intolerance is not among them.

Notes

1   It is often argued that *Birth of a Nation* was merely a product of its time, but this is demonstrably false. Objections to Griffith's racism were raised even then. Arguing otherwise, silences the voices of African-American critics who, even then, considered it racist, as did many others.

2   Paul McEwan, *The Birth of a Nation (BFI Film Classics)* (London: BFI/Palgrave, 2015), p. 14.

3   Martin Scorsese, 'Un'incredibile bellezza', *Martin Scorsese presenta Cabiria di Giovanni Pastrone*. Turin Museo Nazionale del Cinema, 2006. Available online: <www.homolaicus.com/arte/cinema/

interviste/fonti/PressbookCabiria.zip> (accessed 19 Dec. 2021).

4   Fritzi Kramer, 'Silent Movie Myth: *The Birth of a Nation* was the first feature and the first film shown at the White House', *Movies Silently* 7 September 2015. Available online: <http://moviessilently.com/2015/09/07/silent-movie-myth-the-birth-of-a-nation-was-the-first-feature-and-the-first-film-shown-at-the-white-house/> (accessed 19 Dec. 2021).

5   Richard Walsh, 'Griffith's Talismanic Jesus', in David J. Shepherd (ed.), *The Silents of Jesus in the Cinema (1897–1927)* (New York and London: Routledge, 2016), p. 192.

Blade af Satans bog (*Leaves From Satan's Book*)
Denmark, 1920 – 130 mins
Carl Theodor Dreyer

DIRECTOR Carl Theodor Dreyer
SCREENPLAY Marie Corelli,
Carl Theodor Dreyer,
Edgar Høyer
MUSIC Philip Carli
PRODUCTION COMPANY
Nordisk Films Kompany
MAIN CAST Hallander
Helleman, Halvard Hoff,
Johannes Meyer, Ebon Strandin,
Jacob Texiere

Carl Theodor Dreyer is revered by many as one of the greatest directors of all time whose bold and uncompromising films, such as *La Passion de Jeanne d'Arc* (1928) and *Ordet* (1954), offer austere, yet beautiful, explorations of human passions kept in check.

In 1920 however, he was still finding his distinctive artistic voice. Dreyer admitted to being 'strongly influenced by Griffith' finding *Intolerance* 'deeply moving'. [1] Yet while *Blade Af Satans Bog* uses a four story structure, the episodes are not intercut and Dreyer develops the Judean story featuring Jesus more fully, offering a subtler, more nuanced portrait of events.

Common to all four stories is Satan, who adopts human form and attempts to trick those around him into betraying their souls. Satan has some success orchestrating the execution of Marie Antoinette, the denouncement of a husband in Russian-occupied Finland, and the persecution of an inquisition-era Spanish astrologer. However, it's the opening segment where he is most successful, tricking Judas and persuading Caiaphas to incite a riot. As with so many Jesus films of this era the Jewish people are portrayed in wizened and grasping antisemitic stereotypes, in contrast to the noble-looking Romans. Later in life Dreyer wrote a script called *Jesus of Nazareth* hoping to undo the antisemitic aspects of *Blade*. Intending to cast a Jewish actor in the title role, he struggled for years to find funding without success.

One of the film's more surprising twists is that the Jesus episode ends shortly after his arrest in Gethsemane, even before he encounters Pilate. Only three episodes from the Gospels feature – the anointing at Simon's house, the Last Supper and Gethsemane. The focus is on Judas and his emotions rather than his master. Having opened with Jesus being anointed, Judas is clearly disappointed with the path Jesus is taking. Satan appears and sympathizes with Judas' disillusionment, eventually luring him into a trap, before leaving him as Judas' remorse escalates and he takes his own life.

The footage of Jesus is distant and remote, often placed close to the top of the frame but shot from a low angle. He constantly peers upwards as if through his brow. The Last Supper is visually striking, but stiff and unimaginative. It's difficult to appreciate what compelled Judas to follow Jesus in the first place.

Whilst it's the first segment that is of most relevance to the present volume, it's the obscure Finnish love story from the margins of World War I that proves most pivotal in the relationship between God, Satan and humanity. There's palpable tragedy in Dreyer's apparent belief that having hit its lowest point with the Great War humanity was, at last, on an upward trajectory.

There are notable touches of Dreyer's future work here. The number of prolonged close-ups, hint at the lengthy, extreme shots of Maria Falconetti's face in *La Passion de Jeanne d'Arc*, and the film's 'foreboding and otherworldly psychological landscape' is reminiscent of *Vampyr* (1932) and *Day of Wrath* (1943). [2] That the earliest of these masterpieces was just seven years away is surprising. In terms of the development of Dreyer's style it somehow seems much further away.

Jesus (Halvard Hoff) in *Blade af Satans bog* (1920).

Notes

1   Jean Drum and Dale D. Drum *My Only Great Passion: The Life and Films of Carl Th.* Dreyer (Lanham, Maryland, Rowman & Littlefield, 2000) p. 59

2   Acquarello, 'Blade Af Satans Bog', *Strictly Film School*, 2003. Retrieved from: <http://web.archive.org/web/20120314034243/https://filmref.com/directors/dirpages/dreyer.html>.

La Sacra Bibbia (*After Six Days*)[1]
Italy, 1920 – 62 mins [2]
Pier Antonio Gariazzo and Armando Vey

DIRECTORS Pier Antonio
Gariazzo, Armando Vey
PRODUCERS Pier Antonio
Gariazzo, Armando Vey
SCREENPLAY Kathryn Stuart
CINEMATOGRAPHY
Ferdinando Martini, Lorenzo
Romagnoli, Aldo Sunel
EDITOR Peter Cartwright
PRODUCTION COMPANY
Appia Nuova
MAIN CAST Bruto Castellani,
Mario Cionci, Ada Marucelli,
Umberto Semprebene

Like so many silent films, much of Armando Vay and Dr Piero Antonio Gariazzo's *La Sacra Bibbia* is lost. Even what remains is left overlain by an earnest, but dull narration and with some shots cropped atrociously. What remains, however, is a testament to the strength of Italian silent epics. Italy was where the historical epic was born (*Gli ultimi giorni di Pompei*, 1908) and grew spectacularly e.g. *Cabiria* (1914). *La Bibbia* retains much of the grandeur and spectacle of those films and augments them by stunningly evoking numerous works of Christian art.

Joseph tests his brothers in *La Sacra Bibbia* (1920).

The early scenes are ripe with visual flourishes. Eve and Adam simultaneously biting into the forbidden fruit. A furious Cain, dominating the front of the shot, forlornly poking his sacrifice and glowering at the camera while, in the background and almost out of the frame, Abel continues contentedly. Victims climbing desperately onto a rock, hoping to escape the flood (evoking Gustave Doré's 'The Deluge') and then piles of bodies and ghostly, floating, corpses. The Tower of Babel is depicted as a soaring ziggurat, so colossal it bursts through the top of the frame even in an ultra-wide shot. Emboldening Pieter Bruegel's famous painting (1563) and Doré's 1865 engraving, it looms above the seemingly minute people milling about below. The spectacular destruction of Sodom ends in brimstone raining down amidst a whirl of sparks and smoke.

In contrast to these brief eye-catching, spectacular scenes, the Joseph episode is longer and deftly emphasizes the female gaze. Potiphar's wife's obsession with her slave is detailed in the voyeuristic pleasure she finds secretly watching him, alone in a darkened room gazing silently through a grill, biting her bottom lip in excitement. The more psychological elements are also apparent when Pharaoh is shown remembering his dreams – a matte shot of running cows shown above his head, before animated stalks of wheat appear. The courtroom scene uses low and high angles to reinforce the power dynamics.

After such a striking beginning the second part of the film is less impressive, seemingly bearing the brunt of the cuts that accompanied subsequent re-releases. The Exodus episodes feature Moses with horns like Michelangelo's statue (1513–15) and whose staff is more reminiscent of a magic wand than the mighty staffs wielded in DeMille's two adaptations. Then a lacklustre crossing of the Red Sea jumps to a pagan orgy featuring the Queen of Sheba and an array of over-the-top headdresses, perhaps the inspiration behind various scenes from *Solomon and Sheba* (1959).

Despite the cuts, the voiceover, the cropped footage and the mediocre acting,[3] there is so much to be appreciated in the rest of the film, so it is a shame that it has received so little attention. Even though what we have is only a pale reflection of what once was, *La Sacra Bibbia* deserves to be better remembered.

Notes

1 Originally released in the UK as *The Dawn of the World*, as advertised in *Illustrated London News*, London. 2 April 1921, pp. 138–9.
2 The original film was advertised as '12 Reels' long (between two and three hours) in *Exhibitors Herald*, 1 April 1922, p. 18.
3 Gariazzo held actors in low regard saying they have 'no soul' ands calling them puppets in his book *Il teatro muto* (Turin: Lattes, 1919), p. 256. Available online: <https://openlibrary.org/borrow/ia/ilteatromuto00gariuoft> (accessed 19 Dec. 2021).

Der Galiläer (*The Passion Play*)
Germany, 1921 – 54 mins
Dimitri Buchowetzki

DIRECTOR Dimitri Buchowetzki
PRODUCERS Adolf Faßnacht,
Georg Faßnacht
SCREENPLAY Dimitri
Buchowetzki, Stats Hagen
CINEMATOGRAPHY
Arpad Viragh
PRODUCTION COMPANY
The Faßnacht Company
MAIN CAST Elsa Dietler, Adolf
Faßnacht, Georg Faßnacht, Eva
Gühne, Ernst Hardt, Heinrich
Spennrath, Ludwig Stiehl

Of all the silent Jesus films, *Der Galiläer* is the most wonderfully composed; it is also the most unmistakably antisemitic. The poisonous atmosphere that developed in interwar Germany, and many other parts of Europe, was fed and watered by works such as these. The tragic conclusion of this trajectory means we should take all the more notice of such a film not less. Had we done so, perhaps church leaders would not have so easily shrugged off *The Passion of the Christ*'s antisemitism.

Producer Adolf Faßnacht as Jesus in *Der Galiläer* (1921).

Der Galiläer is all the more pernicious for its seductively beautiful images. The film cuts between artful close-ups and perfectly composed wide shots.[1] The close-ups are all the finer for being wordless, pausing for enough time to give proper consideration to the characters' thoughts. The wider shots, often featuring hundreds of extras, are grand, vibrant and chaotic. By the time Kaiphas whips up the Jewish crowd in the marketplace and leads them to appeal Pilate's initial decision, such that a riot seems imminent. Pilate's fear is evident, his capitulation made all the more comprehensible by such distortion.

As with many other biblical films, many compositions echo Christian art, but here, each pose is held for a little more time, the pace is a little more stately and the tone is a little more graceful. Yet even this has its dark side, suggesting continuity between the historic church and the depiction before us.

The antisemitic elements build as the film goes on, but the emphasis on the crowd is there from the start. The film begins with celebrations on the street at the news that Jairus's daughter has been healed and Jesus' triumphal entry meets with huge acclaim. The crowd follow Jesus to the temple but are cowed by Kaiphas and his high priests reasserting their authority.

Visually the depiction of Kaiphas and these other Jewish leaders underlines what the film suggests throughout. Not only are they often shot from below, allowing their faces to loom over the camera, but the actors themselves seem to comply with numerous antisemitic stereotypes. The actors distort their wizened features arching eyebrows, flaring nostrils and rubbing their hands.[2] Their headwear is topped with horns, visually reproducing the 'children of the devil' accusation that has proved so troublesome.[3]

Following the Last Supper Jesus is arrested, tried and brought before Pilate. When Pilate fails to deliver the required verdict, Kaiaphas takes to the streets and 'whips' the 'crowd into a blood-thirsty frenzy' to pressure Pilate into giving them the verdict he wants.[4] The ease with which Kaiphas is able to manipulate the Jewish crowd, and the fear they evoke in hardened soldiers like Pilate, is deeply troubling as is the way the crowd calls down Jesus' blood on them and their children. The crowd remains on the verge of a riot all along the road to Golgotha, only dispersing when the earth quakes and the temple curtain is torn asunder. Compared to all this, the crucifixion itself is curiously brief, further suggestion as to the filmmakers' intentions.

In some ways the Holocaust seems so distant it's difficult to believe it occurred in the middle of cinema history and that film became a tool which perpetuated and intensified stereotypes, contributing to the dehumanisation of Jewish people that led to this most horrific act of violence against them. Films like *Der Galiläer* were part of this awful process. It is critical that such lessons are learned.

Notes

1   Reinhold Zwick , '*Der Galiläer* (1921) and *I.N.R.I.* (1923)' in David J. Shepherd (ed.), *The Silents of Jesus in the Cinema (1897–1927)* (New York/London: Routledge, 2016), p. 213.

2   Adele Reinhartz, *Jesus of Hollywood*. (Oxford/New York: Oxford University Press, 2007), p. 13.

3   Though Katie Turner demonstrates the horned hat evolved from a 'split' bishop's mitre in *Costuming Christ: Re-dressing First-Century 'Jews' and 'Christians' in Passion Dramas* (London: Bloomsbury 2022).

4   Reinhartz, *Jesus of Hollywood*, p. 239.

Salomé
USA, 1922 – 72 mins
Charles Bryant and Alla Nazimova

DIRECTORS Charles Bryant, Alla Nazimova
PRODUCER Alla Nazimova
SCREENPLAY Alla Nazimova, Natacha Rambova, Oscar Wilde
CINEMATOGRAPHY Charles Van Enger
MUSIC Carlos U. Garza, Richard O'Meara
PRODUCTION COMPANY Nazimosa Productions
MAIN CAST Nigel De Brulier, Rose Dione, Mitchell Lewis, Alla Nazimova

Alla Nazimova was a leading figure of 1920s cinema, not just in her native Russia, but throughout the film-viewing world. An actor of some repute, she also wrote, edited, produced and directed. Indeed, whilst her husband Charles Bryant took the directing credit for *Salomé*, many consider Nazimova at least a co-director. Certainly she and her friend Natacha Rambova oversaw the film's art-direction and design of the sets, costumes and remarkable headpieces which were based on Aubrey Beardsley's original illustrations of Oscar Wilde's play.

Nazimova (second right) as *Salomé* (1922).

Whilst the film lacks Strauss' music and omits most of Wilde's text, it is very much an adaptation of Wilde's 1891 play, itself influenced by works from the New Testament to Flaubert and Moreau. Nazimova called her film 'a pantomime of the play' and Wilde's plot and sense of decadence are clearly at the forefront.[1] Much of the film's dialogue belongs to him, and the film retains the occasional Wilde innovation, such as calling John the Baptist 'Jokanaan'.

Furthermore, the play's embrace of diverse genders and sexualities is continued. Sources testify to Nazimova as lesbian or bisexual,[2] and her bold choices of costume and set design created one of the earliest pioneering works of queer cinema.[3] With its androgynous characters, stylized costumes and phallic props, *Salomé* is arguably the most camp of all biblical films and countless subsequent productions suggest its influence, from 1933's *Lot in Sodom*, through to more macho efforts such as *The Passion of the Christ* (2004).

The visual impact of Navimova's work is breathtaking, with avant-garde, art deco sets and strangely alien-esque costumes. Herod looks like a cross between Bacchus and a circus clown; Herodias like one of Macbeth's witches; and Nazimova like she had stepped off the set of *Metropolis* (1927), itself still five years from completion.

At the heart of the film are themes of desire, rejection and unrequited love. Herod desires his step-daughter, oblivious to the pain this causes Herodias. But Salomé has no eyes for him, only for John, who considers himself too pure for the sultry dancer, gazing only towards the heavens. Meanwhile two of Herod's servants (Narraboth the Syrian guard and Herodias's unnamed page) are similarly entangled. Narraboth has eyes only for the moon – which looms large in numerous shots. The page keeps an overly-attached eye on the princess. Salomé is oblivious to both. In a desperate attempt to keep her away from the Baptist, Narraboth takes his own life, but when his body falls at Salomé's feet, she barely even notices, stepping over his corpse in her futile attempt to win a kiss from the prophet. Only after Jokanaan's head has been removed from his shoulders does the princess finally steal her kiss, an act which so enrages Herod that he immediately has her executed.

Sadly, the film's pioneering expression of sexuality proved similarly fatal to its performance at the box office. Its unconventional style, tales of off-set gatherings and rumours that it had 'employed only homosexual actors',[4] hurt the film while the industry was still reeling from the Arbuckle accusations.[5] Yet somehow it was this film, rather than some of Nazimova's more commercially successful films, that survived. Perhaps this was because it became cherished by a community that was still very much underground in the early 1920s, but perhaps it was also because this film, more than any of her others, best expressed her purity of artistic vision and single-minded determination to make a film the way she imagined it.

Notes

1 David Thomson, *The New Biographical Dictionary of Film* (London: Little Brown, [1975] 2002), p. 624.

2 Gavin Lambert, *Nazimova: A Biography* (New York: Alfred A Knopf, 1997), p. 162

3 While not all those of gender and sexual minorities are happy with the use of the word 'queer'. Nevertheless, 'Queer Cinema' has become the dominant term used to label the movement by GSM filmmakers and critics.

4 Kenneth Anger, *Hollywood Babylon* (London: Arrow Books, [1975] 1986), p. 113.

5 Roscoe Arbuckle was an actor who was accused of rape and murder. By the time he was acquitted the papers had ruined his career and weaponized the case in their fight against the movie industry.

Sodom und Gomorrha (*The Queen of Sin*)
Germany/Austria, 1922 – 124 mins
Michael Curtiz

DIRECTOR Michael Curtiz
PRODUCERS Alexander Kolowrat, Arnold Pressburger
SCREENPLAY Michael Curtiz, Ladislaus Vajda
CINEMATOGRAPHY Franz Planer, Gustav Ucicky
MUSIC Kazimir Boyle, Bernd Schultheis, Stefan Traub
PRODUCTION COMPANY Sascha-Film
MAIN CAST Lucy Doraine, Georg Reimers, Victor Varconi, Erika Wagner

The 1920s witnessed two rivals battling for supremacy of the biblical epic. These days it's Cecil B. DeMille who is most associated with the genre, but in as the silent era drew to a close, his output was overshadowed by another: a Hungarian named Mihaly Kertesz.

Today Kertesz (who changed his name to Curtiz when the Warners brought him to Hollywood) is remembered for *The Adventures of Robin Hood* (1938) and *Casablanca* (1942), but he was involved in four 1920s

Lucy Doraine from the modern story in *Sodom und Gomorrha* (1922).

biblical epics including *Sodom und Gomorrha* (1922).[1] As with much of Curtiz's biblical and non-biblical output at this stage, the film used the multiple connected time periods format that had been popular since *An Unsullied Shield* (1913). *Sodom und Gomorrha* bears the strongest structure, producing a series of concentric circles by placing each new storyline as a dream inside the previous one, almost ninety years before *Inception* (2010).[2]

The structure is reinforced by Curtiz's repeated use of iris shots,reflecting both its concentric nature and its relation to sleep/dreams. The iris shots often anticipate a coming dream, or remind us that what we are witnessing is a dream not a (past) reality, but it also signifies the audience, literally sat in the darkness outside the circle, looking in. The initial transition from modern 'reality' to modern 'dream' is facilitated by a priest (Victor Varconi) lecturing the film's anti-hero Mary (Curtiz's wife Lucy Doraine).[3] Just as Varconi's priest wishes Mary to reform, so the film urges its audience to do likewise.

As the expressionist modern dream sequence dissolves into the spectacular sets of Sodom, Doraine is now recast as Lia, Lot's wife, and Varconi as the avenging angel. The film tweaks the original text to heighten the parallels between the modern and biblical stories. In the Bible, two angels visit Sodom and Lia is less amourous than her movie counterpart. Indeed, the arbitrary nature of God's punishment of her is one of the more shocking aspects of the text.

Indeed, it's this episode which provides one of the film's most outstanding moments. An intertitle boosts the tension by announcing the tragedy fully three minutes before it occurs. Eventually, Lia looks back, there's a sudden flash and she is turned into a pillar of salt. Smoke masks the jump-cut, but it's deftly executed and demonstrates Curtia's ability to produce a powerful visual sequence. Other moments similarly stand out, the smoke billowing through Astarte's temple, the water sploshing as sulphur rains down on Sodom.

The size and scale of the sets, and the scenes of their ultimate destruction are particularly remarkable and Curtiz's handling of crowds of extras hint at his future achievements in *Robin Hood* and his later swashbuckling films. Yet overall the film drags and it's hard to imagine its Roaring Twenties audience finding the harsh, angry, priest particularly appealing. *Sodom und Gomorrha* is notable for its sets, effects and structure, but it pales in comparison to Curtiz's later, greater, achievements.

Notes

1   Curtiz also directed *Die Sklavenkönigin* (The Moon of Israel, 1924) about Moses, *Noah's* Ark (1929) and was involved in Alexander Korda's *Samson und Delila* (1922).
2   Österreichische Filmarchiv have released a shorter 90-minute DVD of this film with an entirely different structure.

3   Fritzi Kramer, '*Sodom and Gomorrah* (1922): A Silent Film Review', *Movies Silently*, 24 November 2019. Available online: <https://moviessilently.com/2019/11/24/sodom-and-gomorrah-1922-a-silent-film-review/> (accessed 19 Dec. 2021).

The Ten Commandments
USA, 1923 – 131 mins
Cecil B. DeMille

DIRECTOR Cecil B. DeMille
PRODUCER Cecil B. DeMille
SCREENPLAY Jeanie Macpherson
CINEMATOGRAPHY Bert
Glennon, J. Peverell Marley,
Archie Stout, Fred Westerberg
EDITOR Anne Bauchens
MUSIC Edward Falck, Karl
Gutman, Hugo Riesenfeld,
Milan Roder, Lazare Saminsky
PRODUCTION COMPANY
Famous Players-Lasky
Corporation
MAIN CAST Julia Faye,
Theodore Roberts, Charles de
Rochefort, Estelle Taylor

In the early 1920s Hollywood was reeling from the Roscoe Arbuckle affair and DeMille was out of ideas. Having appealed to magazine readers to submit ideas one suggestion stood out 'You cannot break the Ten Commandments, they will break you'.[1] Arbuckle was cleared, but DeMille was inspired. Trusted screenwriter Jeanie MacPherson began writing the script.

The Commandments sharing the spotlight in *The Ten Commandments* (1923).

The film ultimately comprised of two halves: an opening prologue depicting the Israelites' exodus from Egypt; and a modern day morality play reinforcing the importance of the Commandments today. Martha MacTavish lectures her two sons about the Commandments, only for the younger one, Dan, to rebel by breaking them all. He, like the Egyptian soldiers, ends up in a watery grave. His more even-handed older brother John is ultimately paralleled with Jesus.

DeMille eventually persuaded his producers to invest in gigantic sets, now buried near Guadalupe in the Californian desert,[2] which are as imposing as Pastrone's and Griffith's. But DeMille's greatest strength in scenes like this is his ability to capture the small stories of individuals and extrapolate them across a crowd of thousands. As the Hebrews left the Promised Land, DeMille's experimented with Two-Strip Technicolor to highlight their emotions, giving the scene extra potency by casting 'orthodox Russian, Polish and Palestinian Jews' as extras.[3] Equally memorable, however, is the pre-production code orgy taking place at the foot of Mount Sinai, which, again, switches between individual narratives and the big picture.

DeMille's legacy was cast forever. Yet his love of orgy scenes, special effects and grand spectacle overshadow his subtler achievements. His use of lighting in the film is particularly effective. For all its size and grandeur, Pharaoh's imposing palace is shot as dark and dingy (despite reproductions of artefacts from Tutankhamun's recently-discovered tomb). In contrast, the children of Israel are predominantly found in the bright sunlight.

Theodore Roberts played Moses, his ninth and final film with DeMille, stretching back to the days of DeMille's own acting career. Roberts portrays Moses as supremely confident, assured in the certain success of his mission. He first appears striding into Pharaoh's throne room in the most positive light possible – far closer to the prince of the realm he was brought up as, than the doubting shepherd at the burning bush. The Bible's complex Moses, an impetuous murderer who gives God a string of excuses when called, is whitewashed with faux-piety. Moses' major function here is that of a lawgiver. The Commandments themselves are the movie's biggest star – the film is, after all, named in their honour.

DeMille's opening titles argue that had humanity followed the Ten Commandments, The Great War might never have occurred. Thus the tablet of stone motif occurs throughout. In addition to their role as actual tablets in part one, they also appear as a backdrop to the intertitles. In a climatic late, scene a tablets-shaped light shines, supernaturally, onto some rocks, both as a warning to, and a judgment on, Dan. Yet God's actions here – drowning thousands of Egyptians and massacring worshippers the Golden Calf – seem no less reprehensible than those in war. John's more humane pleading for moderation and DeMille's penultimate scene of Jesus, defuse this to some degree. Nevertheless, the modern story misfires compared to the film's spectacular prologue.

Nine years later Paramount produced a film called *Forgotten Commandments* around a third of which was lifted from DeMille's film.[4] Almost twenty-five years later, DeMille would remake the story to produce his best-known movie. Yet, even given the remake's fame, many still regard his silent version to be the greater film.

Notes

1   Cecil B. DeMille, *Autobiography*, edited by Donald Hayne (Englewood Cliffs, New Jersey: Prentice-Hall, 1959), p. 228.

2   DeMille, *Autobiography*, p. 231.

3   Charles Higham, Cecil B. DeMille (New York: Dell, 1976), p. 97.

4   Richard C. Campbell and Michael R. Pitts, *The Bible on Film: A Checklist, 1897–1980* (Metuchen, NJ, and London: Scarecrow Press, 1981), pp. 21–2.

Ben-Hur: A Tale of the Christ
USA, 1925 – 143 mins
Fred Niblo and Charles Brabin

DIRECTORS Charles Brabin,
Fred Niblo
PRODUCERS Samuel Goldwyn,
Louis B. Mayer, Irving Thalberg
SCREENPLAY Lew Wallace,
June Mathis, Katherine Hilliker,
Carey Wilson, H.H. Caldwell
CINEMATOGRAPHY
Clyde De Vinna, René Guissart,
Percy Hilburn, Karl Struss,
Paul Kerschner
EDITOR Lloyd Nosler
MUSIC William Axt, David
Mendoza
PRODUCTION COMPANY
Metro-Goldwyn-Mayer
MAIN CAST Betty Bronson,
Francis X. Bushman, May
McAvoy, Ramon Novarro

For many, Fred Niblo's 1925 version is the best of several adaptations of General Lew Wallace's nineteenth-century novel. At the time, Wallace's story of a Jewish prince condemned to slavery by his childhood friend was the biggest-selling North American novel. Despite its weaknesses, the novel's popularity led to a sensational, long-running stage show and a 1907 film which, while little more than a chariot race, was sued for breaching copyright. Abraham Erlanger acquired the film rights and eventually the Goldwyn Company adapted it.

Francis X. Bushman and Ramon Novarro in a still from *Ben-Hur* (1925).

Aiming for prestige, Niblo utilised the emerging Two-Strip Technicolor process. Most of the film is black and white, but colour was used for key sequences, including some featuring Jesus. However, the film stuck with black and white for Jesus' sentencing, and his walk to the cross, as if stressing the sombreness of these moments.

Two scenes stand out for particular brilliance. The first features a sea battle between pirates and a Roman slave galley, filmed during a legendarily disastrous shoot in Mussolini's Italy. It used life-sized, seaworthy boats in an audacious piece of film-making, but may have cost the lives of desperate-for-work Italian extras who were unable to swim. The other is the equally staggering chariot race, begun in Italy, but reshot from scratch when production retreated to California's Culver City. A team of 800 took four months to build the set; 42 camera operators were employed on the first day alone; and around 200,000 feet of film were recorded.[1]

The sets are astounding, both in their size and their detail. The groundbreaking use of miniatures in combination with the life-size sets, enabled the camera to pan rather than remain static. Yet the tension is ratcheted up by a variety of close-ups, cut into the wide shots by Lloyd Nosler's note-perfect editing. The low shots, looking up from the ground are particularly striking. The chariot scene is 'among the most valuable in motion picture history': the first time a director not only realized 'the potential of the cinema', but also 'possessed the courage and skill' to fulfil it.[2]

In contrast to some of the more racist biblical films of the era, it's noticeable how this film emphasizes the Jewish elements of the story, such as Ben-Hur wearing a skull cap in the opening scenes. Similarly, it's noticeable that when Pilate blames 'the mob' for Jesus' death, they self-identify as being from many nations, deftly avoiding culpability being placed on 'the Jews' alone. It also retains significantly more of the biblical material from Wallace's novel than the 1959 version, citing verses from the Gospels in the intertitles.

The film is not without its weak points. Many biblical moments are marred by piety, notably stipulations originating from Wallace himself requiring Jesus to be depicted as a beam of light.[3] The scenes of the Last Supper and Jesus' trial particularly suffer in this respect, as if all the available creativity was poured into working out how to hide Jesus' face. More critically, the final half hour drags, a problem with bringing Wallace's *story* to life, as opposed to one circumventing his aesthetic objections.

Nevertheless, the story's reputation, enhanced by the success of Wyler's 1959 version has led to something of a rebirth in the 21st century with a mini-series adaptation in 2010 and a further cinematic adaptation in 2016. Neither are a patch on Niblo's version, however, which remains captivating today and endures as one of silent cinema's greatest achievements.

Notes

1   Kevin Brownlow, *The Parade's Gone By* (London: Columbus Books, 1989), pp. 408–9.

2   Brownlow, *Parade*, p. 409.

3   Ray E. Boomhower, *The Sword & the Pen: A Life of Lew Wallace* (Indianapolis: Indiana Historical Society Press, 2005) p. 140.

The King of Kings
USA, 1927 – 155 mins/112 mins*
Cecil B. DeMille

DIRECTOR Cecil B. DeMille
PRODUCER Cecil B. DeMille
SCREENPLAY
Jeanie Macpherson
CINEMATOGRAPHY
J. Peverell Marley
EDITORS Anne Bauchens,
Harold McLernon
MUSIC Hugo Riesenfeld
PRODUCTION COMPANY
Modern Sound Pictures Inc.
MAIN CAST Dorothy Cumming,
James Neill, Joseph Schildkraut,
Joseph Striker, Ernest Torrence,
H. B. Warner

By the time *The Kings of Kings* was released in 1927, cinema had been around for thirty years. It was Cecil B. DeMille's fifty-first film, though incredibly, at this point in his career, he was known mainly for melodramas and westerns.[1]

DeMille was one of the most pivotal characters in the early studio era and an unusual talent. He could oil-up Charlton Heston, stick him in chains and claim he was Moses; or begin a film about Jesus with Mary Magdalene in a gold coiled-bra, stroking her pet leopard. It's easy to deride DeMille's mix of titillation and

Still from The King of Kings (1927) showing Jesus on the Via Dolorosa.

piety, or see it as being cynical, but he saw little contradiction. The son of a 'flamboyant actress' and 'bookish lay minister' DeMille's 'conflict between faith and trash was very real for him; he loved both'.[2] Indeed DeMille was critical of those who read the Gospels 'through the stained glass telescope … between us and the men and women of flesh and blood who lived and wrote the Bible'.[3]

The screenplay was written by one of DeMille's most trusted collaborators, Jeanie MacPherson. It begins neither with Jesus birth, nor his baptism, nor even at the start of Holy Week, but in the midst of his ministry. In that sense it's different from any of the Gospels, or the earliest creedal confessions. MacPherson's screenplay blends elements of all four gospels together citing each in the various subtitles, though often wildly out of context. It opens with reference to the Great Commission (from Matthew's Gospel); focuses its portrayal on Jesus-the-healer of Luke's Gospel; and depicts a young boy called Mark, who, it implies, will write the earliest Gospel. Meanwhile, its lighting emphasizes John's 'Light of the World' motif. Our first sighting of Jesus comes through the eyes of a blind girl as her eyes, miraculously, begin to open.

Another DeMille's regular, H.B. Warner, played Jesus. At fifty-one he remains the oldest actor to play the lead in a major Jesus movie. Modern audiences find him overly paternal but at the time he was significantly more human and approachable than any previous celluloid Jesus. DeMille, however, insisted Warner remained in character during his time on set, wary of bad publicity were Warner caught on a drinking spree. After some Jewish groups voiced concern over antisemitism, DeMille made changes, placing culpability for Jesus' death solely with Caiaphas, although some elements remain concerning.

It's easy to dismiss the film's soft-focus piety or moments of over-the-topness, but as a filmmaker DeMille doesn't get the credit he is due. The picture is full of memorable images: Magdalene's zebra-powered chariot; the little girl's doll which Jesus fixes with a piece of reed; an awe inspiring sequence *en route* to Gethsemane, where coloured flames lap against a blue-toned background; and the expressionistic portrayal of various miracles. DeMille reproduced 300 paintings in the film going to huge lengths to perfect the lighting and used Two-Strip Technicolor in the opening and penultimate scenes. The shot of the sandstorm as Jesus dies required considerable technical expertise and the intricate designs of the massive sets still impress.

The film's box office success meant screenings continued for years, well into the sound era. Missionaries took it with them abroad leaving a delighted DeMille boasting that 'more people have been told the story of Jesus of Nazareth through *The King of Kings* than through any other single work, except the Bible itself'.[4] DeMille donated his entire earnings to charity.[5]

Just months after the release of *The King of Kings* talking pictures enveloped the movie industry, yet DeMille decision not to introduce sound for the film's 1928 re-release perhaps explains why it is fondly remembered as one of the silent era's final classics.

Notes

1   The original 155 minute 1927 release was cut to 112 minutes the following year and only recently reissued in full.
2   Fritzi Kramer, '(@MoviesSilently) On Cecil B DeMille', *Twitter* 12 August 2016. Available at <https://twitter.com/MoviesSilently/status/764197127815692288> (accessed 19 Dec. 2021).

3   Cecil B. DeMille, *Autobiography*, edited by Donald Hayne (Englewood Cliffs, New Jersey: Prentice-Hall, 1959), p. 365.
4   DeMille, *Autobiography*, p. 258.
5   DeMille *Autobiography*, p. 252n1

Noah's Ark
USA, 1928 – 100 mins
Michael Curtiz

DIRECTOR Michael Curtiz
PRODUCER Darryl F. Zanuck
SCREENPLAY De Leon Anthony,
Anthony Coldeway,
Darryl F. Zanuck
CINEMATOGRAPHY
Barney McGill, Hal Mohr
EDITOR Harold McCord
MUSIC Alois Reiser
PRODUCTION COMPANY
Warner Bros.
MAIN CAST Noah Beery,
Dolores Costello, Louise
Fazenda, George O'Brien

Noah's Ark arrived just as the silent age was drawing to a close, accompanied by a pitter-patter of talkies which became a deluge. To bridge the gap, studios revamped any incomplete silent productions to utilise the new technology. Like Hitchcock's *Blackmail* (1929), director Michael Curtiz added several lines of spoken dialogue and synchronized sound effects to complement the visuals.

As with previous 1920s epics, the historical footage is just a fantasy sequence, re-emphasizing the modern story. While a brief prologue features footage of Noah, a statue of Jesus and a montage of stock market

Still from Hebrew Bible sequence in *Noah's Ark* (1928).

clips, the story proper starts in 1914 with a train crash – the first of three catastrophes. Marie, a young German, is pulled from the wreckage by buddies Travis and Al. Travis and Marie fall instantly in love and marry, but the war separates them. When, four years later, a Russian passenger from the train recognizes Marie she finds herself in front of Travis' firing squad, but an explosion intervenes leaving them trapped by the rubble alongside an old preacher who retells the story of Noah.

As with Curtiz's *Sodom und Gomorrha* (1922) The actors from the film's first half take similar roles in the second, so the same actor plays Noah and the old preacher; Al and Travis pair up as Ham and Japheth; Marie doubles as Japheth's sweetheart, Miriam; and the Russian spy becomes the evil, idol-worshipping, King Nephilim. Miriam is chosen as a sacrifice to Nephilim's God, Jaguth. When Japheth attempts a rescue he is enslaved, only to be freed by the flood's arrival. Once the pair are safely aboard the ark, the film reverts once again to the modern story.

Curtiz's three previous biblical movies, along with other 1920s epics,[1] set new standards for production scale, and *Noah's Ark* follows suit. The size and detail of the sets is magnificent and the flood scenes, with torrents of water appearing from above and below, are truly momentous.[2] The animals rush towards the ark in a masterful sequence which captures the chaotic urgency, while remaining natural and realistic, as if the animals are individually responding to God rather than Noah.

Curtiz draws on an array of visual and textual references to other stories involving biblical characters such as Jesus, Moses, Lot, Samson and Elijah. Golden calves, burning bushes and blinded slaves heaving millstones appear with surprising regularity in Curtiz's 'pastiche of the best-known spectacles of the biblical tradition'.[3] At one point Noah watches God words appear on a huge stone book, recalling DeMille's *Ten Commandments* (1923). As temples crumble and water drops from above like lava, words taken from the Lord's Prayer appear the intertitles.

Unfortunately, in the midst of the biblical allusions, heroic rescues and destruction of pagan temple, the actual story of Noah is left somewhat high and dry. Aside from Japheth's rescue of Miriam, there's little characterization or human interest, the Noah episode just gets buried under its own technical proficiency. It's a shame because some sequences are incredibly well-executed. It was to be Curtiz's final biblical epic and the last Hollywood feature solely about Noah for over 85 years.

Notes

1   Curtiz also directed *Sodom und Gomorrah* (1922), Moses film *Die Sklavenkönigin* (The Moon of Israel, 1924) and was involved in Alexander Korda's *Samson und Delila* (1922).

2   Tragically this archetypal disaster movie went too far and several extras drowned whilst filming these scenes.

3   David J. Shepherd, *The Bible on Silent Film: Spectacle, Story and Scripture in the Early Cinema* (Cambridge: Cambridge University Press, 2013), p. 288.

Lot in Sodom
USA, 1933 – 28 mins
Melville Webber and James Sibley Watson

DIRECTORS Melville Webber, James Sibley Watson
PRODUCERS Bernard O'Brien, James Sibley Watson, Melville Webber, Alec Wilder, Remsen Wood
CINEMATOGRAPHY James Sibley Watson
EDITORS Jolanda Benvenuti, Laurent Quaglio
MUSIC Louis Siegel
MAIN CAST Friedrich Haak, Dorthea House, Hildegarde Watson, Lewis Whitbeck

Both *Lot in Sodom* and Webber and Sibley Watson's *The Fall of the House of Usher* (1928) were significant contributions to the avant-garde/early experimental movement of the late 1920s and early 1930s which rejected narrative as oppressive. Relatively little material remains regarding their life and work, but *Lot in*

Gazing on the male body in *Lot in Sodom* (1933).

Sodom was arguably 'the most commercially successful avant-garde film of the era'.[1] Furthermore, they were pioneers in queer cinema in an age when homosexuality was still illegal.

Lot in Sodom is essentially a silent film, originally available with atonal music by Louis Siegel and today with an excellent alternative modern soundtrack by Hands of Ruin. It's marked by expressionistic sets, superimposed shots, strange camera angles, floating text, kaleidoscopic images and various other experimental techniques. Cuts are often abrupt, and often the connection between the two shots is not immediately obvious. The editing is reminiscent of *Man with a Movie Camera* (1929). The sets of *Das Cabinet des Dr. Caligari* (1920). The filmmakers often superimpose the same symbolic image onto a shot several times, such as an array of naked Sodomite torsos. Indeed, just as Watson and Webber's film is a celebration of the formal potential of cinema, it's also a loving tribute to the human – and predominantly male – form which has fascinated for artists for as long as art has existed.

While *Lot in Sodom* ultimately ends with the fiery destruction of its inhabitants, clearly the filmmakers are rooting for the losing team. The contrast between Lot and the Sodomites, both in terms of looks and of how they are filmed, is stark. The Sodomites are all youthful, dynamic and attractive. In contrast, Lot looks like a cross between an Assyrian Bas Relief and an antisemitic stereotype. He is comparatively old and unattractive, heavily clothed in contrast to his townspeople and the camera spends far less time lingering on him, than it does on his neighbours. Alina Dunbar points out that 'in contrast to the angels and the Sodomites, who are nearly always featured in either medium or full-shots, Lot is frequently cast on either the right or the left side of the frame, in such as way as to suggest that he does not have the power to fill the screen by himself'.[2]

Lot himself appears somewhat conflicted. At one point the film cuts from a shot of Lot in the dark to an intertitle that reads 'How long shall I take counsel in my soul, having sorrow in my heart?', yet, as Grossman observes Lot 'never moves his mouth, in defiance of silent film conventions...the film "speaks" through an intertitle while the character remains totally silent, splitting in a surprising way the cinematic soul'.[3]

As events come to a head, Lot raises his hands to God in desperation, only to receive the terrifying answer 'withhold not even thy daughter', shown not as an intertitle, but superimposed over the image. An array of Latin phrases follow in similar fashion, as if floating on the screen, their meaning unclear: *Non Tacta* (untouched), *Mulier* (woman), *Templum Est* (the temple).

Given the most famous element of the story from Genesis, it is no surprise to find that this sense of internal conflict also extends to Lot's wife. Eventually an angel steps in to intervene, rays of light shine from his chest and Lot and his wife and daughter escape, but of course Lot's wife looks back and turns into a pillar of salt. As she undergoes her metamorphosis, images of the tormented Sodomites are superimposed over her, linking her punishment with her sympathy for the city. As an image it's provocative, challenging and one that only unveils the fullness of its meaning on multiple viewings, so typical of the film itself.

Notes

1   Jan-Christopher Horak, 'A neglected genre: James Sibley Watson's avant-garde industrial films', *Film History*, vol. 20, 2008, p. 41.

2   Alina Dunbar, 'Lot in Sodom: Reading Film Against the Grain', *CurnBlog* 16 May 2014. Available online: <http://curnblog.com/2014/05/16/lot-sodom-reading-film-grain/> (accessed 19 Dec. 2021).

3   Andrew Grossman, 'Tomatoes Another Day: The Improbable Ideological Subversion of James Sibley Watson and Melville Webber', *Bright Lights Film Journal* 28 November 2014. Available online: <http://brightlightsfilm.com/tomatoes-another-day-improbable-ideological-subversion-james-sibley-watson-melville-webber/> (accessed 19 Dec. 2021).

Golgotha (*Behold the Man*)
France, 1935 – 95 mins
Julien Duvivier

DIRECTOR Julien Duvivier
SCREENPLAY Julien Duvivier
CINEMATOGRAPHY
Jules Kruger
EDITOR Marthe Poncin
MUSIC Jacques Ibert
PRODUCTION COMPANY
Ichtys Films
MAIN CAST Harry Baur, Jean
Gabin, Charles Granval, Robert
Le Vigan

Golgotha, the first major Jesus film of the sound era, was produced on a grand scale, yet captures something deeper, mysterious and more spiritual than its silent predecessors.[1] The opening scene, of Jesus' triumphal entry, typifies the difference. Duvivier teases the audience showing the hustle and bustle of the crowd, Jewish leaders discussing recent events, the action at a distance, and even a shot of the crowd from Jesus' point-of-view, but delays showing Jesus himself. This intriguing choice draws the audience into the story, involving them in the crowd straining to see him.

The camera amongst the crowd in *Golgotha* (1935).

When Jesus finally appears on camera, ten minutes into the film, he is at a distance, shot from a low angle, almost obscured by his disciples. The momentary confusion gives the viewer the impression of being present, as if discovering Jesus for the first time. Caught in the crowd, nudging ineffectively towards the action, hoping to catch a glimpse of the man everyone is chattering about. His distant figure can only be made out seconds before he disappears into the temple.

Once inside, Duvivier delivers the film's finest sequence, and one of the most memorable scenes of any Jesus film, as Jesus drives out the money-changers. Several, quick, intercut shots prefigure the action as coins are swept from an off-screen table and crash onto the floor. Action and reaction shots follow swiftly, before the sequence culminates in a single, long take where camera weaves through the palisades of the temple in Jesus' wake, straining to catch him as he zigzags between stalls. Jesus himself is only rarely within the frame as the camera tracks round capturing the buzz, and chaos, of the incident, in a way which no other Jesus film has managed.

Like the earliest filmed passion plays – *Golgotha* focuses on the events immediately before Jesus' death. Most of the dialogue is amongst the Jewish authorities, or between them and Pontius Pilate (played by French superstar Jean Gabin).[2] Released during the rise of Nazism there are various indications of the film's antisemitism,[3] not least the presence of Nazi-esque salutes and the casting of fascist party member Robert Le Vigan as Jesus.[4]

Yet despite the film's other title *Ecce Homo* (Behold the Man),[5] Duvivier emphasizes the mystery around Jesus, focussing on his divinity more than most Jesus biopics, investing beautifully understated events with a deep sense of transcendence. When soldiers arriving in Gethsemane confirm they are seeking Jesus, his calmly spoken 'I am he' gently bowls them over, an understated, low-key, indication of his divinity.

Such subtlety manifests elsewhere, in the range of reactions shown to Jesus' torture; or the muted indications in Herod's ruthless mocking of his desperate desire to gain the approval of his (already pliant) courtiers. On the *Via Dolorosa*, the camera again focuses on diverse reactions amongst the crowd. Even as he stumbles towards the cross, Jesus is both hassled by children throwing stones at him and pressed by the sick for healing. Once there, he is crucified, dies and is buried. The sealing of the tomb is shown from the inside, thus completing Jesus' passion the way it began – from Jesus' point of view. A beautiful but effective shot of the risen Jesus closes the film, embodying the way *Golgotha* combines the ordinary with the extra-ordinary, downplaying the moments where many other Jesus films have opted to ratchet up the spectacle, and investing them with a credibility which witnesses to the reality of the world in which we live.

Notes

1   Franco Zeffirelli said of 'all the films on Jesus' *Golgotha* was 'the most beautiful'. *Franco Zeffirelli's Jesus: A Spiritual Diary*. Trans. by Willis J. Egan, S.J. (New York: Harper & Row, 1984), p. 4.

2   Peter Malone, *Screen Jesus: Portrayals of Christ in Television and Film* (Lanham/Toronto/Plymouth, UK: Scarecrow Press, 2012), p. 32.

3   Aaron McMullan, 'Episode Two: "It Is Accomplished!"' *Mondo Christ Almighty* [podcast]. 26 April 2020. Available Online: <https://mondochristalmightypodcast.blogspot.com/2020/04/episode-two-it-is-accomplished.html> (accessed 19 Dec. 2021).

4   Carol Hebron, J*udas Iscariot: Damned or Redeemed – A Critical Examination of the Portrayal of Judas in Jesus Films (1902–2014)* (London: Bloomsbury T&T Clark, 2016), p. 88.

5   Malone, *Screen Jesus*, p. 30.

The Last Days of Pompeii
USA, 1935 – 96 mins
Ernest B. Schoedsack and Merian C. Cooper

DIRECTORS Ernest B. Schoedsack, Merian C. Cooper
PRODUCER Merian C. Cooper
SCREENPLAY Melville Baker, James Ashmore Creelman, Boris Ingster, Ruth Rose
CINEMATOGRAPHY J. Roy Hunt, Jack Cardiff
EDITOR Archie Marshek
MUSIC Roy Webb
PRODUCTION COMPANY RKO Radio Pictures
MAIN CAST Preston Foster, Alan Hale, Basil Rathbone, John Wood

Following their success with *King Kong* (1933), Ernest B. Schoedsack and Merian C. Cooper, teamed up for another display of iconic spectacle and ominous destruction with this somewhat overblown conflict between material wealth and spiritual salvation. The film's resemblance to either Edward Bulwer-Lytton's popular novel, or the historical events which it supposedly retells, are minor, but in the immediate aftermath of the Great Depression, its lessons about the tempestuous relationship between money and one's soul cut to the thematic heart of the biblical epic like no other.[1]

The film's protagonist, Marcus, transitions from a poor-but-good-hearted blacksmith; to a gladiator who retains enough compassion to adopt one of his foes' orphans; to someone who trains and promotes gladiators; before finally descending into capturing slaves for the arena. His downward journey is typified by slippery, small, steps of compromise, born out of desperation to pay his debts and provide for his adopted son Flavius. Heading to Judea to trade horses, Marcus befriends Pontius Pilate (Basil Rathbone) and makes his fortune, only for Flavius to suffer a near fatal accident.

In desperation, Marcus brings Flavius to Jesus. Seeking to avoid showing Jesus' face, the filmmakers shoot much of the healing sequence from Jesus' point-of-view. Marcus carries Flavius to the front of the crowd with his eyes, and those of the crowd, all transfixed on the camera/Jesus. The heavenly music swells, then a wide, reverse shot, from behind the crowd, captures the crowd with Jesus obligingly wandering off camera, leaving Marcus on his knees and Flavius back on his feet. By the time Marcus returns to Jerusalem Jesus is already being tried. A shell-shocked Pilate washes his hands and murmurs 'What have I done?'

The conflict between money and morality comes to a head in the final act back in Pompeii, where Marcus now enjoys a wealthy lifestyle, unaware that Flavius is secretly aiding runaway slaves. When Pilate visits on the eve of the great eruption, Pilate's shame re-surfaces, liberating Flavius' own ethereal recollections of Jesus and his anger at his father's lifestyle.

In the finest photographed scenes of entire film, Flavius visits the slaves' hiding place. The tight compositions and moody lighting perfectly supplement the slaves' fear and paranoia. Some are about to turn on him when the guards arrive and drag them all to Marcus' arena for the film's climatic disaster. If the film's title gives away the ending, the spectacular scenes of Vesuvius' eruption more than compensate, not least for the sheer scale of the destruction. While somewhat lacking in meaningfully human interactions, the shots of people drowning in the choppy waters as they attempt to escape the lava pouring down the mountain are nevertheless chilling. Wood describes such scenes of destruction as 'a ritual expression of lack of need' continuing 'having all that cash to throw away is a sign of (apparent) financial health. But actually throwing it away is a sign of moral health'.[2]

Flavius' accident causes Marcus to seek out Jesus in *The Last Days of Pompeii* (1935).

The impressive nature of these few final spectacular scenes is not enough, however, to rescue the film from its overly earnest performances, paper-thin characterizations and its extraordinary manipulation of the past'.[3] Making a giant gorilla both terrifying and sympathetic is one thing. Making a slave-trader appear human is entirely another. *Last Days* is ultimately more giant turkey than great ape.

Notes

1   Gerald E. Forshey, *American Religious and Biblical Spectaculars* (Westport, CT: Praeger, 1992), pp. 22–5.

2   Michael Wood, *America in the Movies*, Second edition (New York: Columbia University Press, 1989), p 178–182.

3   Maria Wyke, *Projecting the Past: Ancient Rome, Cinema and History* (London/New York: Routledge, 1997), p. 177.

The Green Pastures
USA, 1936 – 93 mins
Marc Connelly and William Keighley

DIRECTORS Marc Connelly, William Keighley
PRODUCERS Henry Blanke, Hal B. Wallis, Jack L. Warner
SCREENPLAY Marc Connelly, Sheridan Gibney, Roark Bradford
CINEMATOGRAPHY Hal Mohr
MUSIC Hall Johnson choir
PRODUCTION COMPANY Warner Bros.
MAIN CAST Eddie 'Rochester' Anderson, Rex Ingram, Oscar Polk, Frank H. Wilson

The Green Pastures was one of the few 1930s Hollywood films starring a solely African-American cast. Released almost twenty years before the civil rights movement it was one of the first films to portray God, so depicting him as an African-American was a radical step: no doubt why the Klu Klux Klan sought to ban the film, persuading many cinemas to boycott it.[1]

Yet for all the filmmakers' good intentions, it's painfully clear that writer Marc Connelly and his co-director William Keighley were white. Connelly's screenplay injects 'tenderness and reverence' into Roark

God confronts Cain in a promotional still from *The Green Pastures* (1935).

Bradford's novel *Ol' Man Adam an' His Chillun*,[2] but even at the time *The Afro-American* newspaper dismissed *Green Pastures* as 'caricature'.[3] Boycotts and protests greeted a 1951 re-release.[4] 'Plantation' movies such as this and *Hallelujah* (1929) 'embodied the paradox of Hollywood liberalism', giving African-American actors a voice, but only in stereotypical roles.[5] *Green Pastures*' reliance on stereotypes and exaggerated accents sticks out when compared to similar 'folk-religion' films made by African-American producers/directors such *as Heaven-Bound Travelers* (1935) and *The Blood of Jesus* (1941).

Green Pastures begins with children attending their 1930s Sunday school in the USA's Deep South. Hearing stories from the Hebrew Bible they re-imagine them in playful and anachronistic fashion. Heaven is transformed into a big fish-fry in the sky, hosted by a white-haired, smart-suited 'Da Lawd' (Rex Ingram). Needing more 'firmament' Da Lawd creates the earth, and takes his first trip there, passing through heaven's simple white fencing, down its grassy slopes, and through fluffy clouds to meet Adam (also Ingram, illustrating his creation in God's image) and Eve (suggesting for audiences today 'Mitochondrial Eve').

Whilst the scenes of Cain and Abel, and Noah are fairly straightforward, the film's handling of the Exodus is hugely disappointing. Moses leading his people to freedom from slavery was fundamental to the spirituals and the accompanying theology, even retaining significance in modern day Black Theology. Here such resonant associations are absent, presumably fearing the implications of associating Black plantation workers with the Hebrew slaves, putting the film closer to the wish fulfilment of white filmmakers than Black viewers. Only 'Go down Moses' rings out as the Exodus sequence draws to a close.

The prophets are condensed into a single incident before a freedom fighter called Hezdrel (also Ingram), tells Da Lawd he must learn mercy through suffering just as his people have. Strangely, Jesus remains off-screen, perhaps suggesting he is white, and that another white Heaven exists elsewhere.

Nevertheless, the fine work by some of the Black performers, which may otherwise have been lost, should be recognized. Eddie Anderson's comic timing as Noah, and Frank Wilson's world-weary dignity as Moses, both impress. Ingram's Da Lawd is the film's emotional core, holding it together while exuding the warmth and quiet authority of his cinematic successor, Morgan Freeman's 'God' in *Bruce Almighty* (2003). Hall Johnson's soundtrack, primarily comprising spirituals, is superb. Johnson's arrangements bring out the soulful, melancholy power of these traditional songs producing poignant dignity. The unified voices of the choir embody a harmony which powers the film's beating heart: the film's celestial vision is powerful because its heaven is expressed in community.

For all its prejudice, *Green Pastures* played a part in the, still ongoing, battle for racial equality. Connelly believed he was furthering the African-American cause and, while flawed, his work was in some senses, progressive. At its best, *Green Pastures* shows us what it means to be human; to hope and to dream of a better, more equal, world.

Notes

1   Richard C. Campbell and Michael R. Pitts, *The Bible on Film: A Checklist, 1897–1980* (Metuchen, NJ, and London: Scarecrow Press, 1981), p. 25.

2   Sterling A. Brown, *Negro Poetry and Drama* (New York: Atheneum, 1972 Reprint), p. 119.

3   Cited in Donald Bogle, *Toms, Coons, Mulattoes, Mammies, and Bucks: An Interpretative History of Blacks in American Films*, Fifth edition (New York/London: Bloomsbury, 2016), p. 59.

4   Ellen Christine Scott, 'Race and the Struggle for Cinematic Meaning: Film Production, Censorship, and African American Reception, 1940–1960', PhD Thesis (University of Michigan, 2007), p. 88.

5   Mark Winokur, 'The Green Pastures as an Allegory of Accommodation: Christ, Race, and the All-Black Musical', *Film & History: An Interdisciplinary Journal of Film and Television Studies, v*ol. 25 no. 1–2, 1995, p. 8.

Jesús de Nazareth (*Jesus of Nazareth*)
Mexico, 1942 – 86 mins
José Díaz Morales

DIRECTOR José Díaz Morales
PRODUCER Ramón Pereda
SCREENPLAY Alfonso Lapeña,
José Díaz Morales
CINEMATOGRAPHY
Víctor Herrera
EDITOR Juan José Marino
MUSIC Howard E. Randall,
Enrique Rodríguez
PRODUCTION COMPANY
Pereda Films
MAIN CAST José Baviera,
José Cibrián, Adriana Lamar,
Aurora Walker

Compared to the affluence of their North American counterparts, Mexico's relative poverty and Catholic history mean their Gospel adaptations have had a distinctly different feel. José Díaz Morales' *Jésus de Nazareth* from 1942 was one of their earliest biblical films, made in the aftermath of the Cristerio War – a Catholic uprising against the anti-Catholic restrictions brought in by President Calles. The war ended in 1929, but restrictions on public expressions of faith remained in place until the late 1930s. While even today, outdoor worship is only permitted with governmental approval in exceptional circumstances, 1940 saw professing Catholic, President Camacho, easing censorship of religious subjects.[1]

Jesus' baptism from *Jesús de Nazareth* (1942).

Seen through this lens, it's interesting that the film –directly supervised by the church – plays down the other-worldly elements of Jesus' life.[2] Jesus' birth and resurrection are omitted. He arrives as a man – initially seen only as a poor reflection on the water rather than a sold figure. His baptism is shot close-up, such that it's impossible to judge if the 'voice of heaven' issues a public pronouncement, or is solely in Jesus' mind. The film's two miracles, the healing of a blind man and the raising of Lazarus, are similarly ambiguous. Similarly, the film's final shot, following straight after the crucifixion, finds Jesus alive and certainly not the dust-covered peasant of before. But does this suggest Jesus has been resurrected or simply reflect his veneration by the church?

The scene with the woman accused of adultery is particularly telling. Initially Jesus is surrounded by the blind and the lame, but the disciples edge them out, physically separating them from him so he is free to tackle her case rather than heal the sick. This typifies how the film prioritizes the stories of women. In addition to this woman, Jesus also encounters the Samaritan woman at the well, and redeems Mary Magdalene (Adriana Lamar). Lamar's Magdalene does not feature particularly prominently, but Lamar gets top billing ahead of the Argentine actor José Cibrián playing Jesus. Here Magdalene is a wealthy woman and significantly not the woman accused of adultery. There are also separate roles for Mary and Martha, Veronica, and an unnamed courtesan. Furthermore, despite the brevity of the road to the cross scene, Jesus stops to deliver the warning to the woman of Jerusalem (Luke 23) and his mother and Magdalene are shown prominently at his crucifixion.

The woman at the well scene is particularly striking with its graceful establishing shot and its combination of close-ups and a variety of shots as the conversation develops. This is typical of the film's beautiful compositions, startling black and white imagery and quietly stripped down sincerity. Moreover, its numerous close-ups are all the more engaging thanks to Cibrián's sensitive but restrained performance. He is not the classically good looking hero that typified so many of the Hollywood Jesus films which followed. Instead there's compassion and a deep mournfulness in the eyes of this rather introverted Jesus. The clearing of the temple scene is another gem: an opening tracking shot captures four or five brief stories in a wordless thirty seconds; a pause to focus on the sounds of the animals rather than the human activity; then, in a moment, Jesus goes from tenderly stroking a tethered lamb, to taking the rope that bound it, fashioning a whip and scattering its abusers.

In a way as much as Morales' film draws on DeMille, it also points the way towards Pasolini. While the revolutionary edge of that film is little more prominent, here it is its quietness and restraint which makes for a more thoughtful approach to the Gospels than many of the films that have followed in its wake.

Notes

1   Francisco Peredo Castro, 'Catholicism and Mexican Cinema: A Secular State, a Deeply Conservative Society, and a Powerful Catholic Hierarchy', in *Moralizing Cinema: Film, Catholicism, and Power*, Daniel Biltereyst and Daniela Treveri Gennari (eds.), (New York: Routledge, 2015), pp. 74–7.

2   Castro, *Catholicism*, p. 76.

Samson and Delilah
USA, 1945 – 133 mins
Cecil B. DeMille

DIRECTOR Cecil B. DeMille

PRODUCER Cecil B. DeMille

SCREENPLAY Fredric M. Frank,
Vladimir Jabotinsky,
Jesse Lasky Jr., Harold Lamb

CINEMATOGRAPHY
George Barnes

EDITOR Anne Bauchens

MUSIC Victor Young

MAIN CAST Hedy Lamarr,
Angela Lansbury, Victor Mature,
George Sanders

PRODUCTION COMPANY
Paramount Pictures Corporation

Samson and Delilah marks the transition point between two of the mid-twentieth century's most dominant genres. Indeed DeMille's genius was transposing onto the biblical epic key elements of 1940s film noir, most obviously Hedy Lamarr's delightful *femme fatale*, Delilah. With the looks that inspired Snow White and the intelligence that inspired wi-fi, Lamarr consistently outshines Victor Mature's muscular lead. Women in biblical epics were essentially restricted to one of two categories, the boringly pious girl-next-door, or

Samson and Delilah (1949).

soul-threateningly-irresistible harlot. Having appeared naked in *Extase* (1932), Lamarr brought certain notoriety to her role. DeMille's imports noirish elements refashioning her as a calculating and devious sexual predator/scheming femme fatale that Samson cannot resist. Her love is 'so obsessive it must destroy and be destroyed by the object of its desire in order to obtain it'.[1] Delilah's sexiness embodies a fear of women; her exotic accent typifies a fear of the outsider.

If Delilah is the film's femme fatale then Samson is refashioned as the male failing to reintegrate into society post-conflict. For a film about a famous warrior, there is surprisingly little fighting. Instead, Samson seems bored and listless. Rather than plotting against the Philistines, he loafs around trying to impress Delilah, her sister Semadar, and the devoted Jewish girl-next-door, Miriam, with feeble wise-cracks. Biblical quips, such as 'if you had not ploughed with my heifer you would not have solved my riddle', fare no better than original ones. 'Hey, one cat at a time' he purrs to Delilah after defeating a lion, in a scene which cobbles together footage of a stuntman wrestling a live lion, with shots of Mature manhandling a stuffed one. Yet aside from some handiwork with the jawbone of an ass, and his revenge when Semadar is impaled by a javelin, Mature's muscular frame is underused.

Mature had starred in noir films in the 1940s such as *Kiss of Death* (1947) and *Cry of the City* (1948), but subsequent years saw him come to epitomize the biblical epic. Not only did he star in *Androcles and the Lion* (1952), *The Robe* (1953) and its sequel *Demetrius and the Gladiators* (1954), but he embodied the genre's tensions between flesh and purity, and between strength and vulnerability.[2]

The film was a labour of love for DeMille. Having begun working on it in the 1930s he famously pitched it to studio execs with a Dan Groesbeck sketch.[3] Having toyed with casting Rita Hayworth and Cary Grant,[4] DeMille opted for the half-Italian Mature and the Jewish Lamarr, lending the film a more Mediterranean feel than many of the resulting Hollywood epics.

The film's final set piece – where Samson brings down the Philistine temple – remains impressive, but the most interesting scene comes shortly before. Fed up with Delilah's pining for Samson, George Sanders' sardonic Philistine king drags her to see how pitiable her former lover looks as he heaves round a millstone to Philistine jeers. Caught between her wish, still, to arouse Samson's interest, and her desire to laud her elevated status over him, Delilah positions herself in his eye-line so he cannot avoid her gaze. 'I will make him see me' she declares. But he cannot. As Samson trudges by the camera stays on her as, for the first time, she truly sees herself.

Struck by the horror of this revelation she repents, prays to Samson's God and seeks Samson out again to make amends. Her prayers are paired with his, her words inspire his final act, and her hands guide him between the temple's load-bearing pillars. Mature's heroics bring down the house – in both senses. Even in the age of CGI, the crashing down of the colossal statue of Dagon remains an indelible image. For the Philistines, not to mention DeMille, Mature and Lamarr, the landscape was never the same again.

Notes

1   Cheryl Exum, *Plotted, Shot, and Painted: Cultural Representations of Biblical Women* (Sheffield: Sheffield Phoenix Press, 2012), p. 236.

2   Bruce Babington and Peter William Evans, *Biblical Epics: Sacred Narrative in the Hollywood Cinema* (Manchester: Manchester University Press, 1993), pp. 227–37.

3   Cecil B. DeMille, *Autobiography*, edited by Donald Hayne (Englewood Cliffs, New Jersey: Prentice-Hall, 1959), pp. 364–5.

4   Robert S. Birchard, *Cecil B DeMille's Hollywood* (Lexington: University of Kentucky, 2004), p. 336–7.

David and Bathsheba

USA, 1951 – 116 mins

Henry King

DIRECTOR Henry King

PRODUCER Darryl F. Zanuck

SCREENPLAY Philip Dunne

CINEMATOGRAPHY
Leon Shamroy

EDITOR Barbara McLean

MUSIC Alfred Newman

PRODUCTION COMPANY
Twentieth Century Fox Film
Corporation

MAIN CAST Susan Hayward,
Raymond Massey, Kieron
Moore, Gregory Peck

David and Bathsheba was one of the few Hollywood Bible movies of the 1950s and 1960s which was pre-pared to eschew scenes of huge battles and tawdry orgies to focus on the stories themselves. Indeed some critics argue this low-key epic belongs as much to the 'women's film' genre. It opens with the briefest of skirmishes, and features an oddly out of place exotic dancer, but is otherwise a downbeat portrayal of David set long after his glory days. Bored and emotionally guarded David (Gregory Peck) lacks the passion of the famed psalmist and the unwavering confidence of the shepherd boy who slew a giant.

Released six years after World War II, many related to this Peck's hero, returning home from the army, having to re-adjust to real life and take his place in society again.[1] Estranged from the faith of his youth, David's former countryside existence is visually contrasted with his new life cooped up in the palace. It's no coincidence then that he first spies Bathsheba (Susan Hayward) while enjoying a refreshing breeze on his palace roof, nor that their relationship only becomes emotionally intimate when they escape to the country.

The text objectifies Bathsheba, discarding her perspective on these events and allowing commentators to cast her as everything from seductress to rape victim. Certainly, the power dynamics suggest it would have been difficult for her to refuse her king. [2] Haywaard's Bathsheba, however, deliberately puts herself in David's view giving her greater agency, but somewhat letting him off the hook. Moreover, David's culpability in her husband death is also toned down when it is revealed that Uriah is an uninterested husband with a martyr complex. When he refuses to visit Bathsheba while on leave, David laments that 'his dreams of glory are his wife in tears'.

The risk to Bathsheba is made starker by a scene where another woman is accused of adultery and stoned to death. It echoes John 8.2–11, yet here there is no reprieve. David – himself compromised – cannot intervene, and his resulting inaction is almost unbearable, prompting questions about judgment, cruelty and mercy which dominate the film.

God's judgment takes various forms: the death of Bathsheba's child; their exposure by the prophet Nathan; and a drought inflicted on David's people, and their resulting displeasure. The arbitrariness of God's nature is highlighted as the Ark of the Covenant is being relocated. One of David's men, Uzzah, reaches out to prevent it from falling and is struck dead (2 Samuel 6). Later, in the film's most powerful scene, David returns to the Ark (still outside the city walls), after Bathsheba has encouraged him to reconnect with his past and his now withered faith.

Once there, he confesses his weakness and pleads to God as if trying to force God's hand into a greater display of mercy. Remarkably God responds to David's almost suicidal effort to obtain divine mercy. As David touches the ark, lightning strikes and his life flashes before his eyes. Yet this is not David's death, but his resusci-tation.[3] The foray into his youth completed, David's release from spiritual drought is mirrored by Israel's release from physical drought. The rain finally pours down, a public declaration to David's subjects of God's forgiveness.

David's voyeuristic gaze in *David and Bathsheba* (1951).

Notes

1   Julie Kelso, 'Gazing at Impotence in Henry King's David and
    Bathsheba', in *Screening Scripture: Intertextual Connections
    Between Scripture and Film*, George Aichele and Richard Walsh
    (eds.) (Harrisburg: Trinity Press International, 2002), pp. 182.

2   Exum outlines a long history of blaming Bathsheba for seducing
    David, even though the original author has little concern for
    Bathsheba's motives. J. Cheryl Exum *Plotted, Shot, and Painted:
    Cultural Representations of Biblical Women*, (Sheffield: Sheffield
    Academic Press, 1996), pp. 19–53.

3   Bruce Babington and Peter William Evans, *Biblical Epics: Sacred
    Narrative in the Hollywood Cinema* (Manchester: Manchester
    University Press, 1993), p. 82.

Quo Vadis
USA, 1951 – 171 mins
Mervyn LeRoy

DIRECTOR Mervyn LeRoy
PRODUCER Sam Zimbalist
SCREENPLAY S.N. Behrman,
Sonya Levien, John Lee Mahin,
Henryk Sienkiewicz
CINEMATOGRAPHY
William V. Skall, Robert Surtees
MUSIC Miklós Rózsa
PRODUCTION COMPANY
Metro-Goldwyn-Mayer
MAIN CAST Leo Genn,
Deborah Kerr, Patricia Laffan,
Robert Taylor, Peter Ustinov

Quo Vadis was an early attempt to give audiences the kind of visually stunning experience that television could not provide. Henryk Sienkiewicz's Roman–Christian novel had already spawned two large scale silent epics – the first of which (1913) deserves some of the praise handed to Griffith's *Intolerance*. Warner's 'new' version would be even more colossal. On-location filming and 30,000 extras provided the kind of spectacle required to entice audiences back to the cinema.

Today *Quo Vadis* is celebrated as a landmark epic. In addition to its size and scale it inspired a string of other 'Jesus cameo' films, perhaps why it has been so mercilessly and specifically targeted in satires such as in *Monty Python's Life of Brian* (1979). Indeed the opening shots of the film-within-the-film in Coen brothers' *Hail Caesar* (2016) is practically a shot for shot homage to *Quo Vadis'* opening. Moreover its story of American values overcoming totalitarianism – be it Nazism,[1] Stalinist communism,[2] or Italian Fascism[3] – is a classic piece of Hollywood mythmaking.

Yet despite its eight Oscar nominations and $20M at the box office; for all its fabulous colours and spectacular crowd scenes, Miklós Rózsa much lauded score, and Peter Ustinov's memorable take on Nero, it is strangely unmoving. Ustinov plays Nero as a vain toddler without anyone to keep him in check. Leo Genn's Petronius peddles a fine line in providing sharp answers that cut both ways, with Nero unable to even conceive the possibility that what sounds like praise might, in fact, be an insult. Both Ustinov and Genn were nominated for Oscars but lost out. Ustinov's performance is memorable, though mainly for its (perhaps justifiable) excess. Ustinov channels Charles Laughton's take on the character from DeMille's *The Sign of the Cross* (1932) but tones down his sexual desire. Nevertheless, Ustinov's performance mocks non-normativity,[4] and is allowed to dominate and overshadow Patricia Laffan's excellently nuanced Poppaea.[5] It is she, after all, who is more instrumental in how events transpire between tribune Marcus Vinicius (Robert Taylor) and Deborah Kerr's Lygia.

Yet Marcus and Lygia's love story lacks the necessary drama and gravitas to hold the film together. Marcus is far from the first hero to begin a film as an ignorant show-off only to reform his ways. Yet his attempt to fan the flames of love in Lygia by forcibly removing her from her home and dragging her into the middle of one of Nero's orgies, beggars belief. Kerr's subtle, blushing performance in the orgy scene is particularly outstanding. As Marcus makes his arrogant, ham-fisted attempts to seduce her, she bristles at the very prospect. Outwardly she remains calm and polite, but she is clearly appalled and horrified at her treatment. But deeper still is the revulsion she feels because she is attracted to Marcus despite his loutish behaviour.

Kerr's talent is wasted here. Marcus's story arc is his conversion; Petronius', his rebellion; but for Lygia (and similarly Paul and Peter) there is nothing. As Christians, their characters have reached before the film begins, and unlike films such as *Demetrius and the Gladiators* (1954), there's no potential for regression post-conversion. Ultimately, *Quo Vadis* is worthy of attention, but mainly as a landmark film, rather than a great one.

Deborah Kerr's Lygia in the arena in *Quo Vadis* (1951).

Notes

1   Martin M. Winkler, 'The Roman Empire in American Cinema after 1945', in Sandra R. Joshel, Margaret Malamud & Donald T. McGuire , Jr. (eds.), *Imperial Projections: Ancient Rome in Modern Popular Culture*. (Baltimore: John Hopkins University Press, 2001), pp. 59–65.

2   Paul V. M. Flesher and Robert Torry, *Film and Religion: An Introduction* (Nashville: Abingdon Press, 2007), pp. 56–60.

3   Maria Wyke, *Projecting the Past: Ancient Rome, Cinema and History* (London/New York: Routledge, 1997), pp. 140–1.

4   Richard A. Lindsay, *Hollywood Biblical Epics: Camp Spectacle and Queer Style from the Silent Era to the Modern Day.* (Santa Barbara, California/Denver, Colorado: Praeger, 2015), pp. 89–99.

5   Lloyd Llewellyn-Jones, *Designs of the Past: How Hollywood Created the Ancient World* (Edinburgh: Edinburgh University Press, 2018), p336.

The Robe
USA, 1953 – 133 mins
Henry Koster

DIRECTOR Henry Koster
PRODUCER Frank Ross
SCREENPLAY Lloyd C. Douglas,
Philip Dunne, Gina Kaus,
Albert Maltz
CINEMATOGRAPHY
Leon Shamroy
EDITOR Barbara McLean
MUSIC Alfred Newman
PRODUCTION COMPANY
Twentieth Century Fox Film
Corporation
MAIN CAST Richard Burton,
Victor Mature, Michael Rennie,
Jay Robinson, Jean Simmons

The Robe is famous for being the first major widescreen film, which brings it far greater attention than the other 1950s Roman-Christian epics but means its other achievements are often overlooked. It is, for example, one of Alfred Newman's greatest scores, a contrast between subtle and subdued spirituality and the bombastic, dominant self-assured pomp of Rome.[1] The refrains weave in and out linking the characters and tracing their journeys.

The robe confronting imperial power in the final scene in *The Robe* (1953).

At times the film is transcendent and superbly executed. The decision not to show Jesus' face results in the most powerful of all the scenes of the *Via Dolorosa*, liberating the camera to focus on the reactions of those watching, haunted by their knowledge of his awful fate. It's also Victor Mature's best moment as the slave-turned-convert Demetrius. The cruel and powerful sounding score commands everything here grinding on mercilessly to the awful, inevitable climax of the following scene.

Moments later the film's other great scene unfolds. Again the camera focuses not on Jesus' face but on the soldiers getting on with their job. Lashed by the wind and rain, and stuck in a part of the world they despise, they care not a bit about the condemned man, they just want to get it over so they can return to their barracks. By deferring the moment when Richard Burton's tribune Marcellus sees the light, the scene regains its tension. Burton is humanized by his desire to be professional though he is not completely unaffected by his prisoner's suffering.

Two other moments linger in the memory. The first occurs as Richard Boone's Pontius Pilate absent-mindedly asks again to wash his hands, moments after he has already done so. The confusion on his face as his servant respectfully reminds him of his error and Boone's 'Did I? So I did.' conjure an image that is no less effective for being historically unlikely.

The other is the film's very final moment. Jean Simmons's Diana chooses to accompany Marcellus to his death for a faith she has discovered so recently that she barely comprehends it. The scene itself is almost spoilt by the worst of Jay Robinson's excesses as an 'absurdly adolescent' Caligula.[2] Even the moment when Diana chooses death with Christ/Marcellus over life without him is unexceptional. Yet somehow, by the time their procession reaches the end of the hall, 'like a married couple',[3] something has changed, and for a moment the viewer is transported.

There are some weaknesses. Unfamiliarity with the new technology results in compositions which are occasionally too cramped in the middle, or too spaced out.[4] And a combination of lumbering dialogue and over-baked performances occasionally produce the kind of moments which bring the genre into disrepute. These aside the film deftly interweaves the fictional story of Marcellus' spiritual death and resurrection with that of the physical death of Jesus, and reflecting too the emergence of new technology and new cinematic possibilities.

Notes

1   Stephen C. Meyer, *Epic Sound: Music in Postwar Hollywood Biblical Films* (Indianapolis: Indiana University Press, 2015), pp. 96–113.

2   Richard A. Lindsay, *Hollywood Biblical Epics: Camp Spectacle and Queer Style from the Silent Era to the Modern Day.* (Santa Barbara, California/Denver, Colorado: Praeger, 2015), p. 101.

3   Bruce Babington and Peter William Evans, *Biblical Epics: Sacred Narrative in the Hollywood Cinema* (Manchester: Manchester University Press, 1993), p. 199.

4   Jonathan Stubbs, *Historical Film: A Critical Introduction* (London/New York: Bloomsbury, 2013), pp. 145–6.

Sins of Jezebel
USA, 1953 – 74 mins
Reginald Le Borg

DIRECTOR Reginald Le Borg
PRODUCERS Robert L. Lippert
Jr., Sigmund Neufeld
SCREENPLAY Richard H. Landau
CINEMATOGRAPHY
Gilbert Warrenton
EDITOR Carl Pierson
MUSIC Bert Shefter
PRODUCTION COMPANY
Sigmund Neufeld Productions
MAIN CAST Eduard Franz,
Paulette Goddard, John Hoyt,
George Nader

Elijah is one of the Bible's most complex characters, a powerful prophet who spins into depression when threatened by Queen Jezebel.[1] For someone who is portrayed so vividly and dramatically in the Bible, it is remarkable that filmmakers have largely ignored him. Even the only significant feature film to cover his ministry – *Sins of Jezebel* – is named after his opponent and sadly little of his fragility remains. Indeed the film eliminates entirely the dramatic passage where Elijah flees to the desert; begs for death; witnesses God's display of earthquake, wind and fire; then hears God's still, small voice (1 Kings 19).

Paulette Goddard in a promotional still for *Sins of Jezebel* (1953).

For her part, Jezebel's reputation has been somewhat rehabilitated in modern times. After centuries of her name being used as the ultimate slur on female morality or as a racist stereotype,[2] she has even been reclaimed by some as a feminist icon.[3] Re-interpretations of the Book of Kings have uncovered a shrewd operator and devoted wife negotiating her way through the turbulent final days of the house of Omri.[4] Moreover, her grim and brutal death at the hands of men she trusted still has the power to shock,[5] even in an age when on-screen violence against women has become commonplace.

Sins of Jezebel ignores such revisionist angles, sexualizing her, particularly regarding costuming, but still treating her more sympathetically than might be expected. Casting Paulette Goddard in the title role makes her character more congenial. Goddard was best known for her work in husband Charlie Chaplin's *Modern Times* (1936) and *The Great Dictator* (1942), both sympathetic roles. She first comes into view here when her future husband, King Ahab, sends his captain of the guard, Jehu, to escort her to the palace. As the curtains on her lounging sedan are parted, it evokes the opening of curtains in the cinema leveraging Goddard's cinematic royalty to enhance her role as queen. Jezebel is instantly attracted to Jehu, flirting with him in sharp contrast to the stiff and formal manner she adopts with the besotted Ahab.

The third male character Jezebel interacts with is Elijah, played by John Hoyt. In addition to his wooden performance as Elijah, Hoyt also plays the film's narrator. The narrator opens the film dressed in a black vestment, carrying both academic and religious connotations, while recounting the stories of creation and Moses receiving the commandments. Three years later Cecil B. DeMille began *The Ten Commandments* in similar fashion.

When Ahab allows Jezebel to erect a temple to her god Baal, Elijah announces God's fury. A drought follows, leading to the famous confrontation on Mount Carmel between Elijah and Baal's prophets. However, rather than a contest, here the confrontation is presented as Elijah's intrusive take-over of a pagan fertility ceremony. When the rain finally arrives the film deftly cuts between a shot of Elijah, arms aloft, declaring 'The Lord, he is God'; and a delighted Jezebel, striking the same pose, similarly claiming 'Baal is God'.

While the script has its good moments ('A hungry rabble can become far more dangerous than a well-fed army' worries Ahab at the height of the drought), it struggles to shape the narrative fragments from Kings' into a fluent story. Hoyt's narrator jumps from the death of Naboth to Elijah's prediction of Ahab's death, then to its fulfilment, and again to Elijah anointing Jehu as the future king. Afterwards Elijah wanders off screen and it's unclear he's being taken to heaven. Presumably the tiny $100,000 budget couldn't accommodate a credible chariot of fire.[6]

Jezebel's death feels similarly disjointed. Jehu is unmoved either by her war-paint, or by her being shot by an arrow, tipped out of a window and run-over by a passing chariot. Even the shocking abruptness of her death is wasted. There's a final cut to Hoyt's preacher who picks up Elijah's staff and walks off declaring 'there will always be the voice of an Elijah'. He considers that a good thing, but the film has demonstrated little reason why.

Notes

1   Jeff Lucas, *Elijah: Anointed and Stressed* (Eastbourne: Kingsway, 1995), pp. 107–16. Also, Dave Burke, *Genesis to Jesus: Making Sense of the Old Testament* (Leicester: Frameworks, 1991) p. 50.

2   Tina Pippin, 'Jezebel Re-Vamped', in Athalya Brenner (ed.) *Feminist Companion to Samuel–Kings* (Sheffield: Sheffield Academic Press, 1994), pp. 196–7.

3   See for example 'Supposedly Feminist Website' <www.jezebel. com> (accessed 19 Dec. 2021).

4   Judith E. McKinlay, 'Negotiating the Frame for Viewing the Death of Jezebel', *Biblical Interpretation* 10 (2002), p. 305–22.

5   McKinlay, *Negotiating*, p. 311.

6   Richard C. and Michael R. Pitts Campbell, *The Bible on Film: A Checklist, 1897–1980* (Metuchen, NJ, and London: Scarecrow Press, 1981), p. 34.

The Prodigal
USA, 1955 – 112 mins
Richard Thorpe

DIRECTOR Richard Thorpe
PRODUCER Charles Schnee
SCREENPLAY Joseph Breen,
Samuel James Larsen,
Maurice Zimm
CINEMATOGRAPHY
Joseph Ruttenberg
MUSIC Bronislau Kaper
PRODUCTION COMPANY
Metro-Goldwyn-Mayer
MAIN CAST Louis Calhern,
Audrey Dalton, Edmund
Purdom, Lana Turner

Jesus' Parable of the Prodigal Son was first turned into a film by Pathé in 1902. The parable's short, punchy, style suited the short length of early silents, such that four more adaptations followed in the next ten years. As runtimes got longer, however, the parable's appeal faded. The story's dramatic snap relies on brevity. Padding out the material enough to fill a feature film proved difficult.

However, in the early 1950s, films that were similarly tangential to Jesus' story were performing strongly at the box office. *Quo Vadis* and *The Robe* topped the charts in 1951 and 1953 respectively whilst William Dieterle's *Salome* (1953) also performed well. In response, MGM converted Jesus' famous parable into *The Prodigal,* investing a similar budget to *The Robe* amid boasts of 'The Biggest Picture Ever Filmed in Hollywood'.[1]

To bridge the gap in the story, the script invents numerous subplots and summoned all the glitz and glamour they could muster. Just as Rita Hayworth had provided *Salome*'s star power, so Lana Turner was brought in as the priestess of Astarte and assigned a fittingly lavish wardrobe. Instead of portraying the Jewish son, Micah, as a party animal who squanders all his wealth, he is re-cast as an essentially moral man whose infatuation with Turner's priestess causes a catastrophic loss of judgment. Bewitched by her beauty he is easily defrauded by the hierarchy in Damascus.

Driven by a need to rehydrate the, finely-distilled, original material, the script resorts to increasingly bizarre moments: a muscular, sacrificial victim dives headlong into a fire pit; a mute slave is magically resurrected; and Micah wrestles with a vulture. Yet much of this new story arc seems designed to comply with the restrictions of the Hays Production Code. While the biblical setting draped a veil of respectability over *The Prodigal*'s revealing costumes, the code also stipulated that 'the sympathy of the audience shall never be thrown to the side of … sin'.[2] Not only did this control which acts could be shown, but it was generally understood that perpetrators of such behaviour ultimately had to die or be punished. The film, then, establishes Micah's goodness in the opening scene, when he saves a runaway slave. His money is not lost on women and parties, but in his obsessive quest for love, and exploitation by his enemies.

Ultimately, this set Hays' rigid code on a collision course: the moral of the Parable of the Prodigal Son is that no act is so horrendous it cannot be forgiven by the Father's unending love. The code outlawed the self-same moral framework it supposedly sought to uphold. The powerful emotions of the original story ended up as diluted mush. Ironically, while *The Prodigal* took the 'Son' out of the picture's title, its biggest error was taking the 'prodigal' out of its script.

Lana Turner's trapped in her role as priestess in *The Prodigal* (1955).

Notes

1   Motion Picture Herald, vol. 199, 2 April 1955 p. 2.
    Available online: <https://ia801306.us.archive.org/13/items/
    motionpictureher199quig/motionpictureher199quig.pdf>
    (accessed 19 Dec. 2021).

2   Michael Brooke, 'The Hays Code', *BFI ScreenOnline*. Available
    online: <www.screenonline.org.uk/film/id/592022/> (accessed
    19 Dec. 2021).

The Ten Commandments
USA, 1956 – 222 mins
Cecil B. DeMille

DIRECTOR Cecil B. DeMille
PRODUCERS Cecil B. DeMille,
Henry Wilcoxon
SCREENPLAY J.H. Ingraham,
Jesse Lasky Jr., Æneas
MacKenzie, A.E. Southon,
Dorothy Clarke Wilson
CINEMATOGRAPHY
Loyal Griggs
EDITOR Anne Bauchens
MUSIC Elmer Bernstein
PRODUCTION COMPANY
Paramount Pictures Corporation
MAIN CAST Anne Baxter, Yul
Brynner, Cedric Hardwicke,
Charlton Heston, Vincent Price,
Edward G. Robinson

The paradox of *The Ten Commandments* is that it is one of the easiest films to mock yet so magnificent that any discussion about biblical epics will inevitably mention it. The more risible moments begin from the start, when director Cecil B. DeMille eschews a conventional opening and steps from behind the curtain to deliver a ten-minute lecture on his film's historical credibility. Ninety minutes of fictional hokum follow. DeMille converts the Exodus story into a Cold War parable,[1] Moses into a Christ figure and strings together invented back-stories and characters with such unintentionally hilarious lines as 'Oh, Moses, Moses, you stubborn, splendid, adorable fool'.[2]

Moses (Charlton Heston) confronts Ramsees in *The Ten Commandments* (1956).

Yet these early scenes also provide some of the film's most stunning moments. When Moses' slaves erect an obelisk, DeMille creates spectacular and dramatic footage from what is essentially a construction scene. Thousands toil in the immense desert heat, orchestrated by one man's monumental vision and expertise, to create an extraordinary masterwork – a description fitting both Moses and DeMille.[3]

DeMille's groundwork during that opening ninety minutes pays off. The burning bush scene may not have aged well, but the scenes where Moses commands his former rival Rameses to let his people go are deliciously taut. Rameses is still trying to win an old argument; his wife Nefretiri, Moses' former love, stokes their conflict hoping to burn both the man who spurned her and the man who did not.

The treatment of the biblical material is no less impressive: the eerie way the Angel of Death creeps through deserted streets is a fitting climax to the preceding nine plagues; an exodus scene which deftly combines sheer scale with the individual and personal (DeMille takes small moments such as an elderly man's dying wish, or a girl's lost dolly, and multiplies them ten thousand times); the unforgettable parting of the Red Sea; and the sparks flying through the air to engrave the Commandments on sheer rock.

The costumes are, of course, fantastic and the immense sets are first class. Heston and Yul Brynner's muscles gleam. Anne Baxter purrs, Vincent Price camps it up, Cedric Hardwicke wryly delivers dry witticisms while Edward G. Robinson scowlingly dismisses Heston's bright-eyed pronouncements. Meanwhile Elmer Bernstein – a relative unknown at the time – underpins the story with his classical score.[4] Amazingly whilst the film lasts for 220 minutes, it never feels like that long, no doubt why it returned ten times its $13 million production costs.

Perhaps what is most striking about *The Ten Commandments* is how it became the definitive film for so many different categories. Despite decades of westerns and parlour comedies, it is this film that comes to mind when people think of Cecil B. DeMille. Regardless of *Ben-Hur*'s eleven Oscars, it's *The Ten Commandments* which is seen as the quintessential Heston performance. And, of course, it stands as the definitive example of the biblical epic. Indeed few films can claim to be so typical of, and central to, their genre as this. *Double Indemnity* (1944) for film noir. *The Godfather* (1972) for the gangster movie. Like them it deserves to be put on a pedestal and celebrated, even if we recognize that part of the reason it is so memorable is because film-making has moved on and we are unlikely to see anything quite like it ever again.

Notes

1   Bruce Babington and Peter William Evans, *Biblical Epics: Sacred Narrative in the Hollywood Cinema* (Manchester: Manchester University Press, 1993), p. 54.

2   Larry J. Kreitzer, *The Old Testament in Fiction and Film: On Reversing the Hermeneutical Flow* (Sheffield: Sheffield University Press, 1994), p. 26.

3   Michael Wood, *America in the Movies* (New York: Columbia University Press, [1975] 1989), p. 173.

4   Stephen C. Meyer, *Epic Sound: Music in Postwar Hollywood Biblical Films* (Indianapolis: Indiana University Press, 2015), p. 121.

The Star of Bethlehem
UK, 1956 – 18 mins
Lotte Reiniger and Vivian Milroy

DIRECTORS Lotte Reiniger,
Vivian Milroy
PRODUCERS Louis Hagen,
Richard Kaplan
SCREENPLAY Elaine Friedrich
EDITOR Reg Spragg
MUSIC Peter Gellhorn
PRODUCTION COMPANY
Cathedral Films
MAIN CAST Anthony Jacobs,
Barbara Ruick

As with many of Lotte Reiniger's pre-World War II animated films, her 1921 *Der Stern von Bethlehem* was lost during the bombing of Berlin. Thankfully though, her 1956 remake, and another film of her from that era, *The Adventures of Prince Achmed* (1926), have survived and, alongside other examples of her work, testify to her outstanding artistry.

Reiniger started her career as an animator working on Paul Wegener's *Der Rattenfänger von Hameln* (The Pied Piper of Hamelin, 1918) aged just seventeen.[1] The film was a live action movie, but when Wegener was struggling to get his rats to follow his piper he turned to Reiniger to produce an animated sequence instead. The year after *Hameln*'s release she directed her own short film *Das Ornament des verliebten Herzens* (The Ornament of the Enamoured Heart, 1919).

The year after *Stern von Bethlehem* she created her oldest known surviving work *Das Geheimnis der Marquise* (The Marquise's Secret) an advert for Nivea face cream in which a woman's radiant skin attracts potential lovers. Then came her silent masterpiece *The Adventures of Prince Achmed* in 1926 with its sense of weightlessness and magic, summoned effortless by Reiniger unique style.

As an artist, Reiniger always gave the impression that she was simply doing what came naturally to her. Having been cutting-out intricate figures from card from almost as soon as she could hold a pair of scissors,[2] she worked at extraordinary speed. The intricacy of her delicate, hand-cut moving images astounds, as does 'her inclusion of delicate little motions that imbue her creations with life'.[3] She also pioneered technology, inventing the multi-planed camera which Walt Disney later patented.

Here, black silhouetted characters move in the foreground contrasting with the film's coloured backgrounds, although when the angels hear of Jesus' birth, the angels light up against a dark background. Throughout, the graceful, skilful movements induce genuine emotion. The birth scene, for example, elicits surprising intimacy. The layered backgrounds, use of colour and smoothness of movement suggest improvements in her technique from her lost original.

While the original *Star of Bethlehem* was only her third film, the remake came during her most productive period. Having fled Germany, Reiniger and her husband and life-long collaborator Carl Koch were eventually forced to return and were pressed into making work for the Nazis. After the war the couple moved to London where they created 22 films in just ten years between 1949 and 1958. As many of these films were based on German fairy tales, this Nativity film was something of an exception. While the majority of its plot is based on the traditional narrative, the most striking sequence harks back to those European Gothic traditions. As the magi make their way towards Jerusalem, 'a swarm of devils rise out of the mouth of hell, causing a landslide, a sandstorm and a sea storm in hope of stopping the journey'.[4] Reiniger returned to the Bible again in 1974 to film *The Lost Son* based on Jesus' parable.

The Star of Bethlehem (1956).

Notes

1   At 60–85 minutes *Der Rattenfänger* is the first feature-length animated film.

2   From a 1976 interview with Reiniger, available online from *Kenneth Clouse Collection*, Hugh M. Hefner Moving Image Archive, University of Southern California School of Cinematic Arts. Available online: <http://uschefnerarchive.com/project/lotte-reiniger-recording/> (accessed 19 Dec. 2021).

3   Fritzi Kramer, 'Cinderella (1922) A Silent Film Review', *Movies Silently* 18 March 2018. Available online: <http://moviessilently.com/2018/03/18/cinderella-1922-a-silent-film-review/> (accessed 19 Dec. 2021).

4   James White, 'Lotte Reiniger and The Star of Bethlehem', *BFI website* 5 June 2017. Available online: <www2.bfi.org.uk/news-opinion/news-bfi/features/lotte-reiniger-star-bethlehem> (accessed 19 Dec. 2021).

Celui qui doit mourir (*He Who Must Die*)
France/Italy, 1957 – 122 mins
Jules Dassin

DIRECTOR Jules Dassin
PRODUCER Henri Bérard
SCREENPLAY Ben Barzman,
Nikos Kazantzakis, André Obey
CINEMATOGRAPHY
Gilbert Chain, Jacques Natteau
EDITOR Ralph E. Winters
MUSIC Georges Auric
PRODUCTION COMPANY
Indusfilms
MAIN CAST Grégoire Aslan,
Gert Fröbe, Carl Möhner, Jean
Servais, Pierre Vaneck

He Who Must Die is an adaptation of Nikos Kazantzakis' novel *Christ Recrucified* by Jules Dassin, best known for classic film noir *Night and the City* (1950) and heist movie *Rififi* (1955). Dassin's eye for stunning black and white photography is in evidence from the first frame, and it's hard not to love this 'striking' film on that basis alone.[1]

The story is essentially that of a passion play within a passion play, a sub-genre which includes films such as *Jesus of Montreal* (1989), *Man Dancin'* (2003) and *Mary* (2005), but of all those films it's here where the story feels most authentic: the confrontations are more political than religious; the isolation of the village and it's closely knitted community create the correct sort of atmosphere; and the divisive issue at the core is one that still draws deep divides even today.

As with *Jesus of Montreal* the film's passion play is initiated by a religious official who fails to appreciate the radical nature of the work he is commissioning. Here division comes when a substantial immigrant community arrives at a village itself facing potential starvation. The town's council hide their prejudice behind concerns about the impact of housing such a large community. By this time, however, council member and patriarch Father Grigoris has already named the actors for the passion play and commissioned them to live out their lives in a manner consistent with their characters. And so they do.

The nature of these films often means that the plot begins to whither once parallels starts to emerge between Jesus and the character playing him. There's a certain inevitability about how things will end. However, because 'the actual passion play is never performed',[2] Dassin detaches the story from its origins, obscuring how various elements will resolve themselves. The 'real story' becomes so compelling that *it* drives the film to a strong conclusion, rather than the more predictable religious parallels.

Dassin's camerawork anticipates Pasolini's *Il vangelo secondo Matteo* which emerged seven years later.[3] The rugged barrenness of the rural landscape, the unpolished look of the actors' faces, the extensive use of outside locations and the black and white photography, mean much of this strongly reminiscent of Pasolini's famous film and one cannot help but wonder if this film influenced some of Pasolini's choices.

With poverty, war and global warming continuing to displace millions, conflict over immigration shows no sign of abating. The issues raised by *He Who Must Die* are as relevant today as they were during the inter-war years in which it is set. Its focus on those suffering is an important reminder as we wrestle with this complex issue. Putting Jesus on side of the oppressed is hardly an unusual choice, but it has rarely seemed quite so politically relevant.

Jean Servais as Father Fotis in *Celui qui doit mourir* (1957).

Notes

1   Peter Malone, *Screen Jesus: Portrayals of Christ in Television and Film* (Lanham/Toronto/Plymouth, UK: Scarecrow Press, 2012), p. 44.

2   Adele Reinhartz, *Bible and Cinema: An Introduction* (Abingdon: Routledge, 2013), p. 119.

3   Roy Kinnard and Tim Davis note the influence of Eisenstein and Pudovkin, see *Divine Images: A History of Jesus on the Screen* (New York: Citadel–Carol Publishing Group, 1992), p. 109.

Solomon and Sheba
USA, 1959 – 136 mins
King Vidor

DIRECTOR King Vidor
PRODUCERS Tyrone Power,
Ted Richmond
SCREENPLAY George Bruce,
Paul Dudley, Anthony Veiller,
Crane Wilbur
CINEMATOGRAPHY
Freddie Young
EDITOR Otto Ludwig
MUSIC Mario Nascimbene,
Malcolm Arnold
PRODUCTION COMPANY
Metro-Goldwyn-Meyer
MAIN CAST Yul Brynner, Gina
Lollobrigida, Marisa Pavan,
George Sanders

'At times, a man feels drawn toward the dangers that confront him, even at the risk of his own destruction'.

Strip away the glamour and glitz of King Vidor's magnificent-looking epic and its heart is pure film noir – *Gilda* in gold-sequinned underwear, featuring the Queen of Sheba as the *femme fatale*. She arrives innocently enough at Solomon's palace, but everyone, including Solomon himself, knows she's trouble.

Away from Solomon's lavishly-rendered court Sheba conspires with his enemies – the Egyptian Pharaoh and Solomon's waspish half-brother Adonijah (George Sanders). Solomon attempts to keep her at arm's length, and then tries to pretend he's invulnerable to her charms, but he's drawn towards her 'like a moth approaches a flame' and when he falls, he exposes his entire kingdom. And then, like a spangly *Vertigo*, there's the twist: Sheba falls for her mark and realizes the enemy she was trying to deceive, seduce and destroy means more to her that her own traditions. Now there's trouble for both of them.

Just as noir's female characters are always the most interesting, so Gina Lollobridgida's Sheba steals every scene she features in. She smoulders, plots and purrs so well that you can easily forget her biblical role was head-of-state of a prosperous country, posing such tough administrative questions that only Solomon's wisdom could answer them. Yet Yul Brynner's passive, subdued, portrayal of Solomon is also classic noir.

With a strong performance by Lollobrigida – besides a curiously unerotic orgy scene where, she seems bored by its banality – the audience sides with her far more than the stoical Brynner. 'Wherever she moves Sheba colonizes her space, dominating' those she talks with, 'her positioning in the frame often prioritises her spatially'.[1] We see both monarchs consulting with their advisors, but gain far more insight into the wranglings of her inner circle than his, even if he has more to lose.

One of *Solomon and Sheba* greatest surprises is its depiction of the Israelites' god, who unexpectedly takes the noirish role of the dark malevolent force conspiring to keep the lovers apart. In contrast to other biblical epics, here it's the deity whom the Israelites worship – yet fail to understand – that is the problem, rather than the Sheban religion or the Egyptian army. (In an improbable, but visually stunning, sequence Egypt's army fall, literally, for Solomon's battlefield genius). Vidor 'splices an Old Testament God … onto a democratic God'.[2] Only pious Abishag realizes God might kill Solomon as punishment for his affair, and so she sacrifices herself to save him.

While Sheba is an intelligent political leader, uncowed by male power (even whipping Adonijah across the face at one point), the film's regressive portrayal of woman is problematic. By the end Sheba has had to surrender her country's system of matriarchal rule and dress down to avoid a stoning.[3]

The lavish costumes, striking sets and fine compositions impress, and the epic/noir crossover aspect is intriguing. Ultimately, though, its attempts to satiate audiences' voyeuristic desire, whilst reassuring them that such displays of female sexuality will succumb to patriarchal dominance, is too much to swallow.

'Sheba' narrowly avoids being stoned to death in *Solomon and Sheba* (1959).

Notes

1   Bruce Babington and Peter William Evans, *Biblical Epics: Sacred Narrative in the Hollywood Cinema* (Manchester: Manchester University Press, 1993), p. 67.

2   Raymond Durgnat and Scott Simmon, *King Vidor, American* (Berkley: University of California Press, 1988), p. 311.

3   Vidor's makeover of Israel as a modern, anti-slavery, democracy is neither accurate nor convincing.

Ben-Hur
USA, 1959 – 222 mins
William Wyler

DIRECTOR William Wyler
PRODUCERS Sol C. Siegel,
Joseph Vogel, William Wyler,
Sam Zimbalist
SCREENPLAY Maxwell
Anderson, S.N. Behrman,
Karl Tunberg, Gore Vidal,
Lew Wallace
CINEMATOGRAPHY
Robert Surtees
EDITORS John D. Dunning,
Ralph E. Winters,
Margaret Booth
MUSIC Miklós Rózsa
PRODUCTION COMPANY
Metro-Goldwyn-Meyer
MAIN CAST Stephen Boyd,
Haya Harareet, Jack Hawkins,
Charlton Heston,
Cathy O'Donnell, Martha Scott,
Frank Thring

Ben-Hur is that rarest of Bible films – a commercial and critical success[1]. The winner of an unprecedented eleven Oscars and still one of the highest grossing films when adjusted for inflation,[2] its achievements are on a par with its eye-popping sets and its humongous four-hour running time.

Much of its success derives from drawing on closely-related prior experience. Lew Wallace's novel had already proved successful on the big screen, indeed director William Wyler had been an assistant director on the 1925 version. Wyler, much underappreciated today, had also worked before with star Charlton Heston on *Big Country* (1958) and Heston's pedigree with epics had already been firmly established in *The Ten Commandments* (1956). Similarly, co-star Stephen Boyd, 'one of the epic's brightest stars',[3] already had experience in a New Testament production, the BBC's *Family Portrait* (1955).

Like *Big Country*, *Ben-Hur* is the story of two feuding men locked into a destructive cycle of revenge, projected on an epic scale across deserts and dusty landscapes. But Heston's previous moral compass is thrown off course by his thirst for revenge, making Heston's Judah more interesting than his one-dimensional Moses. The darkest moment arrives just as Judah visits Boyd's beaten Messala, minutes before he dies. Heston's frame stands menacingly in the iron doorway blocking out the light, like the angel of death collecting a prisoner, the music underscoring the moment's gravity.

Yet a more literal thirst drives so many of the film's pivotal moments. Having (accidentally) almost assassinated the new governor of his home town of Jerusalem, Judah is enslaved and dragged through the desert to Nazareth, almost dead from dehydration. Only when a mysterious villager defies Judah's captors and gives him a cup of water is he saved. Later, having escaped from the sinking Roman ship on which he served, he finds himself trapped on the open sea, his thirst only worsened by the dangerously undrinkable water that surrounds him. Eventually freed, he treks back to Jerusalem, meeting chariot-racing enthusiast Sheik Ilderim while refreshing himself. The ensuing chariot race leaves Judah's enemy dead, but his thirst for revenge remains unquenched. Yet somehow, he finds himself on a road in Jerusalem, compelled to offer that same mysterious stranger a cup of water.

Jesus has appeared, fleetingly, throughout the film, but not until the closing scenes does he take centre stage, despite already being under arrest. Having contracted leprosy, Judah's mother and sister are hiding, near death, in a colony. Stories about Jesus inspire a desperate Judah to carry his sister into the centre of Jerusalem as Jesus is sentenced. Despite good intentions, these final scenes dissipate the dramatic tension. Only now does the film drag, betraying its length.

In contrast, the chariot race stands out as one of cinema's greatest ever moments. Allowing Judah to prove his mettle, and Messala his villainy, before bringing them head to head, the stunts push the boundaries of believability without quite vaulting over them. Messala's comeuppance is so all-encompassing that it

Charlton Heston as Judah Ben-Hur in 1959's *Ben-Hur*.

generates compassion in spite of his previous misdeeds. Almost as good is the sea battle – the pinnacle of the film's opening half.

Yet for all its splendid sets, costumes and stunts, (not to mention its homo-erotic subtext),[4] it's the pain of betrayal, Judah's determination to survive, the fickleness of victory, and the anger at loss which provide the film's beating heart. It's not merely that *Ben-Hur*'s setpieces are underscored by these emotions, rather, that the sheer size of these dramatic events is what is required to truly express such depth of feeling.

Notes

1 W.Barnes Tatum, *Jesus at the Movies* (California: Polebridge Press, [1997] 2013), pp. 76–7.

2 'Top Lifetime Adjusted Grosses' at *Box Office Mojo*, Available online: <www.boxofficemojo.com/chart/top_lifetime_gross_adjusted/?adjust_gross_to=2020> (accessed 19 Dec. 2021). See also Tim McMahon, 'Highest Grossing Movies Adjusted for Inflation', at *Inflationdata.com*, 16 May 2013. Available online: <https://inflationdata.com/articles/2013/05/16/highest-grossing-movies-adjusted-for-inflation/> (accessed 19 Dec. 2021).

3 Lloyd Llewellyn-Jones, *Designs of the Past: How Hollywood Created the Ancient World* (Edinburgh: Edinburgh University Press, 2018), p. 327.

4 Ina Rae Hark, 'The Erotics of the Galley Slave: Male Desire and Christian Sacrifice in the 1959 a Film Version of *Ben-Hur*' in Barbara Ryan and Milette Shamir (ed.) *Bigger than Ben-Hur: The Book, its Adaptations, & their Audience* (New York: Syracuse University Press, 2016), pp. 162–78).

Ester e il re (*Esther and the King*)

Italy/USA, 1960 – 109 mins

Raoul Walsh and Mario Bava

DIRECTORS Raoul Walsh,
Mario Bava
PRODUCERS John Twist,
Raoul Walsh
SCREENPLAY Ennio De Concini,
Michael Elkins, Raoul Walsh
CINEMATOGRAPHY
Mario Bava
EDITOR Jerry Webb
MUSIC Angelo Francesco
Lavagnino, Roberto Nicolosi
PRODUCTION COMPANY
Galatea S.P.A. Rome
MAIN CAST Rick Battaglia,
Joan Collins, Denis O'Dea,
Richard Egan, Sergio Fantoni,
Daniela Rocca

Joan Collins stars in *Esther and the King* (1960).

Raoul Walsh had been directing movies for almost fifty years when *Esther* was released. If the string of 1950s biblical epics were typified by Godly male heroes torn between dull, overly pious woman on the one hand, and threateningly hyper-sexualized temptresses on the other, then Walsh, assisted by upcoming horror maestro Mario Bava,[1] forged a new approach. Both *Esther and the King* and *The Story of Ruth* launched the same year, starred a female lead and omitted the potential partner's name from the title.

Persian King Ahasuerus returns from way only to hear of the unfaithfulness of his queen, Vashti, in his absence. His informant, Haman, neglects to mention it was he with whom she was having the affair, though their relationship was driven purely by power. This establishes Haman's character while providing mitigating circumstances for Vashti's deposal. The biblical text is somewhat more unpalatable: the king's request would humiliate Vashti and sexually objectify her in front of his guests.[2] Here however, having already been banished, Vashti turns up at Ahasuerus' gaudily overdone throne room and desperately attempts to win him back by performing a, surprisingly graphic, striptease. The film softens the blow by suggesting Vashti's 'burlesque' was a misguided act of repentance.[3] Moments later, Haman's assassin murders her. The film, therefore, justifies Ahasuerus' actions, allowing the audience to sympathize with his plight; have some sympathy for Vashti; and despise Haman. While Haman is depiction as a power-crazed sexual predator, his primary crime in the film is not the attempted massacre of the Jews, but treason and the attempted regicide.

The film's portrayal of Haman as an evil but ineffectual villain,[4] and the queen's tacky striptease, are just two examples of the film's staggering campiness. It begins in the very first scene where, on their return home from battle, Ahasuerus insists his Jewish best friend Simon replaces his rusty dagger with the king's own, greatly enlarged, golden dagger named 'the sword of the golden *rooster*'.

As the film unfolds, the feelings Ahasuerus and Simon have for each other always seem far stronger than either man has for Esther (Joan Collins). When Esther is snatched by the king's soldiers, moments before her marriage to Simon can be completed, Simon fights back, However, the film soon loses interest in Simon, focussing instead on affairs inside the palace. For his part, Ahasuerus appears unattracted to any of the beautiful potential queens paraded in front of him. Indeed he is only drawn to Esther after he has a chance to save her. His attraction is sparked more by his own 'heroics' than Esther herself. Even after she becomes Queen there is no indication they ever consummate the marriage.

Remarkably, the portrayals of Esther and her uncle Mordecai remain relatively refined, all the more surprising given Collins' subsequent career. While her costumes are fabulous and her performance is a little over-earnest, the role is nevertheless treated respectfully. She is, after all, the hero named in the title. Almost fifty years later, *One Night with the King* (2006) framed the story as a romance, as if Esther's wildest dreams were all coming true.[5] On that occasion the camp was not quite so intentional. The Jewish queen still awaits a truly feminist cinematic adaptation.

Notes

1   Mary P. Wood, 'Italian Film Genres and Mario Bava', in Peter Bondanella (ed.), *The Italian Cinema Book* (London: BFI/Palgrave–MacMillan, 2014), p. 303.

2   Maxine E. Garrett, 'Raising the Bar – The Story of Queen Vashti' *Tabitha's Daughters*, 9 May 2015. Available online: <https://tabithasdaughters.com/2015/05/09/queen-vashti-you-must-not-know-bout-me/> (accessed 19 Dec. 2021).

3   Adele Berlin, *The JPS Bible Commentary: Esther* (Skokie, Illinois: Varda Books, 2004), p. 10.

4   Barry Atkinson, *Heroes Never Die: The Italian Peplum Phenomenon 1950–1967*, (London: Midnight Marquee, 2018), p. 175.

5   Deborah W. Rooke, '"What Shall we do with the Tainted Maiden?" Film Treatments of the Book of Esther', in Richard Walsh (ed.), *The T&T Clark Companion to the Bible and Film* (London: Bloomsbury, 2018), p. 327.

The Story of Ruth
USA, 1960 – 131 mins
Henry Koster

DIRECTOR Henry Koster
PRODUCER Samuel G. Engel
SCREENPLAY Norman Corwin
CINEMATOGRAPHY
Arthur E. Arling
EDITOR Jack W. Holmes
MUSIC Franz Waxman
PRODUCTION COMPANY
Twentieth Century Fox Film
Corporation
MAIN CAST Elana Eden, Viveca
Lindfors, Tom Tryon, Stuart
Whitman, Peggy Wood

Many see Ruth as a relatively late addition to the Hebrew Bible, added to balance or rebuke the rise of anti-gentile sentiment.[1] Henry Koster's 1960 adaptation can be read as a similar rebuff to mid-twentieth century society, particularly Hollywood's biblical epics. Whereas DeMille' *Ten Commandments* paralleled the Cold War, casting the Israelites as proto-Americans liberated from a dictator, *Ruth* puts a non-Israelite/foreigner centre-stage. Norman Corwin's 'pithy' script frequently references Israelite laws about care for aliens as if challenging nationalist paranoia.[2]

Elana Eden breaking epic stereotypes in *The Story of Ruth* (1960).

While *The Story of Ruth* is hardly the first Bible film to extrapolate a few verses into a two-hour plus film, the biblical text comprises just four short chapters, and some of the most pivotal figures are dead almost before the story has begun. The film, however, takes time establishing this pre-story, notably Ruth's love affair with Naomi's son Mahlon. Ruth is a Moabite, indoctrinated from childhood into the worship of Chemosh and its accompanying practice of child-sacrifice, yet Ruth herself is portrayed as good-hearted. When she meets Mahlon her interest in his 'invisible God' piques and her religion begins to trouble her faith.

The ensuing conflict with the priests of Chemosh see Mahlon, his brother and Naomi's husband die, and Naomi and Ruth return to Bethlehem. McCarthyism references abound,[3] Naomi's return to Bethlehem mirrors the many leftist screenwriters returning to Hollywood. Once in Israel Naomi and Ruth try to navigate 'anti-Moabite feelings' and some of the Bible's strangest customs such as gleaning practices, inheritance laws, remarriage arrangements and the curious symbolism of exchanging sandals.[4] Naomi is not on good terms with her relative, Boaz. Much changed from his youth, Boaz is torn between politics, the law and, eventually, his love for Ruth. When the two first meet, he is rude to Ruth and remains distant for some time. In contrast, his kinsman, Tob, initially appears helpful, though his façade masks ulterior motives.

The film subverts the typical biblical epic by minimizing battles, orgies and falling masonry; with its positive view of outsiders; and its echoes of Austen's *Pride and Prejudice*. A feminist impulse governs the film. The title indicates Ruth as its hero; no man is even mentioned. Furthermore, Ruth is married to two men during the film and it is her intelligence that means she end up married to the man she wants, rather than accepting societal norms that view her as property. While its star, Israeli actress Elana Eden, is beautiful, she is not heavily sexualized nor clothed in revealing costumes. Moreover, she fits neither of the two extremes usually assigned to women in biblical epics (pious-but-unenticing or seductive-and-dangerous).

A sub-plot concerning two Moabite soldiers hunting Ruth unnecessarily lengthens the film, while a closing scene features an angel/prophet figure predicting Ruth's place in both the ancestry of King David and one 'who some say will be the messiah'.

Shorn of battles and overt displays of sexuality, Koster's anti-epic is able to take a more serious look at some of the important issues raised by the text. At a time when attitudes to immigrants are hardening, its negative portrayal of those mobilizing against immigrants, emphasis on Hebrew laws to protect outsiders, and its reminder of Jesus' own mixed ancestry was a powerful testament to those in the 1960s and still challenges attitudes today.

Notes

1   Margaret Beeching, 'Ruth, Book of', in *The Illustrated Bible Dictionary*, Part 3 (Leicester: Inter-Varsity Press, 1980); Rpt, (1994), p. 1354.

2   Barry Atkinson, *Heroes Never Die: The Italian Peplum Phenomenon 1950–1967*, (London: Midnight Marquee, 2018), p. 314.

3   Jeffrey Richards, *Hollywood's Ancient Worlds* (London: Continuum UK, 2008), p. 118.

4   Jon Solomon, *The Ancient World in the Cinema* (New Haven: Yale University Press, [1978] 2001), p. 173.

Barabbas (1961)
Italy/USA, 1961 – 132 mins
Richard Fleischer

DIRECTOR Richard Fleischer
PRODUCERS Dino De Laurentiis,
Luigi Luraschi
SCREENPLAY Nigel Balchin,
Diego Fabbri, Christopher Fry,
Pär Lagerkvist, Ivo Perilli
CINEMATOGRAPHY
Aldo Tonti
EDITORS Raymond Poulton,
Alberto Gallitti
MUSIC Mario Nascimbene
MAIN CAST Katy Jurado, Arthur
Kennedy, Silvana Mangano,
Anthony Quinn
PRODUCTION COMPANY
Columbia Pictures Industries Inc.

By the time Dino De Laurentiis hired Richard Fleischer to adapt Pär Lagerkvist's 1950 novel, a Swedish version had already been filmed by Alf Söjberg in 1953. Beginning on the first Good Friday both book and film follow Barabbas rather than the Nazarene as he struggles to come to terms with the fact that he was saved at Jesus' expense.

Barabbas' finest moment is the crucifixion scene, shot during an actual solar eclipse, a decision taken just 48 hours beforehand as Fleischer and director of photography Aldo Tonti drove into uncharted territory. Ultimately, working in the dark (literally and metaphorically) Tonti stripped off any filters, opened the lens wide and placed the camera so the sun shone directly into the lens' centre.[1] Even if based on historical speculation, the results are powerful, comprising one of the earliest movie recordings of an eclipse and giving the scene an eerie feel, far superior to equivalent moments from other biblical epics of the era. The strange atmosphere during an eclipse seems perfectly suited to the death of God's son.

The eclipse scene has been perfectly teed up by the disdain with which Flesicher's camera treats Jesus, stripping him of any significance. He first appears as the camera begrudgingly nudges left to incorporate him into the fringes of the opening shot. Beginning by focussing up a set of steps towards Pontius Pilate, highlighting his power; Jesus appears, almost incidentally around the frame's edge, emphasizing his weakness. Positioning the camera amongst the crowd alongside those rooting for Barabbas, associates the viewer with him, making them complicit in Jesus' death. Jesus is flogged – in shots indebted to Caravaggio and Diego Velázquez – and Barabbas stumbles away, dazzled by a bright light that appears almost to emanate from Jesus himself. Here, as elsewhere, he seems haunted by Mario Nascimbene's unusual *'suoni* nuovi' soundscape.[2]

Yet Barabbas (Anthony Quinn) cannot escape the 'prophet'. He returns to his friends only to find his girlfriend now follows Jesus. As he tries to laugh off his experiences, Jesus passes by his window *en route* to Golgotha. When he tries to sleep he awakes during the eclipse, fearing the light even as the darkness begins to envelop him. Barabbas spends twenty years in the sulphur mines, with a stately montage marking his gradual descent deeper and deeper under the earth, and then in the gladiatorial arena. Impervious to his opponents, and lucky, it begins to look like Barabbas *cannot* be killed,[3] as if sentenced to wander, unable to find peace.

However, just as Quinn's Zampano fails to comprehend the pure-hearted Gelsomina in *La Strada* (1954), so too Barabbas fails to comprehend what God desires from him. He seeks out Peter and the early church, but misunderstands, helps burn Rome and gets arrested.

The film ends on an ambiguous note. Barabbas is finally is crucified, but it's unclear whether his dying words 'Darkness. I give myself up into your keeping' are an affirmation of faith or a denial of it. Of all the biblical epics it's *Barabbas* that leaves itself most open to interpretation. A 2012 remake starred Billy Zane in the title role.

The real-life eclipse from *Barabbas* (1961).

Notes

1   Joel K. Harris, 'Totality, cinema, and crucifixion', in *Astronomy* vol. 22 Iss. 11 (Milwaukee, November 1994), p. 18.

2   Stephen C. Meyer, *Epic Sound: Music in Postwar Hollywood Biblical Films* (Indianapolis: Indiana University Press, 2015), p. 198.

3   Meyer, *Epic Sound*, p. 208.

King of Kings
USA, 1961 – 171 mins
Nicholas Ray

DIRECTOR Nicholas Ray
PRODUCER Samuel Bronston
SCREENPLAY Ray Bradbury,
Philip Yordan
CINEMATOGRAPHY
Manuel Berenguer, Milton
R. Krasner, Franz Planer
EDITORS Harold F. Kress,
Renée Lichtig
MUSIC Miklós Rózsa
PRODUCTION COMPANY
Samuel Bronston Productions
MAIN CAST Brigid Bazlen,
Hurd Hatfield, Jeffrey Hunter,
Siobhan McKenna,
Ron Randell, Robert Ryan,
Carmen Sevilla, Frank Thring,
Orson Welles (narrator)

King of Kings should have been one of the best Jesus films ever made. Producer Samuel Bronston assembled an illustrious team including Nicholas Ray director of *Rebel Without a Cause* (1955), writer Philip Yordan and the incomparable composer Miklós Rózsa. The cast was equally experienced featuring great stage actors such as Robert Ryan, Hurd Hatfield, Ron Randell and Frank Thring

Unfortunately, Bronston and Ray were very different styles of filmmakers. Bronston set up operations in Spain and produced a series of opulent epics such as *El Cid* (1961). Ray directed intimate, personal films such as *In a Lonely Place* (1950) and *Johnny Guitar* (1954). Clashes between their artistic visions left the film in a mess. Extra scenes and additional characters were introduced and then removed again, requiring further new scenes to be shot to patch up the gaps.[1] Ray was unable to 'undo the havoc wrought on Jeffrey Hunter's diction by studio staff' and left production before the final cut.[2]

However, in spite of the final production's patched-together feel, there is much to admire, particularly Ray's visual flair. The bright and vivid exteriors contrast with the darker, foreboding interiors, most notably those in the city. Outdoor scenes constantly take place under a bright blue sky. Despite Hunter's laboured delivery of the Sermon on the Mount, Ray creates a lively choreography and spontaneity as Jesus wanders among friends, foes, and curious neutrals, answering their questions with sound-bites from the Gospels.

Equally enjoyable is Ray's use of colour and costumes. While many Jesus films focus on Jesus' eyes, Ray repeatedly uses intense close shots of Hunter's azure blue irises, immense on a big screen.[3] Prior to his ministry, Jesus wears a plain brown robe, contrasting with power-signifying red of the ruling Romans. Once Jesus' mission begins he switches to white robes. At key points, however, Jesus appears in red, highlighting his opposition and challenge to Roman rule.[4]

Those pursuing power are often framed climbing up stairs or walking up hills. The treacherous Herod Antipas, and Judas, are both shown clambering up steps immediately before betraying those closest to them. This symbolic connection is inverted as Jesus ascends through Jerusalem's streets *en route* to his crucifixion. The scene also reproduces shots from DeMille's 1927 *The King of Kings*. Indeed, Ray delights in experimenting with traditional Christian imagery. The Last Supper scene eschews Leonardo's painting preferring a God shot of a Y-shaped table with Jesus at the centre not only emphasizing his importance, but also suggesting greater intimacy and community. Later in the scene, a light behind Jesus' head gives Jesus a halo.

It wasn't only Ray's masterful visuals that encouraged the viewer to look at Jesus in a new way. Yordan's script enables the audience to look at proceedings through the eyes of two opposite characters. Judas' journey from trusted disciple to betrayer is well known, and whilst the script humanizes him and makes his betrayal more understandable, his naïvety is still considered unforgiveable. In contrast, Yordan develops the semi-fictional Roman character, Lucius, who makes the opposite journey. Initially just one of the hated Romans, he ultimately becomes the centurion who declares Jesus as the Son of God having presided over his crucifixion.[5]

Unfortunately the film gets too entangled in a zealot subplot, such that Jesus is only on screen half the time. Redubbing Jesus made his scenes dull compared to the swordplay, and the chopping and changing of episodes and characters destroyed its narrative flow. It's unlikely that a director's cut of *King of Kings* will ever turn up in a vault somewhere, but we can only hope somehow it does.

The Sermon on the Mount scene from *King of Kings* (1961).

Notes

1   Bernard Eisenschitz, *Nicholas Ray: An American Journey*, trans. Tom Milne (London: Faber & Faber, 1993), pp. 360–75.
2   Bernard Eisenschitz, *Nicholas Ray: An American Journey*, trans. Tom Milne (London: Faber & Faber, 1993), p. 374.
3   Richard C. Stern, Clayton N. Jefford and Guerric Debona, *Savior on the Silver Screen* (New York/Mahwah NJ: Paulist Press, 1999), p. 75.
4   Richard Walsh, *Reading the Gospels in the Dark: Portrayals of Jesus in Film* (London and New York: Trinity Press International, 2003), pp. 132–3.
5   W. Barnes Tatum, *Jesus at the Movies* (California: Polebridge Press, [1997] 2013), p. 85–6.

Il vecchio testamento (*The Old Testament*)
Italy/France, 1962 – 115 mins[1]
Gianfranco Parolini

DIRECTOR Gianfranco Parolini
PRODUCERS Mario Maggi,
Mario Damiani
SCREENPLAY Ghigo De Chiara,
Luciano Martino, Giorgio
Prosperi, Giovanni Simonelli
MUSIC Angelo Francesco
Lavagnino
PRODUCTION COMPANY
Cinematografica Associati
MAIN CAST Brad Harris,
Mara Lane, Franca Parisi,
Ivano Staccioli

The two Books of the Maccabees are tucked away amongst the 'deuterocanonical' books of the Bible (sometimes called the Apocrypha), which perhaps explains, why filmmakers have struggled to find them. Aside from Enrico Guazzoni's 1911 *I Maccabei* the only significant treatment is another Italian movie, Gianfranco Parolini's *Il Vecchio Testamento* .

Illustrated film booklet for the German release of *Il vecchio testamento* (1962).

While both books tell the story of how Mattathias and his five sons led the Maccabean overthrow of the Seleucid Empire, book two zooms in on the third son, Judas – nicknamed 'The Hammer'. None of this translates particularly easy into a screenplay, not least because the ruling Maccabee keeps getting killed and replaced by another of his relations.

Parolini's adaptation gets around this problem by making Simon, rather than Judas, the lead character. As the last of the brothers to die, the deaths of Simon's various family members become tragic moments in his story. The film culminates not with Judas' restoration of Jerusalem's temple in 164BC, but with Jonathan and Simon's victory at Joppa seventeen years later.

These decisions enable a more fluid screenplay, but they also Christianize texts that have greater significance in Judaism than Christianity. These problems start with titling the film as '*The* Old *Testament*' and extend to the final scene where Jews essentially crucify their enemies. In-between Judas' celebrated restoration of the temple, and the miracle that enabled it, are largely ignored. Indeed the Bible's primary hero, Judas (played by Serbian Djordje Nenadovic) is portrayed, without nuance, as a violent zealot, whose ideology is surpassed by his more three-dimensional, blond, peace-seeking brother (the USA's Brad Harris).

Two cuts of the film survive. The shorter omits much of the nuance around Simon. Initially Simon seems almost like a Hellenized Jew, representing a more appeasing, moderate approach to Seleucid rule.[2] He socializes with, and dresses like, Seleucid friends (here called Syrians) each of whom are horrified when their countrymen inflict suffering on their friends, especially when Simon's Syrian best friend Antenone is executed by Jewish forces. Significantly, of all the deaths in this film, only the spirit of non-Jewish Antenone is shown rising up in bodily form. He appears later as a Christ figure.

Without these moments the story becomes little more than that of a series of battles. Judas' violent tactics lend a certain inevitability to his untimely death, as if the film is demonstrating how it considers his violent approach to be incompatible with true faith. Yet Antenone's and Judah's deaths make Simon realize that he must use limited force against the Syrians. This could be read as being about post-Fascist Italian politics, the brewing Israeli-Palestinian conflict, USA foreign policy or simply the filmmakers' desire to include crowd-pleasing battles without facing criticism. Either way 'the set design of Old Jerusalem … is fantastic' and better prints reveal some accomplished cinematography.[3]

Rumours continue to circulate about Mel Gibson film about the Maccabees. Given the source's guerrilla violence, determination amidst persecution and unlikely victories, a Hasmonean *Braveheart* seem plausible, though equally unlikely to reflect the source material.

Notes

1   Currently only an 89-minute cut of the English version is available. German version 115 minutes.
2   Whilst the film calls them Syrians and the text calls them *ethnon* (nations/gentiles) the opening prologue to Maccabees makes clear they were from the Syrian/Northern Greece part of Alexander the Great's former empire, typically known as Seleucids.
3   Barry Atkinson, *Heroes Never Die: The Italian Peplum Phenomenon 1950–1967*, (London: Midnight Marquee, 2018), p. 182.

Il vangelo secondo Matteo (*The Gospel According to Matthew*)
Italy/France, 1964 – 127 mins
Pier Paolo Pasolini

DIRECTOR Pier Paolo Pasolini
PRODUCER Alfredo Bini
SCREENPLAY Pier Paolo Pasolini
CINEMATOGRAPHY
Tonino Delli Colli
EDITOR Nino Baragli
MUSIC Luis Bacalov
PRODUCTION COMPANY
Arco/Lux Procuction
MAIN CAST Margherita
Caruso, Enrique Irazoqui,
Marcello Morante,
Susanna Pasolini

Many consider *Il vangelo secondo Matteo* to be both the finest biblical film ever made and Pier Paolo Pasolini's greatest work. Pasolini, a self-described '*pasticheur*' delighted in mixing 'the most disparate stylistic material' in unusual combinations.[1] His love of mixing or 'contaminating' (to use his term), high culture with low culture saw him prosecuted for his bawdy 1963 crucifixion-themed tragi-comedy *La Ricotta*.

Il vangelo secondo Matteo (1964).

Here, his adaptation of Matthew's Gospel places neorealist techniques alongside documentary-type footage.[2] Costumes evoke historic art rather than history itself and images from classical painters such as Piero della Francesca sit alongside the rugged faces of rural farm workers. The soundtrack famously combines 'high' culture music, such as Bach's baroque aria from 'St. Matthew Passion', with grassroots forms such as Odetta and Blind Willie Johnson, alongside music with Russian Marxist connotations.

Fired by a conviction that his people ought to run their own affairs, rather than be subject to a political elite, Pasolini's Jesus is a fired-up revolutionary. He marches round the jagged, southern Italian countryside like Rossellini's Garibaldi spitting pithy aphorisms over his shoulder and unleashing his ire on the ruling classes. 'I did not come to bring peace, but a sword' he fires back at his disciples as they hurry to keep up.

The focus on the men and women working in the agricultural south is one of the most arresting aspects of the whole film. Not only were the Hollywood Jesus movies of the era filled with perfect smiles and finely chiselled features, they also tended to focus on the story's leading characters. Pasolini opts for ordinary people with little or no acting experience whose faces are not classically attractive, encompassing a wider spectrum, old, young, male, female, attractive and ugly. Pasolini favoured lingering close-ups of faces and black and white film stock as opposed to colour. The result is a gritty feel which captures the poverty of those among whom Jesus ministered, bringing them out from the margins.

Pasolini consistently refuses to sexualize the women in the narrative. A plain-faced, teenage Salome dances without eroticism. The woman who anoints Jesus in Bethany is not young and exceptionally beautiful but normal-looking and middle-aged. As with others, Enrique Irazoqui had little acting experience when cast as Jesus. His Jesus is often thought of as the 'angry Christ' and indeed the words of the seven woes, or even the Sermon on the Mount, have rarely been spoken so forcefully. Yet on closer investigation, Irazoqui is a prayerful Jesus who smiles and emits warmth when surrounded by children. In truth, Jesus is stranded halfway between the intellectuals and the Jewish peasants. The camera often separates him from his countrymen as if, despite his desire to be one of the people, he cannot bridge the gap.

The film's stark, black and white cinematography, innovative hand-held camera-work, elegant compositions and dreamy, meditative feel, combine to create a host of strikingly memorable images. Similarly the eclectic blend of music imparts the film with a deeply spirituality. Whether these images and sounds denote a temporary embrace of Christianity or loss of faith in communist ideals, it's their beauty that makes Pasolini's *Gospel According to (St) Matthew* such a moving and memorable work.

Notes

1   Oswald Stack, *Pasolini on Pasolini* (London: Thames and Hudson/British Film Institute, 1969), p. 28.

2   The film is not simply neorealist as often claimed; rather neorealism is just one of many elements Pasolini uses in his pastiche.

The Greatest Story Ever Told
USA, 1965 – 191 mins
George Stevens

DIRECTOR George Stevens
PRODUCERS Frank I. Davis,
George Stevens, Antonio Vellani
SCREENPLAY James Lee
Barrett, Henry Denker, Fulton
Oursler, George Stevens
CINEMATOGRAPHY
Loyal Griggs, William C. Mellor
EDITORS Harold F. Kress, Argyle
Nelson Jr., J. Frank O'Neill
MUSIC Alfred Newman
PRODUCTION COMPANY
Metro-Goldwyn-Mayer
MAIN CAST Michael Anderson
Jr., Pat Boone, José Ferrer,
Charlton Heston, Angela
Lansbury, David McCallum,
Dorothy McGuire, Donald
Pleasence, Telly Savalas,
Max von Sydow, Shelley Winters

Just as the comic book genre has dominated the twenty-first century box-office, so too the biblical epic dominated mid-century cinema. When United Artists gave celebrated director George Stevens control of an array of star talent, a limitless supply of celluloid and a colossal $20 million budget, they hoped for the kind of success enjoyed by modern movies such as *Avengers: Endgame* (2019). Instead Stevens' box office disaster almost killed the biblical epic and remains widely derided for its plodding pace, catastrophically corny conclusion to the first act and misfiring cameos (particularly John Wayne's drawling centurion).

Yet, in an age where the film is more likely to be viewed from the comfort of home, in instalments, by an audience increasingly unfamiliar with the likes of Telly Savalas, Shelley Winters and Pat Boone, its strengths are beginning to re-emerge. In contrast to most of the cast list, the relatively unknown Max von Sydow plays Jesus. Having proven his ability to play introverted philosophical characters in numerous Ingmar Bergman films, von Sydow gives Jesus an understated determination and a quiet authority.[1] The screenplay, adapted from a post-war radio series and Fulton Oursler's resulting novel, stays close to John's Gospel – the opening shot accompanied by John's prologue, the pivotal raising of Lazarus, the greater emphasis on Jesus' words rather than miracles, and the interior spirituality. Von Sydow encapsulates John's mystical, other-worldly saviour.[2]

But perhaps what most impresses these days is the photography. Initially Stevens had scouted out Israel, but ultimately opted for the southwestern United States,[3] enabling Stevens and cinematographer William Mellor to capture some astounding images, even if they bear little relation to first century Judea. As with *Shane* (1953), Stevens uses the visual language of the western to tell the story of Jesus.[4] The film's mood, and its Jesus, seems far more at home in the desert, and the open spaces. Jesus and his disciples move about within shots dominated by the sparse natural beauty of the landscape, such that at times it feels as if God-incarnate is dwarfed by his creation.

The lighting of the similarly imposing interior shots contrasts greatly with these bright exteriors. The dark, shadowy images reflect Jesus' disdain for those who can afford to live inside them – separated from creation and detached from the suffering of the poor, reflecting the Gospels' ambiguity about Jerusalem. While the long running-time is sometimes considered off-putting, it allows time to inhabit these images, and enjoy them for what they are. It gives the film a meditative feel where the viewer allows the beauty and perfection of the images to wash over them.

Yet this is not empty spirituality. A verse from the prophet Hosea – 'I desire mercy not sacrifice' – is repeated three times in the film, summing up this Jesus' message. Right attitude is more important than hollow actions. Mercy rather than sacrifice, teaching rather than miracles, devotion rather than spectacle and artistic purity rather than box office success. While this might not be the greatest version of the greatest story ever told, it is undoubtedly one of the most devout.

The quiet authority of von Sydow's Jesus in *The Greatest Story Ever Told* (1965).

Notes

1   Tim Cawkwell, *The Filmgoer's Guide to God* (London: Darton, Longman and Todd, 2004), p. 148.

2   Richard Walsh, *Reading the Gospels in the Dark: Portrayals of Jesus in Film* (London and New York: Trinity Press International, 2003), p. 152

3   William R. Telford, 'The Greatest Story Ever Told', in Adele Reinhartz (ed.), *Bible and Cinema: Fifty Key Films* (London/New York: Routledge, 2013), p. 122.

4   Bruce Babington and Peter William Evans, *Biblical Epics: Sacred Narrative in the Hollywood Cinema,* (Manchester: Manchester University Press, 1993), p. 141.

I grandi condottieri (*Samson and Gideon*)
Italy/Spain, 1965 – 86 mins
Marcello Baldi and Francisco Pérez-Dolz

DIRECTORS Marcello Baldi,
Francisco Pérez-Dolz
PRODUCER Toni Di Carlo
SCREENPLAY Marcello Baldi,
Tonino Guerra, Ottavio Jemma,
Flavio Niccolini
CINEMATOGRAPHY
Marcello Masciocchi
EDITOR Carl Pierson
MUSIC Teo Usuelli
PRODUCTION COMPANY
San Pablo Films
MAIN CAST Ivo Garrani,
Anton Geesink, Rosalba Neri,
Fernando Rey

The success of Pietro Francisci's 1958 film *Le fatiche di Ercole* (Hercules) resulted in the *peplum* era during the late 1950s and early 1960s which saw vast numbers of B-grade Italian sword and sandal epics reaching cinemas on both sides of the Atlantic. *Pepla* featuring supernatural heroes such as Hercules, Goliath and Machiste – the hero created by the 1914 silent *Cabiria* – proved particularly popular. Indeed, rather than re-working the traditional myths, the majority of these films were based on entirely invented stories, meaning often the name of the lead character varied from country to country. 1961's *Maciste contro il vampire* (Machiste against the Vampire), was rebranded in the UK and the USA as *Goliath and the Vampires*.

Still from *I grandi condottieri* (1965).

Unsurprisingly Samson was a frequent choice. At least fifteen films were named after Samson in just seven years. But Marcello Baldi, director of *I grandi condottieri* takes a less 'superficial' approach than films like *Samson in the Wax Museum* (1963) and *Samson vs. the Giant King* (1964), which 'draws on the viewer's curiosity'.[1] Moreover, Samson shared the billing with another Hebrew 'judge', Gideon, whose story cinema has largely bypassed.

The film is the last of four biblical *pepla* made by the much underappreciated Baldi, following *I patriarchi* (*The Patriarchs*, 1962), *Giacobbe, l'uomo che lottò con dio* (*Jacob, the Man Who Fought with God*, 1963) and *Saul e David* (1964). Working with Spaniard Francisco Perez Dolz, much of the film (including the Gideon episode) was shot in Spain, with some parts being shot in Italy's Cinecittà studios.

The first part of the film stars Ivo Garrani as an affable, 'folksy' Gideon and Fernando Rey as 'the Stranger'.[2] The two form an unlikely friendship such that having delivered God's initial message, Rey's character stays on to help Gideon slim down his burgeoning volunteer army, advise on strategy and give Gideon much needed encouragement. There are moments of humour (having reduced his army again Gideon quips 'I wonder why we don't charge the Midianites, just the two of us') and the initially grumpy Gideon become a more relaxed and inspiring leader. The lesser known part of the story, where Gideon pursues, captures and kills the Midianite leaders, also features.

Part two, is more self-serious, even including moments of pathos. This section of the film is more typical of the mythical muscleman *pepla*. Whereas Gideon remains fully clothed, Samson is frequently shirtless. While Gideon's messenger remained present throughout, Samson experiences God as a voice or a billowing wind. Even when God appears at the end of the film, Samson does not perceive him.

The film's strength, though, is its host of memorable images, testifying to Baldi's eye for striking compositions such as Midianites burning Israelite fields; Garrani's face superimposed over a montage of Israelite victories; the flames enveloping the Midianite camp; the moment of realization when Samson spots the ass' jawbone; and the shot of the upper echelons of Dagon's soon-to-be-destroyed temple.[3] 'Teo Usuelli's reverberating score' also impresses.[4]

Sadly though, the main versions of the film available for home viewing are blighted by poor image quality, so not only is it hard to appreciate *Grandi condottieri*'s strengths, but consequently it gets less attention than it merits. Hopefully, one day the film will get a decent release, so Baldi and Dolz's contributions to the *pepla* genre and the Bible on film can be appreciated and re-evaluated.

Notes

1   Massino Giraldi and Laura Bove, *Marcello Baldi: cinema, cattolici e cultura in Italia*, (Trento, Italy: Fondazione Museo Storico del Trentino), p. 36. Translation my own.

2   Jon Solomon, *The Ancient World in the Cinema* (New Haven: Yale University Press, [1978] 2001), p. 166.

3   Christopher Mulrooney, 'Marcello Baldi', *Pix*. Available online: <https://cmulrooney.tripod.com/baldimarcello.html> (accessed 19 Dec. 2021).

4   Barry Atkinson, *Heroes Never Die: The Italian Peplum Phenomenon 1950–1967*, (London: Midnight Marquee, 2018), p. 185.

The Bible: In the Beginning...
Italy/USA, 1966 – 167 mins
John Huston

DIRECTOR John Huston
PRODUCERS Dino De Laurentiis, Luigi Luraschi
SCREENPLAY Orson Welles, Mario Soldati, Ivo Perilli, Christopher Fry, Vittorio Bonicelli, Jonathan Griffin
CINEMATOGRAPHY Giuseppe Rotunno
EDITORS Ralph Kemplen, Alberto Gallitti
MUSIC Toshirô Mayuzumi, Ennio Morricone
PRODUCTION COMPANY Dino Di Laurentiis Cinematographica
MAIN CAST Ulla Bergryd, Stephen Boyd, Ava Gardner, Richard Harris, John Huston, Peter O'Toole, Michael Parks, George C. Scott

John Huston was one of the great figures of Hollywood, bursting onto the scene in 1941 with *The Maltese Falcon* before creating a series of front-line World War II documentaries. His catalogue of hits extended well into the 1980s. Meanwhile he furthered the Hollywood dynasty founded by his father Walter – his children Anjelica, Tony and Danny gained prominent Hollywood roles, and his grandson Jack took the lead in *Ben-Hur* (2016).

Houston acted too. Here he narrates Genesis' opening chapter over a stunning collection of images of the natural world: molten lava bubbles and flows as the land is separated from the sea; a gigantic sun rises, and moves across the skies, as the greater light is brought forth; and swarms of fish burst through the waters of the deep, as the creatures of the seas are created. In addition to the jaw-dropping beauty of the creation sequence, which even after numerous nature documentaries still creates a sense of awe, Huston skilfully pilots a course between literal and more metaphorical readings. Like the written text, the viewer applies their own interpretation to the raw material.

Following the creation of Adam, and then Eve – where the actors cavort around behind a series of strategically-placed plants – the fall, and the scenes where Cain (Richard Harris) kills his brother, are accompanied by dissonant music (the soundtrack excels throughout). This, combined with the bizarre poses Harris strikes and the low, then high, camera angles make this whole sequence strange and disorientating. Whilst the narration keeps rigidly literal to the text, the film uses the more cinematic elements of image and sound to provide a more mythical reading.

The exception is Huston's 'folksy' Noah segment,[1] whose lighter comedic touch, inter-family dialogue and looser adherence to the text seems out of place with the broody, otherworldly tone struck by the rest of the film. However, the pre-historic feel soon returns at the Tower of Babel, where high contrast lighting contributes to the eerie aura. Stephen Boyd's Nimrod, complete with a painted-on mono-brow, shoots his arrow into the sky only to find that, suddenly, no-one can understand him.

The second half begins with George C. Scott's Abraham leaving Ur. Again the film adapts the stories (Ishmael's birth, the angelic visitation, the fall of Sodom and the cancelled sacrifice of Isaac) in biblically-'faithful' fashion whilst simultaneously questioning the legitimacy of such a presentation. Particularly strange is Peter O'Toole's head switching between Abraham's three ethereal visitors and an orgy scene in a 'dark, labyrinthine' Sodom that is more creepy than arousing.[2]

These scenes present Abraham's story, as some sort of hope for humanity, even as it hints of the rocky, traumatic road ahead. The scene of Abraham and Isaac walking stealthily through the charred remains of Sodom, jumps to Abraham preparing to kill his child, often provoking anger rather than reverence. Abraham is troubled, but also haunted by his temperamental God. His willingness to sacrifice his son is an act of fear of rather than faithful service.

Director/Noah-actor John Huston surveys his team's work on/in *The Bible: In the Beginning...* (1966).

It's a fitting end to Huston's 'personal film on a gigantic scale'.[3] Huston's film appreciates Genesis's transition from the broad scale of chapter one to the story of God's relationship with a string of individuals – Adam, Cain, Noah, Abraham and Isaac. Its literal narration, in tandem with its dark, primitive feel, underlines the mythological nature of the texts imbibing the film with that strange sense of the dawn of time, and the primitive nature of early humanity. While the tone of the Noah sequence is occasionally misplaced, the overall boldness of Huston's vision is hard to deny.

Notes

1   Jeffrey Richards, *Hollywood's Ancient Worlds* (London: Continuum UK, 2008), p. 119.

2   John Huston, *An Open Book* (London: Macmillian, 1981), p. 322.

3   Gerald E. Forshey, *American Religious and Biblical Spectaculars* (Westport, CT: Praeger, 1992), p. 146.

Les Actes des apôtres (*Acts of the Apostles*)
France/Italy/Spain/West Germany/Tunisia, 1969 – 340 mins
Roberto Rossellini

DIRECTOR Roberto Rossellini
PRODUCERS Vittorio Bonicelli,
Renzo Rossellini
SCREENPLAY Roberto
Rossellini, Vittorio Bonicelli,
Luciano Scaffa, Jean-Dominique
de la Rochefoucauld
CINEMATOGRAPHY
Mario Fioretti
MUSIC Mario Nascimbene
PRODUCTION COMPANY
RAI/ORTF/TVE Studio Hamburg
MAIN CAST Malo Brass,
Jacques Dumur, Zignani
Houcine, Mohamed Kouka,
Edoardo Torricella, Enrico
Osterman

'Cinema is dead' claimed the great Roberto Rossellini in 1963, just eighteen years after his *Roma, citta aperta* had thrust Italian neo-realism into the spotlight.[1] Instead he proceeded to make didactic, historical, television films aiming to promote rational thought amongst 'the masses'. After the success of his 1966 *Rise to Power of Louis XIV*, he moved onto the Book of Acts.

The series' five-hour runtime enables all Acts' major episodes to be included whilst allowing them space to breathe. Using ultra-long takes, most scenes are filmed in single, extended, *plan-séquence* shots, though some scenes are presented in montage. This implied neutrality and its understated acting, suggest historical

Les actes des apôtres (1969). (Courtesy of Tag Gallagher).

reliability, yet these scenes remain emotionally powerful. The subtleties of the performances are particularly moving. For example, shortly before the Council of Jerusalem, Peter is shown waiting for the other delegates, capturing his anticipation and joy at being reunited with his friends and brothers in Christ.

The film's quiet restraint proposes a simpler age. Moments of space, often at the beginning or end of a shot, are the very essence of Rossellini's film. The disciples' mundane, everyday existence is spent in manual labour, Peter dyeing cloth, Paul weaving and Stephen serving food. The disciples spread the gospel as they work, an idea Rossellini repeated in *Il Messia* (1975). The protracted timescale stresses the apostles' geographic isolation from each another, and their lack of awareness about the speed and progress of Jesus' message. When Paul meets Priscilla and Aquila he is amazed to discover both Jesus and he himself, are already well known. Elsewhere a trademark Rossellini 'Pan Cinor' shot very gradually zooms out from a close-up of a deserted dust track.[2] The masterful shot, gradually incorporates, and eventually dwarfs, Paul and Barnabas as they trek up the road to Pisidian, epitomizing so many long quiet walks along deserted roads.

Rossellini communicates significant quantities of contextual historical information. In particular, during the opening half hour a Roman noble is given social and historical commentary during a tour of Jerusalem, which places the narrative in a broader context, including explaining that Christianity was only one of numerous Jewish sects. Elsewhere, another character offers an exposition of the rise and fall of the various Caesars. Rossellini shows a great respect for the Judaism of the period, stressing the Judaism of the early apostles. Prior to his conversion Saul is shown sitting in the Sanhedrin, and even after his trip to Damascus he retains his *payot* (side curls).

Yet Rossellini's primary concern is to minimize that which Hollywood epics sought to exaggerate. Rossellini omits romantic sub-plots and underplays the persecution of leading figures. Acts' many sermons are not rousing speeches but low-key affairs, delivered 'in a flattened, often completely uninflected way'.[3] Moreover, large crowd scenes and onscreen miracles are kept to a minimum, relying on characters recounting supernatural occurrences. Not only is this the way these stories been heard ever since, but it sets them in a fresh context so that, once again, they become as startling as they were for their original audiences, liberating viewers from the confines of over-familiarity. Seven years later, Rossellini would adopt a similar approach when filming the Gospels in his final film *Il messia*.

Notes

1   Tag Gallagher, *The Adventures of Roberto Rossellini: His Life and Films* (New York: Da Capo Press, 1998), p. 538.

2   Rossellini's long Pancinor shots zoomed in and out, typically changing the point of focus before zooming in, keeping different pockets of action within the same shot.

3   Peter Brunette, *Roberto Rossellini* (Berkeley/Los Angeles/ London: University of California Press, 1996), p. 262.

La Voie lactée (*The Milky Way, 1969*)
France/Italy/West Germany, 1969 – 97 mins
Luis Buñuel

DIRECTOR Luis Buñuel
PRODUCERS Anna Muzii,
Serge Silberman
SCREENPLAY Luis Buñuel,
Jean-Claude Carrière
CINEMATOGRAPHY
Christian Matras
EDITOR Louisette Hautecoeur
MUSIC Luis Buñuel
PRODUCTION COMPANY
StudioCanal Image/Fraia Film
– Rome
MAIN CAST Alain Cuny,
Paul Frankeur, Edith Scob,
Laurent Terzieff

As an irreverent religious satire, Luis Buñuel's *La Voie lactée* (The Milky Way) makes for easy comparison with *Monty Python's Life of Brian*. Both films are the product of well read, subversive artists,[1] who incorporate short sections of the Gospels into a more extensive filmic collage of humour, surrealism and hyper-articulate discussions.

Mary and Jesus in *La Voie lactée* (1969).

The film follows the bizarre encounters surrounding two impious pilgrims journeying along Camino de Santiago, featuring numerous Catholic-related characters from through the ages: an eloquent, but insane, priest; waiters debating theology, philosophy and heresy; a dogma-drenched school speech day; a revolutionary firing squad shooting the pope; a duel between a Jansenist and a Jesuit; and the Marquis de Sade. Sometimes the pilgrims interact with the characters and events they encounter, other times they simply witness them.

The biblical material is used in varying ways. The opening scene finds the pilgrims asking a stranger for alms. Discovering the younger man is penniless, the stranger gives him nothing, yet when the older man admits having money, he receives a crisply-folded banknote. The stranger then commands them to 'go and find a harlot, and have children by her' naming them 'You Are Not My People' and 'No More Mercy'. These jarring re-contextualizations of Jesus' conclusion to the Parable of the Talents, and God's instructions to Hosea, are typical of Buñuel's forensic approach. After they part, the pilgrims observe a child and a dove alongside the stranger completing the Trinity.

The more classical appearances of Jesus follow from chance remarks. The pilgrims conclude that the stranger favoured the older man because of his beard, so Buñuel flashes back to the first century with Mary persuading Jesus not to shave off his beard. When one of the philosophical waiters claims Jesus 'must've walked like anyone one', Buñuel cuts to Jesus running to greet his disciples, late for the Wedding at Cana. Once there, he begins the Parable of the Shrewd Steward, but tantalizingly the scene ends before we see if the water has turned into wine. There's something fresh and exciting about the way Jesus enters the scene running, even if it is because he is late.

Further enigmatic vignettes follow, but when the pilgrims finally arrive at Santiago they are greeted by a woman who takes them into the woods for a 'frolic in the grass', and repeats Hosea's quotation. The camera pans from them to two blind men who encounter Jesus and ask for healing. Jesus rubs mud on their eyes, prays and walks on with the disciples and the men in tow. The film's final shot shows the feet of Jesus and his disciples walking through the grass. As they step over a ditch the camera fixes on it, waiting for the blind men to approach it. The film ends abruptly before the miracle is proved/disproved.

Buñuel claimed his road-movie through heresy and orthodoxy was 'neither for nor against anything at all', except the kind of 'fanaticism, where each person obstinately clings to his own particle of truth'.[2] It's the product of 'a lifetime deeply marked by Catholicism and surrealism',[3] more damning about Catholicism specifically than Jesus himself. The two miracles are left open-ended, the refusal to conclude them left in the realm of faith. It's an ambiguity typified by Buñuel's famous quip, 'Thank God I am an atheist'.[4]

Notes

1   Peter William Evans, *The Films of Luis Buñuel: Subjectivity and Desire* (Oxford: Clarendon Press, 1995), p. 160.
2   Luis Buñuel, *My Last Breath* (London: Jonathan Cape, 1984), p. 245.
3   Ian Christie, 'Buñuel against "Buñuel": Reading the Landscape of Fanaticism in *La Voie lactée*', in Peter William Evans and Isabel Santaolalla (eds.), *Luis Buñuel: New Readings*, (London: British Film Institute, 2004), p. 140.
4   For context and later misgivings about this quote see Philippe Theophanidis, 'On Luis Buñuel's aphorism: "Thank God I'm an Atheist"', *Aphelis*, 5 February 2012. Available online: <https://aphelis.net/luis-bunuels-aphorism-god-im-atheist/> (accessed 19 Dec. 2021).

Son of Man
UK, 1969 – 90 mins
Gareth Davies

DIRECTOR Gareth Davies
PRODUCER Graeme MacDonald
SCREENPLAY Dennis Potter
PRODUCTION COMPANY BBC
MAIN CAST Colin Blakely, Brian
Blessed, Edward Hardwicke,
Robert Hardy, Bernard Hepton

Dennis Potter's play was filmed by the BBC in 1969 and its initial broadcast, featuring Colin Blakely as a fiery, working-class, messiah left many shocked. Potter chose Blakely for the role because of his 'marvellous pent-up hatred'.[1] It works well for Blakely whose roughly-hewn Jesus is brilliant, passionate and unpredictable. In contrast to the BBC's first attempt at the Gospels, the eight-part, location-shot, *Jesus of Nazareth* (1956), *Son of Man* was filmed in a studio in just three days. Director Gareth Davies' stripped down, low-budget feel, shot with a bobbing camera circling the crowds, recalls Pasolini's *Il vangelo secondo Matteo* (1964).

Colin Blakely's working-class messiah in *Son of Man* (1969).

The roughness of the production, which Potter claimed looked 'as though it's trembling and about to fall down',[2] only enhances its raw power, aligning it with 1960s British social realism films such as *This Sporting Life* (1963). 'You bastard' sneers Brian Blessed's Peter as Judas betrays their master.

Potter's everyday English was groundbreaking, and more realistic than other such attempts, enabling Blakely to make Jesus come alive, while retaining a dangerous edge so often absent in Jesus films. Occasionally interjecting humour ('Give to Caesar what belongs to Caesar. Give to God what belongs to God… and shut up.') or pathos ('Good timber this. I could fill a room with tables and chairs with wood like this', mutters Jesus as he affectionately pats a recently vacated cross). Potter's words on Blakely's lips are dynamite. When he first encounters Peter and Andrew they dismiss him as a 'loony' and a 'madman'. Two minutes later they abandon their nets to follow him.

Indeed the spectre of mental instability haunts the entire production, from the opening shot of a huddled Blakely crying out 'Is it me?', through to when Robert Hardy's Pilate yells 'take the idiot away' after Jesus' beatific smile deeply unnerves the governor. Hardy plays Pilate more like a working-class soldier who has progressed through the ranks, than part of the imperial elite. He slurps his food, cheers on with almost sexual excitement at residential wrestling bouts and letches over his servant girl. What frightens him is not violence but 'ideas'.

In contrast, only Caiaphas and Judas are recognizably middle-class. Caiaphas is elegantly dressed with a crisp, well-spoken accent and physical poise, suggesting an in-built sense of superiority. When he dismisses Pilate as having 'the manners of a carpenter', he links Rome's physical empire to Jesus' spiritual kingdom. Elsewhere Potter puts Jesus' declaration 'He is coming' from the end of scene one, onto the lips of a revolutionary at the start of scene two.

But whereas Pilate can put down revolutionaries like Barabbas, he's right to fear Jesus' ideas. When Pilate beats his slave girl, she repeats Jesus' teaching 'love your enemies', a message first unleashed immediately after the Romans have butchered a village of insurrectionists.[3] Potter's script delivers best when reworking Jesus' actual words and Blakely's electric delivery here converts an angry and sceptical crowd to the path of love in the face of suffering and atrocity.

Of course, such influence cannot stand and Blakely's charismatic preacher dies in the bleakest of all on-screen crucifixions. There's a brief flashback to the wilderness where he once again writhes with fear howling 'Is it me?' Then we are back at the cross, its low height and the shot's tight composition emphasizing the Romans' utter dominance. There's no music forcing emotion, just a depressing silence and the desperate cry of 'why have you forsaken me?' The play offers little hope of a resurrection, and for once we understand how the first Good Friday felt to those unfortunate enough to have been there.

Notes

1   W.S. Gilbert, *Fight, Kick And Bite: Life and Work of Dennis Potter* (London: Sceptre, 1996), p. 180.

2   Dennis Potter, *Potter on Potter* (London: Faber and Faber, 1993), p. 40.

3   Philip Yancey, *The Jesus I Never Knew* (London: Marshall Pickering, 1995), p. 129.

Jesús, nuestro Señor (*Jesus, Our Lord*)

Mexico, 1971 – 115 mins
Miguel Zacarías

DIRECTOR Miguel Zacarías
PRODUCER Alfredo ZacarÃas
SCREENPLAY Alfredo Zacarías
CINEMATOGRAPHY
Eduardo Rojo
EDITOR Federico Landeros
MUSIC Enrico C. Cabiati
PRODUCTION COMPANY
Panorama Films, S.A.
MAIN CAST Claudio Brook,
Narciso Busquets, Carlos East,
Rita Macedo

Mexico may be geographically close to the United States, but their religious landscapes and cinematic aesthetics are markedly different, amply demonstrated by Miguel Zacarías' *Jesús, nuestro Señor*. Clearly there's a gulf in budgets, resulting in ill-fitting beards and significantly smaller crowd scenes. More significant, though, is the film's use of the camera, including shots which deliberately draw attention to themselves. Occasionally the camera zooms into a scene quickly and sometimes unevenly, resisting movement at a gradual pace, contrary to mainstream Hollywood aesthetics. Shots from low angles (emphasizing Jesus' power) and high shots abound, including the 'God shot' that introduces Herodias' daughter's dance of the seven veils.

There are also marked visual differences. After Jesus' baptism he transforms into a dove.[1] During the nativity, the angels wear school play-style costumes. Aside from Satan's 'Dracula-like cape',[2] bright colours feature prominently throughout in costumes and decor, recalling High Renaissance era paintings by Raphael and Michelangelo. Indeed the film opens with a montage of famous paintings from Filippo Lippi's 'Adoration of the Child' to El Greco's 'Disrobing of Christ'.

Zacarias was 'a pioneer of film-sound' so unsurprisingly, there are differences in terms of sound.[3] Whilst the film's main theme remains essentially orchestral, brass instruments dominate and are joined by less-familiar instruments. We also hear the voice of Jesus inside the heads of those accusing a woman of adultery, suddenly giving the viewer a range of different perspectives.

The most startling difference, however, is the inclusion of two incidents which feel more typical of horror movies than biblical films. When John the Baptist is executed, his head is placed before Herod, eyes still open. Herod attempts to evade its stare, even walking out of its direct gaze, only for the Baptist's head to rotate following a terrified Herod back and forth. Not dissimilarly when Jesus dies, previously-dead bodies arise from the ground and start walking about in a highly literal take on Matthew 27. Indeed *Nuestro Señor* is particularly pre-occupied with the re-animating miracles, including all three of those Jesus raised from death, the widow of Nain's son, Jairus's daughter and Lazarus. These contribute to the significant screen time given to women.

Such scenes perhaps explain Zacarías' choice of Claudio Brook as Jesus. Brook made his name in a string of films with Luis Buñuel, including the title role in *The Exterminating Angel* (1962), the lead in *Simon del Deserto* (Simon of the Desert, 1965) and a minor role as a bishop in *La Voie Lactée* (The Milky Way). *Jesús, nuestro Señor* is more reverential than Buñuel's work, but one cannot help wondering if Buñuel might have enjoyed these moments.

Brook carried on working until his death in 1995. His work on *Cronos* (1993) with Guillermo del Toro, means he is probably the only actor to have worked with Mexican cinema's two greatest directors. Zacarías, released two other adaptations of the Gospels: *Jesús, el niño Dios* (Jesus the Child of God, 1971) and its sequel *Jesús, María y José* (Jesus, Mary and Joseph, 1972).

Claudio Brook in *Jesús, nuestro Señor* (1971).

Notes

1   Carol Hebron, *Judas Iscariot: Damned or Redeemed – A Critical Examination of the Portrayal of Judas in Jesus Films (1902–2014)* (London: Bloomsbury T&T Clark, 2016), p. 146.

2   Peter Malone, *Screen Jesus: Portrayals of Christ in Television and Film* (Lanham/Toronto/Plymouth, UK: Scarecrow Press, 2012), p. 97.

3   Hebron, *Judas*, p. 145.

Jesus Christ Superstar
USA, 1973 – 102 mins
Norman Jewison

DIRECTOR Norman Jewison
PRODUCERS Norman Jewison,
Patrick J. Palmer,
Robert Stigwood
SCREENPLAY Tim Rice, Melvyn
Bragg, Norman Jewison
CINEMATOGRAPHY
Douglas Slocombe
EDITOR Antony Gibbs
MUSIC Andrew Lloyd Webber
PRODUCTION COMPANY
Universal Studios
MAIN CAST Carl Anderson,
Barry Dennen, Yvonne Elliman,
Ted Neeley

Tim Rice and Andrew Lloyd Webber's rock opera reworked the story of Jesus' death with electric guitars and theological angst, having developed from a handful of songs into a triple-platinum album. Following successful runs on Broadway and London's West End, Norman Jewison took charge of making *Superstar* into a film.

Jewison combined Roman ruins, tanks and aeroplanes with costumes evoking both biblical and modern eras, giving *Superstar* a distinctive, deliberately anachronistic, look to accompany its memorable score. While today its deliberate camp seems somewhat dated,[1] it captures both the story's ancient and modern significance.

Ted Neeley as Jesus in a still from *Jesus Christ Superstar* (1973).

Having enjoyed critical and financial success with another musical, *Fiddler on the Roof* (1971), Jewison prioritized singing ability over cinematic experience, meaning that while the actors have formidable voices, most were unknown beforehand. Ted Neely (Jesus) and Carl Anderson (Judas) give formidable performances in vocally demanding roles. Anderson's vocal power gives his role a striking vitality. Judas (the opera's unexpected hero) realizes Jesus has fallen prey to his popularity, and so acts to save the people.[2] Anderson's performance, both physically and vocally, not only overturned centuries of caricatures of Judas, but also upended the stereotypical roles usually given to Black actors.

Moreover, the filmmakers' desire for greater inclusivity is apparent throughout. Mary Magdalene, Simon the Zealot and many of Jesus' other followers were played by non-white actors,[3] similarly several shots of men with their arms around one-another, suggest greater positivity towards same-sex relationships. Yet disconcertingly the film does little to counter the musical's inherent antisemitism,[4] particularly apparent when the Jewish crowd bully a reluctant Pilate into crucifying Jesus.

Rice's libretto replaces a single narrative viewpoint with the internal monologues of the leading characters, harnessing the emotionally powerful music to express their inner feelings in a series of solos, dialogues or consecutive monologues. This enables the audience to temporarily adopt the soloists' point-of-view and glimpse inside their minds. For the first time we hear the 'thoughts' of Judas, Mary, Pilate and Caiaphas. As each character tells the story from their own perspective we not only see what they say and do, but also to what they think and feel.

Judas worries that Jesus' claims of divinity and growing popularity, will undo all their previous good work. Determined not to give the Romans another opportunity to crush his people, Judas hands Jesus over, fulfilling both their destinies. Realizing he has been used by both God and the priests, he kills himself, but returns in the glittering finale to quiz Jesus about his motives.

What enables these solos to be so powerful is the emotion in the music. Lloyd-Webber's use of rock smashed the conventions of the day, but nevertheless produced the same stirring impact of its predecessors. The radical nature of the production rubs off on the characters. Like Rice and Lloyd Webber, Jesus and his band of disciples are youthful outsiders taking on the establishment, perhaps why subsequent adaptations have lacked the original's impact.

The cinematography and Israeli locations are stunning; from the opening moments (when an axial cutting series of zooms captures Judas alone on top of a mountain) through to the hazy sunset of the deeply moving, closing shot. A masterful and technically outlandish slow zoom links the final moments of Judas' life on a mountain top, to Jesus' trial far below. Neeley and Anderson continued playing their roles for decades, forever changed by their experience. *Superstar* endures today, a pertinent reminder that musicals can be revolutionary, poignant, artful, hugely entertaining and deeply affecting.

Notes

1   Richard A. Lindsay, *Hollywood Biblical Epics: Camp Spectacle and Queer Style from the Silent Era to the Modern Day.* (Santa Barbara, California/Denver, Colorado: Praeger, 2015), p. 156.

2   Mark Goodacre, 'Do You Think You're What They Say You Are? Reflections on Jesus Christ Superstar' Journal of Religion and Film: Vol 3, no. 2 (1999). pp. 14–15. Available online: <https://digitalcommons.unomaha.edu/jrf/vol3/iss2/2/> (accessed 19 Dec. 2021).

3   Richard C. Stern, Clayton N. Jefford and Guerric Debona, *Savior on the Silver Screen* (New York/Mahwah NJ: Paulist Press, 1999), p. 192.

4   Adele Reinhartz, *Jesus of Hollywood. Oxford* (New York: Oxford University Press, 2007), pp. 241–2.

Godspell
USA, 1973 – 102 mins
David Greene

DIRECTOR David Greene
PRODUCERS Edgar Lansbury,
Kenneth Utt, John Van Eyssen
SCREENPLAY David Greene,
John-Michael Tebelak,
Stephen Schwartz.
CINEMATOGRAPHY
Richard G. Heimann
EDITOR Alan Heim
MUSIC Stephen Schwartz
PRODUCTION COMPANY
Columbia Pictures Industries Inc.
MAIN CAST Victor Garber,
Katie Hanley, David Haskell,
Lynne Thigpen

Released the same year as the hugely popular *Jesus Christ, Superstar*, *Godspell* tends to suffer in comparison, despite the two being very different productions in style and genre. While both were based on hit musical versions of the Gospels, *Godspell* (written by Stephen Schwartz) is more concerned with Jesus' life and ministry – passing quickly over his death – whereas *Superstar* skips over Jesus' ministry to focus on the events leading to his crucifixion. While *Superstar* poses more controversial questions, *Godspell* took a more creative and innovative approach to the material.

Garber's Jesus with David Haskell's Judas/John the Baptist in *Godspell* (1973).

The flavour of 1970s student movements is strong in both. *Godspell* is set in 1970s New York with John the Baptist calling Jesus' disciples from mundane jobs in the city, towards a deserted Central Park where they encounter Jesus, dressed in a Superman T-shirt and clown shoes. They proceed to follow him around New York locations, including a now eerie sequence on top of the World Trade Centre's twin towers.

Looking back, neither the original musical nor the film have dated well. Decisions that were bold at the time, now look overly kitsch, and its flaws have become more obvious. The costumes and the interplay between the characters have particularly failed the test of time. However, its biggest flaw is the presentation of the events leading to Jesus' death. Re-contextualizing the story as 1970s New York 'American street theatre',[1] extracts Jesus from his original political and religious context, but fails to find a fresh alternative. By removing any tangible disagreements with Jesus' teaching, the film creates a bizarre robot to be his primary antagonist. Judas' betrayal lacks any motivation and Jesus' 'crucifixion' upon an electric fence also weakens what should be a powerful conclusion. Jesus' death feels tacked on and lacking in motive and significance.

Yet the finished film still has its strengths, notably the way it re-invigorates Jesus' parables. After 2000 years of church history, it is easy to forget that the parables were once unknown. To us they have lost their element of surprise and their creativity. *Godspell* counteracts that, giving them fresh vitality and restoring their original challenge and 'social discontent'.[2] While *Godspell* claims to be based on Matthew's Gospel, it pulls in Luke's most vivid and memorable parables: the Good Samaritan; the Pharisee and the Publican; the Rich Man and Lazarus; and the Prodigal Son.

In contrast, miracles are largely absent from the film.[3] Even the resurrection is depicted simply by Jesus' (still lifeless) body being carried victoriously into the city by his now reinvigorated disciples. If the intention was to portray the resurrection as a metaphor then the bizarre sight of Jesus' followers victoriously carrying his corpse into central New York rather undermines it. If those who truly loved him thought his death was permanent, how could they be this joyful so soon afterwards? Conversely, the moments when *Godspell* most resembles cinema, rather just a filmed musical, occur during the film's prologue when the John the Baptist character 'magically' appears in several places at once.[4] This, very self conscious, use of camera trickery represents the supernatural aspect of Jesus' ministry, though it ends just as Jesus' ministry begins.

Whether the film is saying that Jesus' miracles were simply a way to gain attention, or that his teaching superseded the need for miracles, is unclear. Nevertheless, it is interesting that the very end of the film provides one final example. Jesus' disciples carry his body round a corner and suddenly the streets are no longer deserted and the disciples and Jesus are no longer visible. The music creates an upbeat and stirring ending which is rather unearned.

Notes

1   Lee Gambin, *We Can Be Who We Are: Movie Musicals from the '70s* (Albany: Bear Manor Media, 2015), p. 175.

2   Richard Walsh, *Reading the Gospels in the Dark: Portrayals of Jesus in Film* (London and New York: Trinity Press International, 2003), pp. 73–7.

3   Tina Pippin '*Godspell* (1973)', in Adele Reinhartz, *Bible and Cinema: Fifty Key Films*, (London/New York: Routledge, 2013), p. 106.

4   Gambin, *Movie Muscials*, p. 173.

Moses und Aron (*Moses and Aaron*)
West Germany/Austria/France/Italy, 1975 – 107 mins
Danièle Huillet and Jean-Marie Straub

DIRECTORS Danièle Huillet,
Jean-Marie Straub
PRODUCERS Danièle Huillet,
Jean-Marie Straub
SCREENPLAY Arnold
Schoenberg, Danièle Huillet,
Jean-Marie Straub
CINEMATOGRAPHY
Renato Berta, Saverio
Diamante, Giovanni
Canfarelli Modica
EDITOR Harold F. Kress
MUSIC Arnold Schoenberg
MAIN CAST Eva Csapo,
Louis Devos, Roger Lucas,
Günter Reich
PRODUCTION COMPANY
Österreichischer Rundfunk (ORF)

Moses und Aron was an adaptation of Jewish-Austrian composer Arnold Schoenberg's unfinished opera by French filmmakers Danielle Huillet and Jean Marie Straub. Having suffered antisemitic abuse in 1921,[1] Schoenberg realized assimilation into German culture was unattainable and re-converted to Judaism. He turned to biblical themes and began arguing for a modern Jewish state. By 1932 'Moses und Aron' was complete, barring its final act. Schoenberg pioneered atonalism, his obscure style giving each of the scale's twelve notes equal prominence.

Schoenberg's opera enabled Straub/Huillet to combine their interest in texts with their interest in stratifications of the past. Rather than creating false versions of the past in the present, their adaptations of

Aron bound-up in the final act of *Moses und Aron* (1975).

Brecht, Bach, Cornille and Kafka display different layers of history without stitching them into the present. Their 1970 film *Othon* features actors dressed as first-century Romans, reciting lines from a seventeenth-century play, amongst Roman remains, while the sounds of modern city continue in the background.

Moses und Aron, allowed Huillet/Straub to adapt an opera, based on the biblical text, which originated from previous written or oral prehistoric texts, and included two layers in Schoenberg's work: two acts completed and honed to perfection, and one incomplete act preserved in the midst of formation.

Schoenberg's libretto omits much of Exodus, and begins with Moses kneeling before the burning bush, charged with persuading his people to follow an 'invisible and inconceivable' God. Aron comes to help, but Moses cannot communicate the depth of his experience. So Aron alters Moses' message so the people can understand.[2] Turning Moses' rod into a snake and showing Moses' infected (and then uninfected) hand, wins the people to this new faith.

Having skipped past Moses' confrontations with Pharaoh, the plagues, the Exodus and the parting of the Sea of Reeds, Act II begins with Moses on Mount Sinai, while rebellion stirs below. Aron, believing the people need a god they can conceive of, casts the golden bull. An orgy ensues. Moses returns, but Act II – and often the entire opera – ends with him in despair, crying 'Oh word, word that I lack'. Once more, the interval skips several key events. When we return, Moses is in charge again and Aron is on trial.

Just as Schoenberg's obscure style is hard to appreciate, so is Straub/Huillet's. Their interest in film as an artistic form produces 'a cinema of withholding,' removing melodrama and overt demonstration of the characters' feelings, even disrupting their cadences.[3] Their diagonal compositions, long takes, natural sound and concern for location create mindful, formal cinema. Here Günter Reich (Moses) and Louis Devos (Aron) are largely stationary. The choir stand in regimented rows, grouped together but distinct from their surroundings. Only during the orgy, when Moses is on the mountain, do characters break from these strictures, signifying their rejection of God's perfect order.

The unscored final act most clearly reveals Huillet/Straub's 'counter-reading' of Schoenberg's ideas.[4] As Marxists they emphasize Moses wrestling back control. Denied a trial, Aron lies bound up in the mud. For them this signifies the defeat of both authority figures: having witnessed this revelation, the people should now lead themselves.

The result is a dense and challenging work which provides a religious angle and a political one. Having witnessed how the more meaningful and spiritual biblical films are often less accessible and entertaining, here the characters wrestle with the same paradox – communicating God's essence results in dilution, if not distortion, of this invisible and inconceivable God. Even those who grasp that may resort to violence to further their aims.

Notes

1   Bluma Goldstein, *Reinscribing Moses: Heine, Kafka, Freud, and Schoenberg in a European Wilderness* (London: Harvard University Press, 1992), pp. 138–41.

2   God's words, which begin the work, follow a pure form of twelve note atonalism. Moses mirrors this but Aron distorts these tonal patterns.

3   Robert Phillip Kolker, *The Altering Eye: Contemporary International Cinema* (Oxford: Oxford University Press, 1983), p. 212.

4   Benoît Turquety, *Danièle Huillet, Jean-Marie Straub: "Objectivists" in Cinema*, trans. by Ted Fendt (Amsterdam: Amsterdam University Press, 2020), p. 93.

Il messia (*The Messiah*)
Italy/France, 1975 – 145 mins
Roberto Rossellini

DIRECTOR Roberto Rossellini
PRODUCERS Tarak Ben Ammar,
Silvia D'Amico Bendicò
SCREENPLAY Silvia D'Amico
Bendicò, Jean Gruault
CINEMATOGRAPHY
Mario Montuori
EDITORS Roger Dwyre,
Pierre Gillette
MUSIC Mario Nascimbene
PRODUCTION COMPANY
Orizzonte 2000
MAIN CAST Fausto Di Bella,
Carlos de Carvalho, Pier Maria
Rossi, Mita Ungaro

Most of the films Rossellini directed during his later historical phase were made for television,[1] but he returned to the cinema because 'RAI had decided to back Zeffirelli's *Jesus of Nazareth* instead of Rossellini's Jesus film.[2] The result remains one of the finest Jesus films ever made. Like Pasolini, Rossellini's *Il messia* aligns Jesus' followers with the rural south, rather than the industrial north and integrates Jesus more completely with his followers. The *mise en scène* treats his disciples almost as Jesus' equals as he carves wood and catches fish alongside them as he teaches.[3] The rural peasant community that forms around Jesus – he is repeatedly shown returning to the heart of the same village – is shown in contrast to the corrupt elite. They are associated with the grand buildings of the city. He is largely shot in the dust and dirt of the open air.

Jesus with fishermen in *Il messia* (1975).

The emphasis on corruption goes right back to the film's unusual prologue, set in the days of the prophet Samuel. Tired of defeats in battle, Israel's leaders press for a king. Samuel's warnings about adopting a monarch go unheard and Saul is anointed king. It is not long until Saul and his army are abusing their power. The film abruptly leaps forward to King Herod, plotting a massacre for the hour of his death so at least the people will mourn for *somebody*.

Jesus and his disciples are ordinary labourers. A series of masterful long takes show Jesus instructing his followers as they work. Jesus teaches the Parable of the Sower as he fashions a plough and delivers another parable about fish as they all haul in a net. It's almost surprising when he arrives in Jerusalem to find a large following.

Rossellini had long perfected his use of dispassionate extended takes which here becomes part of his critique of power. His refusal to manipulate his viewers' emotions through editing and camera tricks embodied his message.[4] The film only depicts three 'miracles', all in characteristically understated fashion. In the first, Jesus suggests that, following an unsuccessful night's fishing, the disciples try again. Jesus rests. There's a cut. Suddenly the disciples return with a 'marvellous' catch, but the interpretation is left to the viewer. Later a blind man recounts to Caiaphas how Jesus healed him, but the miracle itself remains off-screen.

The low-key approach continues to Jesus' crucifixion. His trial is restrained and downplayed. The crowd numbers around twenty in a vast courtyard stressing how Caiaphas' supporters are not representative of the Jewish people. Later shots are composed like a modern courtroom only with Jesus, rather than Pilate, in the position of judge.[5] There is no procession to the cross, indeed, the two Marys and John witness the trial, but only arrive once Jesus is on the cross. A short while later he dies. No signs or special utterances mark his passing. In the background children continue chanting the Seder prayer *Had Gadyo* unaware of what has happened.

The focus of the closing scenes is on Jesus' mother, played by seventeen-year-old Mita Ungaro. In one of the film's most memorable moments she holds the body of her son, perfecting recreating Michaelangelo's *Pietà*. Two days later when she discovers Jesus' tomb is empty she kneels on the ground, looks skyward, and worships. As before, this final miracle is ambiguous. Mary's tears and her serenity provide an uplifting moment, even if her experience remains open to interpretation.

Notes

1   For an overview of religious and biblical themes in Rossellini's work, see my chapter 'Roberto Rossellini: From Spiritual Searcher to History's Documentarian' in Rhonda Burnette-Bletsch (ed.) *The Bible in Motion: A Handbook of the Bible and Its Reception in Film*. vol.2, (Berlin/Boston: Walter de Gruyter, 2016), pp.623–34.

2   Tag Gallagher, *The Adventures of Roberto Rossellini: His Life and Films* (New York: Da Capo Press, 1998), p.669.

3   Peter Brunette, *Roberto Rossellini* (Berkeley: University of California Press, 1996), p343.

4   Lloyd Baugh, *Imaging the Divine: Jesus and Christ Figures in Film* (Franklin, Wisconsin: Sheed & Ward, 1997), p.90.

5   Tag Gallagher, 'The Messiah' [video essay]. Available online: <https://vimeo.com/48501880> (accessed 19 Dec. 2021).

The Passover Plot
Israel/USA, 1976 – 108 mins
Michael Campus

DIRECTOR Michael Campus
PRODUCERS Menahem Golan,
Wolf Schmidt
SCREENPLAY Millard
Cohan, Paul Golding, Patricia
Louisianna Knop, Hugh J.
Schonfield
CINEMATOGRAPHY
Adam Greenberg
EDITOR Reg Spragg
MUSIC Alex North
PRODUCTION COMPANY
Atlas Film
MAIN CAST Harry Andrews,
Hugh Griffith, Zalman King,
Donald Pleasence

A generation before Dan Brown's *The Da Vinci Code* there was another implausible, best-selling book whose controversial claims proved popular: Hugh Schonfield's 1965 *The Passover Plot*. Following the success of 1973's *Jesus Christ, Superstar* and *Godspell*, Schonfield's book was adapted into a movie. However, whereas *The Da Vinci Code* claimed Jesus died at the crucifixion but his blood line lived on, *The Passover Plot* has Jesus 'fake his death on the cross' so he could pretend to have been resurrected.[1]

Given this premise, Michael Campus' adaptation is better than might be anticipated. A reasonably solid cast, Alex North's score, Oscar-nominated costumes and the Israeli locations raise the film above its source material. Zalman King, who became a pioneering producer of 'softcore films and television',[2] is probably the first Jewish actor to play Jesus, here known as Yeshua. The disciples are likewise known as Yohanan, Yaocov and Yudah, rather than John, James and Judas. Indeed the Jewish origins of the gospel narratives are heavily emphasized: the prayers around the Last Supper rely more on traditional *seders* than the New Testament; other Jewish rituals are shown such as the celebration of Bartholomew's son being born; and the recital of the Shema. Jesus and his disciples are even shown wearing *tefillin* at one point. There's a strong emphasis on the hopes for a Jewish messiah and Yeshua repeatedly stresses his work is reforming and fulfilling Judaism, rather than launching a new religion. However, some of these traditions emerged well after Jesus' death.

In contrast to Dafoe's controversial Jesus in *The Last Temptation of Christ* (1988), King's Yeshua is a 'political radical' who initially appears well-rounded and easy to relate to.[3] The pivotal moment arises when a fraudster claiming to be blind begs for money. Jesus spits in his face to expose him, but the disciples interpret his new-found vision as a miracle and onlookers quickly form a crowd. Campus allows plenty of time to relate to this devout, dancing, smiling Jesus, but gradually he becomes more unstable, yelling his message at night and claiming to be the messiah. At times Jesus whispers with his friends. Moments later he yells with all his might to a crowd in the open air.

Omitting all Jesus' other miracles, the film features long periods of quiet while the camera pans round to capture the atmosphere, giving the piece a rhythm and mood quite unlike any other Jesus film. Moreover, there is relatively little teaching. Yet therein lies the main problem with Schonfield's theory and Campus's adaptation. Without Jesus' resurrection, miracles or teaching he is reduced to a nice, but misguided, individual whose ideas about loving enemies may be part of his delusion. The odd story about a sower, and turning a few tables in the temple do not even make someone particularly interesting, let alone significant enough to inspire their followers to found one of the world's largest religions.

The Passover Plot (1976).

Notes

1 W. Barnes Tatum, *Jesus at the Movies* (California: Polebridge Press, [1997] 2013), p. 141.

2 Peter Malone, *Screen Jesus: Portrayals of Christ in Television and Film* (Lanham/Toronto/Plymouth, UK: Scarecrow Press, 2012), p. 86.

3 Roy Kinnard and Tim Davis, *Divine Images: A History of Jesus on the Screen* (New York: Citadel–Carol Publishing Group, 1992), p. 184.

Jesus of Nazareth
Italy/UK/USA, 1977 – 382 mins
Franco Zeffirelli

DIRECTOR Franco Zeffirelli
PRODUCERS Bernard J. Kingham, Vincenzo Labella, Tarak Ben Ammar, Lew Grade, Dyson Lovell
SCREENPLAY Suso Cecchi D'Amico, Anthony Burgess, David Butler, Franco Zeffirelli
CINEMATOGRAPHY Armando Nannuzzi, David Watkin
EDITOR Reginald Mills
MUSIC Maurice Jarre
PRODUCTION COMPANY ITC Entertainment Limited and Radio-Televisione Italiana
MAIN CAST Anne Bancroft, Ernest Borgnine, Claudia Cardinale, James Farentino, Ian Holm, Olivia Hussey, James Earl Jones, James Mason, Laurence Olivier, Donald Pleasence, Robert Powell, Anthony Quinn, Michael York

Franco Zeffirelli's six hour *Jesus of Nazareth* is arguably the most iconic of all Jesus films. The different film-making traditions of its Italian, USA and UK funders combined well: its Italian/Roman Catholic familiarity with Christian art and its veneration of Mary; its Hollywood stars; and its dialogue, at times, akin to a British soap opera. The tendency is exemplified in lead actor Robert Powell. His blue-eyed Jesus is so typically North-European, yet nevertheless, reflects the Christ of Italian Renaissance art.

Robert Powell in *Jesus of Nazareth* (1977).

The supporting cast featured 'an avalanche of' household names.[1] Laurence Olivier, Michael York, Anne Bancroft, James Mason, James Earl Jones, Anthony Quinn, Christopher Plummer, Donald Pleasence and Ian Holm all had starring roles, not to mention Olivia Hussey's youthful, unageing, Mary. But it was Robert Powell's mesmerizing performance as Jesus that became the major talking point. Even today, people tell him how moving they found the film and how touched they were by his portrayal.[2] Powell's piercing, blue, unblinking eyes and his slow, measured delivery, gave his character a sense of awe which some adored, but others found lifeless or dull.

The reverence for Jesus gives an impression of other-worldliness, but also makes him somewhat detached. Low, close shots emphasize his stately grace and authority suggesting his divinity. Zeffirelli's stated intention to portray a more human Jesus caused a storm of outrage and lost him a major sponsor,[3] but bears little relation to the final product, especially when compared to the film's contemporaries such as *Jesus Christ Superstar* or *Il messia*.

However, Zeffirelli creates a sense of intimacy verging on the romantic by repeating the same combination of shot selection, blocking and physical touch. Each follows the same classic Hollywood formula: an array of establishing shots from different angles captures a sense of the space and those present; then closer, more intimate shots of Jesus and the person he is connecting with. Eventually, the camera lands on a two-shot with the characters looking deep into one another's eyes, followed by alternating point-of-view or over the shoulder shots. Inevitably, the viewer is drawn towards Powell's unflinching eyes. At a pivotal point in the scene, Jesus reaches out and places a reassuring hand on their shoulder, or holds their hand comfortingly, their togetherness captured in a final two shot. Interestingly two major deviations from this formula are Jesus' encounter with the rich young man (Mark 10) and his first meeting with Judas. The pattern is largely the same, but Jesus never reaches out and touches either man.

The series' lengthy running time enables development of both the story's background and its characters. Perhaps its greatest sequence portrays the newly converted tax collector Matthew throwing a banquet. He invites his friends from his former life as well as Jesus and the harrumphing disciples. Jesus tells the Parable of the Prodigal Son and, from across the room, melts Peter's heart, and ours, ably assisted by Maurice Jarre's stirring score. Moreover, the crucifixion material is incredibly poignant. Jesus' belief in his mission falters, injecting occasional hints of desperation and uncertainly as those in power move to crush him.

Even if passages emphasizing the extremes of Jesus' humanity and divinity are excluded,[4] and the resurrection sequence feels strangely rushed,[5] the sheer length of the production means enough gospel material is included to make it feel comprehensive. For many it remains the definitive adaptation and when they picture Jesus, Powell's face is still the one they imagine.

Notes

1 Franco Zeffirelli, *The Autobiography* (London: Arrow Books, 1986), p. 280.
2 Powell to author, London, 28 February 2008.
3 W. Barnes Tatum, *Jesus at the Movies* (California: Polebridge Press, [1997] 2013), p. 153.
4 Lloyd Baugh, *Imaging the Divine: Jesus and Christ Figures in Film* (Franklin, Wisconsin: Sheed & Ward, 1997), p. 74.
5 Franco Zeffirelli describes problems filming this scene including a sandstorm *Franco Zeffirelli's Jesus: A Spiritual Diary*. Trans. by Willis J. Egan, S.J. (New York: Harper & Row, 1984), pp. 93–97.

Karunâmayudu (*Man of Compassion*)
India, 1978 – 142 mins
A. Bhimsingh and Christopher Coelho

DIRECTORS A. Bhimsingh,
Christopher Coelho
PRODUCER Vijayachander
SCREENPLAY Johnson
Modukuri, Christopher Coelho
CINEMATOGRAPHY
K. S. Prasad
MUSIC Joseph (Krishna)
Fernandez, B. Gopalam
PRODUCTION COMPANY
Radha Chitra
MAIN CAST Chandramohan,
Thyagaraju, Rajasulochana,
Vijayachander

Karunamâyudu's portrayal of the Gospels is thoroughly non-Westernized.[1] Whilst not technically a Bollywood film,[2] its actors are almost entirely Indian, including Vijaychander who is the first actor from Jesus' own continent to portray him in a major film. Stylistic similarities to other Indian cinema are very apparent. The film is packed with an array of bright colours, quite unlike anything found in most films from Europe and the USA, and features major open-air dance sequences, most notably that accompanying Jesus' triumphal entry into Jerusalem.

Karunamayudu (1978).

The project became personal for Chander having witnessed the producers early efforts flounder, he took on the role of producer. *Karunamâyudu* debuted in cinemas in India just before Christmas 1978. A year after a successful run at the box office, Chander sold the film to the missionary organization Dayspring International who still screen it throughout India today.

Whilst singing is hardly alien to Jesus films, here there are only a few such routines. Some western viewers may consider the change in sound production and the transformation of the characters unfamiliar, but it is no further from 'real life' than the conventions of Hollywood and Broadway musicals and here the musical numbers stand amongst the film's greatest moments.

The wordless ten-minute opening number covers Jesus' birth and childhood with skilful brevity, capturing the essentials without bogging the story down in cloying religiosity. The third song/dance routine covers Jesus' triumphal entry into Jerusalem. As with *Jesus Christ, Superstar*, the setting of this moment lends itself to a large chorus scene. Here a spectacular portrayal wonderfully captures the episode's mood.

Chandar's portrayal of Jesus is strong, particularly compared to his Hollywood counterparts at the time. Convincing both when smiling and when angry, his strong sense of compassion is evident in numerous scenes, without him ever appearing weak or tediously pious. The film gives him a healthy balance of humanity and divinity. Scenes of Jesus teaching high above his audience are balanced with those of him amongst the people, reacting and interacting, rather than remaining emotionally distant. One scene starts with him teaching from high up, but stops to descend to the rocks below to heal someone with leprosy. This consistent balance marks Chandar's Jesus out, both as a man of the people and as someone who still has important ideas. He draws people to himself to hear his vital message.

To stress Jesus' divinity, and the supernatural events around him, the film utilizes numerous special effects. While in a CGI-dominated era these lack gloss and seem somewhat kitschy, they emphasize the 'otherness' of these events; their extra-ordinary nature. Indeed, the film's most dazzling and memorable image is just such a shot, Jesus' ascension. So often awkwardly literal, or simply omitted, here a simple double exposure is used as Jesus' body rises above the disciples, and then proceeds to grow until it is many times their size. Stars and coloured clouds of gas punctuate the night sky, the semi-transparent nature of Jesus' body give the shot a supernatural feel as if breaking through to another reality. Meanwhile the composition evokes a host of images of Hindu deities particularly 'Krishna's return to the abode of the gods'.[3]

While the production values are not those of contemporary western cinema, *Karunamâyudu* turns this to its advantage, disregarding realism to maximize visual impact and powerful emotional responses. Chander went on to play the role of St. Paul in a 1987 biopic *Dayamayudu*, while his film's success led to a 52 episode spin off TV series, *Daya Sagar* (Oceans of Mercy, 1996–97) twenty years later.

Notes

1   *Karunamâyudu* (which can also be translated 'The Compassionate One') is the title in its original Telegu language. In other parts of India it was called *Karunamoorthy* or *Dayasagar*.

2   Technically speaking, Bollywood films come from Mumbai, whereas *Karunamâyudu* originated in India's Telugu-speaking region.

3   Dwight H. Friesen, 'Analysis of the production, content, distribution, and reception of *Karunamayudu* (1978), an Indian Jesus film', unpublished PhD Thesis (University of Edinburgh, 2009), p. 152.

Jesus
USA, 1979 – 117 mins[1]
John Krish and Peter Sykes

DIRECTORS Peter Sykes,
John Krish
PRODUCER John Heyman
SCREENPLAY Barnet Bain
CINEMATOGRAPHY
Mike Reid
MUSIC Luigi Patruno,
Luciano Salvemini
PRODUCTION COMPANY
Inapirational Films, Inc.
MAIN CAST Brian Deacon,
Rivka Neuman, Niko Nitai,
Alexander Scourby

Jesus was made outside of Hollywood, with a cast of almost entirely non-professional actors, and a shoestring budget. More often than not, it has been viewed on *ad hoc* cinema screens, set up specifically for the occasion, in remote villages across the developing world. It contains no CGI, memorable performances or hi-tech special effects and dialogue is dubbed rather than subtitled. When a new translation is made, native speakers of that language voice the various parts.

Yet a generation later, *Jesus* is arguably the most watched film in history. Its distributors Campus Crusade for Christ claim 8.1 billion viewings in around 1850 different languages.[2] The story started with producer John Heyman whose plan to film the entire Bible, word for word, was struggling financially before he had completed Genesis. Unperturbed, Heyman approached Campus Crusade about filming Luke's Gospel and releasing it to cinemas in order to bankroll the rest of his project. *Jesus* flopped and Heyman's *Genesis* remains the only word-for-word adaptation of an entire book from the Hebrew Bible. However, just as many

Jesus (1979).

of the earliest biblical filmmakers were driven by cinema's evangelistic potential, so Campus Crusade adopted it for their missionary efforts, beginning a project that has taken the film to practically every nation on earth.

Having limited dialogue almost entirely to the biblical text, *Jesus* also attempted stringent historically accuracy.[3] It was shot using the exact locations in the Holy Land and aside from the white Englishman playing Jesus (Brian Deacon) almost all the actors were Yemenite Jews – supposedly the least altered Jewish racial group over the last 2000 years. Deacon even contracted pneumonia after spending hours waist-deep in the Jordan waiting for a dove to land on his seed-covered shoulders. The desire not to 'add to existing anti-Semitism' has the narrator introduce Pontius Pilate as 'the most vicious of all Roman procurators, alone responsible for the crucifixion of thousands' in a rare addition to Luke's text.[4] The film also shows Jesus reciting the Lord's Prayer whilst wearing a prayer shawl, or reciting a Passover *Seder* prayer before feeding the 5000.

Earnestness plays badly these days, however, leaving the film suffering from its slavish reliance on a somewhat stilted text, the rambling nature of the screenplay and poor acting in minor roles. Yet surprisingly the film is a relatively strong piece of visual cinema. The attention given to composition, long tracking shots and diagonal camera positions provide a rich aesthetic which has suffered from its previous circulation on full-frame VHS cassettes. Part of the reason it has often got its message across – in addition to the warmth Deacon injects into his portrayal – is its ability to communicate through its images. Deacon's terrible bobbed hairstyle aside, high density versions of the film now available reveal a far better-looking film than was ever apparent twenty years ago.

Campus Crusade have continued to evolve their operation. Child friendly versions, editions with an opening creation narrative, a retelling of the story from a female perspective and even an attempted anime version can all be downloaded via apps on mobile phones. Meanwhile teams continue touring remote parts of Africa and Asia armed with little more than a generator and a sheet. The cultural appropriateness of that is questionable, but it's hard to imagine another film, past or future, will ever be able to make the same kind of claims about audience reach.

Notes

1   Original cut. Numerous subsequent versions have added or deleted scenes.

2   Figures include repeat viewers and are not entirely accurate. From 'Official Jesus Film Project Ministry Statistics' *Jesus Film website*, 27 May 2020. Available online at: <www.jesusfilm.org/about/learn-more/statistics.html> (accessed 19 Dec. 2021).

3   One section of footage was even re-filmed after it was discovered that they showed Eucalyptus trees which had not reached the Holy Land until a few centuries after Jesus.

4   Paul Eshleman, *I Just Saw Jesus* (San Clemente, CA: The 'Jesus' Film Project, [1985] 1994), p. 47.

Monty Python's Life of Brian
UK, 1979 – 94 mins
Terry Jones

DIRECTOR Terry Jones
PRODUCER John Goldstone
SCREENPLAY Graham
Chapman, John Cleese, Terry
Gilliam, Eric Idle, Terry Jones,
Michael Palin
CINEMATOGRAPHY
Peter Biziou
EDITOR Julian Doyle
MUSIC Geoffrey Burgon
PRODUCTION COMPANY
Python (Monty) Pictures
MAIN CAST Graham Chapman,
John Cleese, Kenneth Colley,
Terry Gilliam, Eric Idle, Terry
Jones, Sue Jones-Davs,
Michael Palin

Life of Brian is not a film about Jesus; it's a film about Brian Cohen – another Jewish man living in the same time and place, but who is clearly revealed, in a pre-credits Nativity sequence, to be a different character. Moments later Brian appears around the fringes as Jesus delivers the Sermon on the Mount. Yet a failure to grasp this basic point generated huge controversy about the film, typified by a tetchy debate where Python's John Cleese and Michael Palin refuted criticisms from Michael Muggeridge and the then Bishop of Southwark.[1]

Still from Monty Python's *Life of Brian* (1979).

Whilst Python's other films like *Monty Python and the Holy Grail* (1975) are essentially a collection of sketches, *Brian* is their most accomplished and normatively coherent film, despite their tweaking of conventional narratives, such as when a spaceship swoops down and scoops Brian into space. Surprisingly, the plot is essentially a boy-meets-girl comedy. Brian spies Judith following the Sermon on the Mount – his gaze accompanied by romantically suggestive music – and then joins the People's Front of Judea to catch her attention. As the film progresses, he tries to impress her by painting political slogans and partaking in a plot to assassinate Pilate's wife. It's only when he is mistaken as the messiah that she falls for him, celebrating his bravery even as he's crucified.

Of course, the reason for the film's enduring popularity is its humour. Analysing, or even just reciting the jokes is like carving open the golden goose. At the heart of the film's success is the sheer range and volume of gags combined with the Pythons' irreverence and gift for sending up the absurd. Yet *Life of Brian* is surprisingly respectful of Jesus himself. While Eric Idle quipped ahead of *Brian*'s release that their next project was *Jesus Christ, Lust for Glory*, such disrespect is absent from the finished film. Once the Pythons took a closer look, they realized that it was his followers they distrusted, not the man himself.[2] The movie's ultimate message is not that religion is necessarily wrong, but unquestioned ideology. It's not so much pointing upward, as inward.

Once the farce and the humour are put aside, there are numerous interesting historical and theological details that subsequent (unsuccessful) biblical comedies assumed they could dispense with.[3] A diversity of Judaisms and apocalyptic preachers are critical to understanding first-century Judea. Even Geoffrey Burgon's overlooked score cites Mozart, Wagner and Monteverdi,[4] though all anyone remembers is the Shirley Bassey-esque theme song and Idle's 'Always Look on the Bright Side of Life'.

It's that final scene which people feel most strongly about, and not for its *Spartacus* parody. Many Christians find it disrespects the most solemn event in history; agnostics and atheists see it embodying the importance of living life in the moment, making it such a popular choice at funerals, it's almost considered cliché. Public screenings of the film often culminate in a sing-a-long which can itself feel almost, well, religious.

Forty years later, many still consider *Life of Brian* to be the greatest comedy film of all time because like all great films it is excellent at one particular thing, in this case humour. Blesséd cheesemakers, ungrateful lepers, bureaucratically obsessed revolutionaries, and men pretending to be women pretending to be men just to attend a stoning, have given the film a large and dedicated following and entered our cultural vocabulary. Even those who don't find it appealing appreciate the fresh perspective it brings to the Gospels. After all, before *Brian*, who ever even considered what things might have been like for those at the back of the crowd, straining to hear the Sermon on the Mount?

Notes

1   *Friday Night, Saturday Morning* [Television Programme], BBC2, 9 November 1979. Available online: <www.youtube.com/watch?v=CeKWVuye1YE> (accessed 19 Dec. 2021).

2   The Pythons with Bob McCabe, *The Pythons The Autobiography* (London: Orion, 2003), p. 278–9.

3   See Joan Taylor (ed.) *Jesus and Brian: Exploring the Historical Jesus and His Times via 'Monty Python's Life of Brian'* (London/New York: Bloomsbury, 2015) for several interesting essays on this.

4   *Silverscreen Beats: Life of Brian* [Radio Programme], BBC Radio 4, 6 July 2006.

Camminacammina (*Keep Walking*)
Italy, 1983 – 171 mins
Ermanno Olmi

DIRECTOR Ermanno Olmi
PRODUCER Ludovico
Alessandrini, Ermanno Olmi
SCREENPLAY Ermanno Olmi
CINEMATOGRAPHY
Gianni Maddaleni,
Ermanno Olmi
EDITOR Giuliana Attenni
MUSIC Bruno Nicolai
PRODUCTION COMPANY
RAI Radiotelevisione Italiana
MAIN CAST Antonio Cucciarrè,
Alberto Fumagalli,
Eligio Martellucci,
Renzo Samminiatesi

At the heart of Ermanno Olmi's films is the reaffirmation of traditional values which society is leaving behind, a celebration of community and ordinary working-class people. His films are considered amongst the finest examples of neorealism even though its popularity was waning before his second film *Il posto* (1961) thrust him into the limelight. Olmi's 'peasant-worker background' enabled him 'to look at the world with others, not as an aristocratic intellectual',[1] and his films adroitly encapsulate the lives of those around the margins of the story with a few scant details. And then there is his Catholicism, the Christian humanism at the core of his work.

Camminacammina (1982) – which Olmi wrote, produced and directed – shifts Mary and Joseph to the sidelines, and focuses instead on the perilous, longer journey made by the wise men, primarily Mel(chior). Typically Olmi's 'narratives are structured around unspectacular dilemmas reflecting ordinary lives',[2] hence the first hundred minutes here focus solely on Mel and his community as he realizes he must respond to what he sees foretold in the skies. This puts Mel's character under the microscope and much of the film's interest comes from understanding his strengths and flaws – his passions, motivation and devotion. Mel is deeply rooted in the Jewish tradition, and so respected by his people that many follow when he announces his mission.

It is relatively late in the film when the three men finally meet up. They are presented as far more lowly than the 'three kings' of tradition. 'Olmi's heroes are always poised between a lifelike, human solitude and membership in some kind of community' here the groups accompanying them are presented as occasionally grumbling followers rather than servants.[3] Some are even of higher social status. The flawed, ordinary protagonists make a less deferential adaptation than most, though Olmi packs their interactions with echoes of Jesus' future teaching. Each character bears distinguishing traits, fleshed out with a typically light-touch economy.

Yet despite Mel's immersion in the scriptures, he fumbles for ideas when the party fails to find the new born king in Jerusalem. It is a young woman in the group who suggests the nearby village (which is never named) and the pilgrims are unsure what they have actually found. Olmi creates an atmosphere suggesting *something* significant has occurred, whilst making it appear utterly unremarkable. The desperate poverty of the holy couple is tempered by the poverty of the pilgrims themselves.

As the film ends it grows increasingly ambiguous. Realizing Herod's murderous intentions Mel's party flees without warning the villagers – a decision a companion criticizes later. Joyous scenes of Mel's pilgrims returning home are blunted by shots from the village showing both children and adults lying murdered.

Eleven years later Olmi would return to the Bible, this time with *Genesi: La creazione e il diluvio* (Genesis: Creation and Flood, 1994) and again, of sorts, in 2007 where his *Centochiodi* (One Hundred Nails), featured a professor as a modern day Christ figure.

The wise men finally gather in *Camminacammina* (1983).

Notes

1   Ellen Oumano, *Film Forum: Thirty-Five Top Film-makers Discuss Their Craft* (New York: St Martin's Press, 1985), p. 97.

2   See Kent Jones's essay 'Handcrafted Cinema', included in The Criterion Collection's 2003 DVD release for Il Posto, 2003. Available online: <www.criterion.com/current/posts/287-il-posto-handcrafted-cinema> (accessed 19 Dec. 2021).

3   *Ibid.*

Je vous salue, Marie (*Hail Mary*)
France/Switzerland/UK, 1985 – 76 mins[1]
Jean-Luc Godard

DIRECTOR Jean-Luc Godard
PRODUCERS Yves Peyrot,
Alain Sarde
SCREENPLAY Jean-Luc Godard
CINEMATOGRAPHY
Jacques Firmann,
Jean-Bernard Menoud
EDITOR Anne-Marie Miéville
MUSIC François Musy
PRODUCTION COMPANY
Gaumont – Pegase Films
MAIN CAST Manon Andersen,
Juliette Binoche, Malachi Jara
Kohan, Philippe Lacoste, Thierry
Rode, Myriem Roussel

Jean Luc Godard had been acknowledged a master of cinema for three decades by the time he wrote, directed and produced this fascinating exploration of the incarnation. Beginning as a writer for *Cahiers du Cinéma* in the early 1950s he soon became the most recognizable name among the French New Wave directors. If, by the time the 1980s arrived, his output had begun to wane and lose a little of its early vitality, there was still no shortage of ideas.

Hail Mary's premise is simply retelling the story of Jesus' Mother Mary/Marie as if it happened today. However, contained within are numerous avenues including Marie's obsession with her changing body, her

Myriem Roussel as Mary in *Je vous salue, Marie* (1985).

struggle persuading Joseph of her baby's divine origin, her continued virginity, the idea of a godly figure born into a lowly background and Marie's struggle to come to terms with her new, constantly evolving, role. Many of Godard's films give an importance to his female leads, occasionally verging on the deification. An examination of the mother of God seemed inevitable.

As ever with Godard's there's no shortage of cinematic conceits: the interplay between the intertitles' written text and visual imagery; Godard's characteristic humour; playing with continuity and editing, by focussing for long stretches on single scenes before jumping ahead days or even years. References abound including Bach, Andrea Mantegna, Dreyer, Pasolini and Bresson.

At the time Godard favoured a 1.37:1 screen ratio and here these more equal-proportions focus attention on an array of circular objects, the full moon, an enlarged sun and the basketballs Marie and her team-mates play with. A glowing spherical light shade sticks out from the edge of one shot like a huge pregnant belly. Reflections of the sun's light are everywhere from the opening shot of sunlight skipping across ripples of the water's surface, to multiple shots of the moon, 'a Marian symbol of virginity and femininity'.[2]

But the film's most central visual theme is Marie herself, as the camera repeatedly focuses on her naked body. Perhaps this to focus on Mary's own confusion and conflicting emotions about her body being taken over by this patriarchal God. Godard wrestles with the question 'How would Mary have felt about the changes to her body throughout her pregnancy?' Having given her consent initially, she swings back and forth. In a later monologue she mutters 'God's a creep, a coward … a vampire who suffered me in him'. Mary's language here is an example of how the film pits the sacred against the profane. Godard later explained his 'purpose was to try and shoot a woman naked and not make it aggressive, not in an X-rated picture way … more the purpose of an anatomical drawing'.[3] 'I was trying to make the audience see not a naked woman, but flesh'.[4] However, the film quickly becomes uncomfortably voyeuristic and given Marie is a teenage schoolgirl these shots are all the more problematic.

The film received heated criticism from many quarters including The Vatican, as well as Brazil and Argentina where it was banned. Godard was attacked with a shaving-foam pie at a screening at Cannes.[5] Yet this constant referencing of, attention to, and subversion of Christianity's visual traditions is what sets *Hail Mary* apart from so many other biblical films. It may have been the ensuing controversy that grabbed the headline, rather than Godard's artistry, but the fingerprints of a great master are all over the film, even if we have to concede it is far from his best work.

Notes

1   The film was released together with the 27 minute *The Book of Mary*, directed by Anne-Marie Miéville

2   Catherine O'Brien, *The Celluloid Madonna: From Scripture to Screen* (New York: Columbia University Press, 2011), p. 137.

3   Katherine Dieckmann's interview with Godard in David Sterritt, *Jean-Luc Godard: Interviews* (Jackson: University Press of Mississippi, 1998), p. 169.

4   Ibid.

5   Aljean Harmetz, 'Godard Has A Bad Day In Cannes…And Tries To Withdraw *Hail Mary* In Italy', *The New York Times*, 11 May 1985. Available online: <www.nytimes.com/1985/05/11/movies/godard-has-a-bad-day-in-cannesand-tries-to-withdraw-hail-mary-in-italy.html> (accessed 19 Dec. 2021).

King David
UK/USA, 1985 – 114 mins
Bruce Beresford

DIRECTOR Bruce Beresford
PRODUCERS Martin Elfand,
Charles Orme
SCREENPLAY Andrew Birkin,
James Costigan
CINEMATOGRAPHY
Donald McAlpine
EDITOR William M. Anderson
MUSIC Carl Davis
PRODUCTION COMPANY
Paramount Pictures
MAIN CAST Richard Gere,
Hurd Hatfield, Alice Krige,
Cherie Lunghi, Denis Quilley,
Edward Woodward

For a film short of two hours long, Bruce Beresford's *King David* manages to cover the material surprisingly thoroughly from Saul sparing Agag in the opening minutes, through to Absalom's rebellion and Solomon's succession; with plenty of time for David's dealings with Goliath, Michal, Bathsheba and Jonathan in-between. It was the film that earned Richard Gere a Razzie for 'Worst Performance of the Year' and the one that steered major studios clear of the Hebrew Bible for almost thirty years.

Gere's award detracts from the film's other strengths. Edward Woodward's performance as David's predecessor Saul impresses, as does Carl Davis' score, and the meticulous costumes and make-up. Director Bruce Beresford puts the Italian locations (Matera) to good use, indeed Stacia Kissick Jones lauds the film's impressive 'right angles and classically symmetrical shots'.[1]

Beresford allows the camera to linger when Jonathan gazes upon Gere and edits together footage of them when they are separated, the only David film to hint at a possible romantic attachment. Later the narrator recalls David's words 'My brother Jonathan, thy love to me was wonderful' at the very moment David strips to begin his infamous dance celebrating the arrival of the Ark of the Covenant. The biblical text describes David's half-naked dancing as being so 'undignified' that his wife Michal disowns him. Gere strips down to his underpants and dances like a monkey, amply meeting the requirements. It was five years before Gere had managed to reassemble sufficient dignity to be a star again, thanks to *Pretty Woman* (1990).

The film re-appropriates the story of Jacob wrestling with God (Genesis 32.22–32). Dreams of this story fuel Saul's mental illness but represent David's desire to see God 'face-to-face' and pursuit of a special relationship with God unrestricted by convention or organized official religion. As a boy he fought Goliath when others refused. As a king he danced half-naked before God. As a father he ignored his advisors to showed mercy to his rebellious son. His final advice to his son Solomon is to trust his heart, rather than the prophets. David illustrates this approach best when he smashes his model of the temple he wants to build. Yet the film uses slow motion to emphasize the moment's significance as the narrator speaks of David having God's favour.

In contrast, the prophets are depicted as 'merciless religious fanatics',[2] notably the dour, harsh, and inflexible Nathan. Even when Absalom is declared dead, he admonishes the grief-stricken David. Yet David remains in favour of one element of organized religion: 'Must you record every word I utter?' he complains in one of the closing scenes. 'It's for the Book of Samuel, my Lord' an advisor replies. 'You ordered it'.

It's moments like these where the occasional ill-judged moment undoes previous good work. Slow motion running; a David who cannot shoot straight; pre-battle 'I'm Spartacus' moments; and, worse of all, managing to strip Richard Gere not only of his dignity, but also, more bafflingly, his sex appeal.

Behind the scenes photo from the set of King David (1985).

Notes

1   Stacia Kissick Jones, 'King David (1985)' at *She Blogged by Night* 2003. Available online: <https://shebloggedbynight. com/2014/king-david-1985/> (accessed 19 Dec. 2021).

2   J. Stephen Lang, *The Bible on the Big Screen: A Guide from Silent Films to Today's Movies* (Grand Rapids, Michigan: Baker Books, 2007), p. 241.

Esther (*1986*)
Austria/Israel/UK, 1986 – 97 mins
Amos Gitai

DIRECTOR Amos Gitai
PRODUCER Ruben Korenfeld
SCREENPLAY Amos Gitai,
Stephan Levine
CINEMATOGRAPHY
Henri Alekan
EDITOR Sheherazade Saadi
MUSIC Claude Bertrand,
Pierre Tucat
PRODUCTION COMPANY
Agav Films
MAIN CAST Mohammad Bakri,
Simone Benyamini, Juliano
Mer-Khamis, Zare Vartanian

Israeli filmmaker Amos Gitai made his name directing documentaries like *Wadi* (1980) and *Field Diary* (1982) investigating issues around the Arab-Israeli conflict. So while nobody expected Gitai's first non-documentary to tackle a biblical subject, it's hardly surprising that he incorporated the story's impact and legacy today.

Gitai situates the film in Wadi Salib, a former Arab neighbourhood of Haifa. Its residents fled the 1948 war and were replaced by Moroccan and Algerian Jewish immigrants, who in turn were displaced in the 1960s. The area, including much fine Ottoman architecture was left to decay uninhabited. Indeed Gitai's team had to scout for a new location at short notice when the roof of their preferred location fell in shortly before filming.[1] The sets mirror these layers of history, reflecting themes of migration and displacement so central to the story.

Simone Benyamini as the title character in *Esther* (1986).

The semi-modernized version of the story deliberately challenges cinematic conventions and typical interpretations of the text. Influences such as Pasolini, Rossellini and Straub/Huillet are apparent, as is inspiration from Persian miniatures and *tableaux vivants*. Gitai captures most scenes in a single shot, typically with a static camera and minimal action. The age of the buildings lends the story a timeless feel, yet elements of the modern world are captured within the frame, an aesthetic emphasized by its natural, on-location sound. Sirens, airplanes and pneumatic drills punctuate the silence at various points, occasionally even accompanying the dialogue. Esther's narrator frequently 'breaks the fourth wall' to directly address the camera, often with comic effect. Gitai repeatedly reminds viewers that this is a film/story, downplaying potential moments of high drama.

Two notable exceptions to these static shots are particularly striking. The first tracks backwards through a harem as women, including Esther, prepare for the king's appraisal. The sweltering heat; the gentle pans; the tight compositions (where the narrator pops up just as respite from the cramped *mise en scéne* appears to be coming); all emphasize the seediness of the whole affair. The other occurs when Esther prepares to go, unbidden, before her husband. From a close-up of Esther, it slowly pulls back as she begins to walk and pans as she moves in front of a mirror. As her maids dressed her, her reflection captures her dual identity (Jew/Queen) as well as a minaret

peaking out among the rooftops. As Esther and her maids depart, again the camera tracks their journey.

Esther's finale uses the kind of long travelling shot that is more typical of Gitai's earlier documentary work. The camera tracks alongside each of the actors in turn, now out of costume, as they explain their own relationship with the text, particularly how they see the story's cycle of revenge continuing today. For them, the narrative epitomizes the Middle East's current problems. Most poignantly Palestinian Mohammed Bakri (Mordecai), talks of his 'hate' and 'fury' for his character – the story's traditional hero – because his fight to survive 'turned into a cruel and bloody war … without justification or end'. Little wonder that Mordecai's outfits grow darker as the film progresses.

The Esther story continues to have an impact today. Purim, the Jewish festival which celebrates the triumph of Esther and Mordecai, is still celebrated, often omitting its beginning (Vashti's refusal to be objectified) and end (Jewish fighters killing 75,000 enemies). For Gitai the story 'is about a cycle of repression. It is about oppressed people who gradually turn into oppressors'.[2] He made two more films looking at migration and displacement, including *Golem: Spirit of the Exile* (1992) which modernized the story of Ruth and combined it with ancient myths.

Notes

1   Richard Ingersoll, 'The Ruins of Esther: Towards an Open Scenography', in Paul Willemen , *The Films of Amos Gitai* (Worcester: Trinity Press/BFI Publishing, 1993), p. 56.

2   Amos Gitai, 'Gitai on Gitai', in Paul Willemen, *The Films of Amos Gitai* (1993), p. 88.

Samson dan Delilah (*Samson and Delilah*)
Indonesia, 1987 – 88 mins
Sisworo Gautama Putra

DIRECTOR
Sisworo Gautama Putra
PRODUCER Raam Soraya
SCREENPLAY Djoko Gautama
CINEMATOGRAPHY
Partogi Simatupang
EDITOR Muryadi
PRODUCTION COMPANY
Intercine Films
MAIN CAST Soendjoto
Adibroto, H. I. M. Damsyik,
Eddy Gunawan, Paul Hay,
Muhammad Rizqy, Suzzanna,
Corbi Vile, Affandi S. Yasin

If Bible films cover a spectrum encompassing profound exploration, propaganda and entertainment then Samson dan Delilah, by Indonesian director Sisworo Gautama Putra, very much falls into the latter category.

Putra's film follows in the tradition of Italian peplum films such as Samson and the Sea Beast (1963) and Samson and the Pirate (1964) which borrowed the names of mythical strong men like Hercules, Odysseus and Goliath and created new fantastical stories for them. Just as the seminal *Hercules* (1958) cast Californian bodybuilder Steve Reeves as its titular strongman, here Samson is played by Australian Paul Hay, whose muscular credentials are listed during the opening credits. As with the pepla, Samson battles fantastical foes such as an unconvincing cyclops, whose pointed shield grinds into Samson's torso without a scratch. Later Samson steals another attacker's weapon and slices him in two from top to bottom, only to see the two halves rejoin so he can redouble his efforts. Moments later, Samson slices clean through his foe's waist, only for his attacker's legs to continue to kick him. Putra, drawing on his better-known work in horror, includes plenty of cartoon gore.

Australian body-builder Paul Hay and Indonesian horror queen Suzzanna in *Samson dan Delilah* (1987).

The film's most telling variation is including several elements of the kung-fu/martial arts genre. The choreographed fights, the exaggerated foley work and poor dubbing are strongly reminiscent of the shenmo TV series 'Monkey' (1978–80) or the films produced by the Shaw brothers. Samson's fight scenes are hardly sophisticated, but are entertaining nevertheless, perhaps because of their sheer over-the-topness.

Yet in contrast to many pepla, Putra's film holds more closely to the biblical material. The key to Samson's strength lies in his uncut hair. He belongs to an invaded and oppressed people and is prepared to give himself up to stop the ruling regime's soldiers attacking his compatriots. He has a thirst for revenge, a motivation many adaptations overlook.[1] Also included are Samson's affair with Delilah (played by 'Queen of Indonesian Horror' Suzanna),[2] her betrayal of him, and his subsequent blinding and enslavement. Like the biblical story Samson regains some of his former super-strength (although bizarrely the film also has him regaining his sight after another woman rubs her breasts in his face). It ends with Samson destroying his captors' temple, killing both himself and his enemies.

Aside from a food-inspired love scene between the two leads, the most interesting deviation from the biblical text involves its time and place. Instead of bronze-age Israel the story relocates to early 1800s colonial Indonesia. The soldiers who plot to destroy Samson are white Europeans wearing tall hats and full length, powder-blue jackets as if picked from a Quality Street tin or a Jane Austen novel. While they are Dutch, they represent a glossed-over, dark, era of European history, one of brutal invasion, colonization, repression and rule of countries around the world. Putra and others from former European colonies doubtless experience this film differently from white Europeans. His film is a reminder of a shameful era in history, and he offers no easy way out.

While *Samson dan Delilah* is a somewhat trashy rather than a profound adaptation, its 'zestful playfulness' is nevertheless strangely-enjoyable.[3] Moreover, by retelling the story in an unfamiliar context, it reminds us that while Samson stood on the side of the oppressed, too often those claiming to be on the side of his god, have not.

Notes

1   The film's French release was titled *La Revanche De Samson* (Samson's Revenge).

2   Ekky Imanjaya, *A to Z about Indonesian Film*, (Bandung: DAR! Mizan, 2006), p. 112.

3   Paul Cooke, '*La Revanche De Samson* aka Revenge Of Samson', *Ballistic Blood Bullets*, 30 January 2011. Available online: <https://ballisticbloodbullets.blogspot.com/2011/01/indonesian-biblical-brawn.html> (accessed 19 Dec. 2021).

The Last Temptation of Christ
Canada/USA, 1988 – 164 mins
Martin Scorsese

DIRECTOR Martin Scorsese
PRODUCERS Barbara De Fina,
Harry J. Ufland
SCREENPLAY Nikos
Kazantzakis, Paul Schrader
CINEMATOGRAPHY
Michael Ballhaus
EDITOR Thelma Schoonmaker
MUSIC Peter Gabriel
PRODUCTION COMPANY
Universal City Studios Inc.
MAIN CAST David Bowie,
Juliette Caton, Willem Dafoe,
Paul Greco, Barbara Hershey,
Harvey Keitel,
Harry Dean Stanton

Many of *Last Temptation*'s critics were unwilling or unable to accept its opening statement 'This film is not based on the Gospels but upon this fictional exploration of the eternal spiritual conflict'. However, director Martin Scorsese and screenwriter Paul Schrader saw it 'as a metaphor for the human condition'.[1] Just as Jesus agonizes over what God wants from him, thirty years later Scorsese's *Silence* (2016) and Schrader's *First Reformed* (2017) suggest they still wrestle with such questions.

The Last Temptation of Christ (1988).

Last Temptation opens with Jesus (Willem Dafoe) writhing on the ground in anguish, and as the film draws to a close the situation has only worsened. Moments from an agonizing death on the cross, Jesus' drifts into his unconscious, trapped by the lure of an ordinary, domesticated life. It's unclear whether this is a dream, a hallucination, or the final fantastical flickers of brain activity, but between 'Why have you forsaken me?' and 'It is accomplished' moments later, an entire forty minute sequence occurs.

Many miss the cinematic aspects of this transition. The camera twists ninety degrees, as if Jesus is lying down, the sound of the scene is muted and the sun brightens to warm Jesus' face. 'It's clichéd' Scorsese explained, 'but after all, it's a scam, it's the Devil'.[2] For the first time we experience Jesus' disorientation – marriage to Magdalene, a bizarre shared life with Mary and Martha, Saul's illogical, empty, preaching. Jesus' mind flits about struggling to comprehend his ordeal.

Just as other Scorsese protagonists are torn between women and friends, here the young girl playing Satan hijacks Judas' role as buddy/confidant and replaces the disciples with Magdalene, Mary and Martha.[3] Only when his disciples' return, exposing Satan's deception, does Jesus revert to his sacrificial death. He dies victorious and, finally, at peace. In the novel Jesus declares '"It is accomplished!"' before it adds 'And it was as though he had said: Everything has begun'.[4]

The image here gets 'edge fog' giving way to flashing bursts of coloured light – the result of light leaking into the canister. The visual distortion combined with the sound of ululations and church bells form a modern expression of the resurrection, typical of *Last Temptation*'s contemporary use of cinematic language. The constantly moving camera gives earlier scenes an unsettling spontaneity. Scorsese's protagonists often find themselves out of their depth. Here long panning shots suggest events moving unavoidably towards their inevitable conclusion. As Jesus is pulled into Lazarus's tomb he is also being pulled towards his destiny.

Initially terrified by the call of God (another complex Scorsese father figure), Jesus constructs Roman crosses, attends Magdalene's brothel and visits a monastery. The film's lack of reverence is refreshing. Jesus films often accuse him of blasphemy, but not of madness. When he preaches love, some laugh, others insult him. When he disrupts a mob stoning Magdalene, rocks are thrown at him. Pilate (an aloof David Bowie) treats him with detached cynicism: he's just another failed messiah to dispatch.

Yet the spontaneity of Jesus' Sermon on the Plain, his forceful exorcisms and his playful transformation of water into wine reverberate with unprecedented energy, as does the much-imitated desert fasting sequence. Jesus is unpredictable, and possibly unstable, but Dafoe's performance is breathtakingly compelling. Contemporary accents and Schrader's fresh paraphrasing liberate the Gospel texts from centuries of tradition.

Peter Gabriel's evocative soundtrack, Thelma Schoonmaker's editing, and its lighting and costuming also contribute to making *Last Temptation* a hugely original piece of work. It's disappointing that it's mainly remembered for being controversial. It deserves to be appreciated for Scorsese's attempt 'to make the life of Jesus immediate and accessible to people who haven't really thought about God in a long time'.[5]

Notes

1   Martin Scorsese and Paul Scharader. DVD Commentary. *The Last Temptation of Christ*. Criterion Collection, 2000.

2   David Thomson and Ian Christie, *Scorsese on Scorsese* (London: Faber and Faber, 1996), p. 143.

3   Other elements typical of Scorsese's work are portraying Jesus as a sexually-repressed loner and his emotional dependence on his buddy, Judas.

4   Nikos Kazantzakis, *The Last Temptation. Translated by Peter A. Bien* (London: Faber and Faber, 1961), p. 575.

5   Thomson and Christie, *Scorsese on Scorsese,* p. 124.

Jésus de Montréal (*Jesus of Montreal*)
Canada/France, 1989 – 115 mins
Denys Arcand

DIRECTOR Denys Arcand
PRODUCERS Roger Frappier,
Pierre Gendron,
Monique Létourneau
SCREENPLAY Denys Arcand
CINEMATOGRAPHY
Francois Aubry, Guy Dufaux
EDITOR Isabelle Dedieu
MUSIC Jean-Marie Benoît,
François Dompierre
PRODUCTION COMPANY
Max Film Productions Inc.
MAIN CAST Lothaire Bluteau,
Rémy Girard, Robert Lepage,
Gilles Pelletier, Johanne-Marie
Tremblay, Catherine Wilkening

In many ways, Denys Arcand's *Jesus of Montreal* is not a Jesus film at all. Rather than being set in first-century Judea, it is set in twentieth-century Quebec. And the film is not so much directly about Jesus as about Daniel, a young actor who plays him in a revised Easter passion play. Daniel has been commissioned by Father Leclerc to revise his church's tired old passion play. Daniel spends hours in research, talks with theologians and gathers a troupe of four fellow actors – Constance (Leclerc's mistress), glamorous model Mirelle, and two voiceover actors Martin and René.

Lothaire Bluteau as Daniel as Jesus in *Jésus de Montréal* (1989).

The play is a tremendous success, but proves highly controversial, so Leclerc and his superiors cancel it. The actors push ahead, but when security guards close the play on its third night Daniel is seriously injured in the ensuing scuffle, dying shortly afterwards. His body parts are used for organ transplants – signifying resurrection – and his followers start a new movement in his name.

Initially, the film is clear that Daniel is simply a struggling actor; however, similarities between Daniel's life and Jesus' soon emerge. Another actor, Pascal, hails Daniel as a greater actor than himself. Shortly afterwards Pascal's head (alone) features in a trite advertising campaign confirming him as a John the Baptist figure. Daniel selects unlikely followers and inspires great devotion. When he 'performs' a miracle during the play, an audience member cries out, thinking Daniel is actually Jesus. Lines are blurring and already some cannot tell them apart. Daniel is welcomed triumphantly into the media world, but clashes with religious authorities. A slick lawyer tempts him with the world from high above the city. After Mirelle's mistreatment at an audition he drives out the executives running it. He is arrested and tried, but his culpability is unclear.

Arcand's earlier works draw 'parallel[s] between the historical fall of a great western empire and that of America, as seen from the gates of Montreal'.[1] The Decline of the American Empire (1986) focussed on a group of academics obsessed by their sexual conquests. Quebec's corruption at the edge of the American Empire is typified by its banal intellectuals, suggesting the glories of the empire are fading. Arcand's interests in eyes, glasses, mirrors, hospitals, unlikely communities, and Quebec itself, all re-occur here. His 2003 film The Barbarian Invasions, nominally a sequel to Decline, also features four of the characters from Jesus of Montreal: Leclerc's world-weary priest, Constance (now helping those in hospital), a security guard, and the detective who arrested Daniel, now a vice-squad lieutenant. Together, these three films compare the USA to Rome with its outpost Montreal representing Jerusalem. This film's climax sees Daniel leave hospital and stumble through the underground, reciting passages from Mark 13 – foreseeing the decline of Quebec, and the American Empire as a whole.

By now, the dividing line between Daniel and Jesus is almost non-existent: when Daniel dies, his 'Jesus' is no more. Daniel's play may have revised the Gospels, but the film's apparently more meaningful allegory relies on them, implying it's 'the story as such, not its historicity, that has the potential to change people's lives'.[2] Daniel/Jesus function as modern-day prophets, pointing out the decline in society and predicting its end. Given Arcand's stinging critique of the empire and its backwaters, it's perhaps unsurprising that Arcand takes a cameo role as a judge.

Notes

1   Réal La Rochelle, 'Sound design and music as tragédie en musique: the documentary practice of Denys Arcand', in André Loiselle and Brian McIlroy (eds.), Auteur/Provocateur: The films of Denys Arcand (Trowbridge: Flicks Books, 1995), p. 44.

2   Adele Reinhartz, Jesus of Hollywood. Oxford (New York: Oxford University Press, 2007), p. 39.

The Garden
UK/Germany/Japan, 1990 – 86 mins
Derek Jarman

DIRECTOR Derek Jarman
PRODUCERS Takashi Asai,
Dagmar Benke, James Mackay
CINEMATOGRAPHY
Christopher Hughes
EDITORS Peter Cartwright
MUSIC Simon Fisher-Turner
PRODUCTION COMPANY
Basilisk Communications
MAIN CAST Pete Lee-Wilson,
Philip MacDonald, Johnny Mills,
Tilda Swinton

Far from the classic Hollywood style, Derek Jarman's non-linear, trance-like *The Garden* mixes the iconographies of Christianity and 1980s/1990s gay subculture. As much at home in an art gallery as a cinema, its avant-garde surrealism recalls Sibley Watson and Webber's *Lot in Sodom* (1933).

Passages from the Bible and Christian imagery feature extensively, but essentially this a frank and profoundly honest attempt to express what it feels to be Derek Jarman, to express his thoughts, anxieties and fears. David Thomson describes Jarman as 'like a prisoner whose ... films may also need an audience of inmates' noting a sense of 'frustration, desperation and 'confinement' running throughout.[1] Scenes of Jarman sleeping emphasize the feeling of fervid hallucinatory dreams.

Upon release, some were horrified by Jarman's mixture of biblical and homosexual imagery, yet the sheer volume of references indicate serious engagement with the material. Indeed, given the toxic attitudes about homosexuality in Britain in the 1990s, it is an incredibly brave film – a genuine reflection on two huge elements of Jarman's psyche, parcelled up with past memories.

The biblical imagery starts with the title. While 'The Garden' refers to the patch of land surrounding Jarman's Prospect Cottage near Scotland's Dungeness beach, it evokes the biblical gardens of Eden, Gethsemane and Paradise.[2] These themes recur throughout as the gay couple who appear regularly during the film, are frequently seen with a baby or being persecuted, but also, at times, expressing a sense of hope.

Beyond this there's the use of the Nativity Story – at one point narrated from Matthew's Gospel as a man in first century dress sits writing the script in his lap. Later, following a stunning montage of blurry fairground lights, two men on a beach uncover a crown. Soon it re-appears upon Tilda Swinton's head, one of several shots linking Swinton to the Madonna.

Elsewhere there are shots of classic paintings (including Piero della Francesca's 'Resurrection'); a resurrected Jesus figure displaying his wounds; giant pages from the Bible flashing in the background; scenes evoking the Last Supper and the breaking of bread. Latterly, a leather-clad Judas dangles from a rope with his blackened tongue hanging down to his sternum.

While *The Garden* contains very little conventional dialogue – in one sense it's almost a silent film – the varied and unpredictable soundtrack combines snippets of monks singing, 1990s synthesizers and mocking laughter. At one point three men dressed as Father Christmas menacingly circle the couple in bed, aggressively singing 'God Rest Ye Merry Gentlemen'.

Perhaps the film's most critical invocation of biblical imagery surrounds the couple's persecution. For much of the film, Jarman's framing and unsteady camera create a sense of danger around them. Soon they appear in front of Roman officials at the public baths, and then bound and gagged surrounded by security guards. Tar is daubed around their foreheads – evoking blood from the crown of thorns – and then feathers stuck on, leaving both men humiliated and dripping with what appears like droplets of blood. Moments later the two are whipped by the demented Santas until their shirts are red with blood. Finally the two carry a cross, eyes closed, along the beach. A man in a dress (previously seen attempting to escape from a stone-throwing mob) kneels and kisses one man's feet.

Jarman was an important and influential figure in the British film scene. His death in 1994 left a legacy of artists who were inspired and profoundly changed by him. Whilst *The Garden* is not his most significant work, it remains a boldly unconventional use of the Bible.

Still image from *The Garden* (1990). Photo Liam Daniel, courtesy & © Basilisk Communications

Notes

1   David Thomson, *The New Biographical Dictionary of Film* (London: Little Brown, [1975] 2002), p. 439.

2   The word 'paradise' originally derived from gardens.

The Visual Bible: Matthew
South Africa, 1993 – 240 mins
Regardt van den Bergh

DIRECTOR
Regardt van den Bergh
PRODUCERS Chuck Bush,
Robert Marcarelli,
Charles K. Robertson
SCREENPLAY Johann Potgieter
CINEMATOGRAPHY
Michael Ferris, Tobie Swanepoel
EDITORS Chuck Bush,
Ronelle Loots
MUSIC Sue Grealy
PRODUCTION COMPANY
Visual Bible
MAIN CAST Richard Kiley,
Bruce Marchiano, Dawid
Minnaar, Gerrit Schoonhoven

The Visual Bible: Matthew
(1993). Courtesy of Bruce
Marchiano.

'No scriptwriter's liberties. No interpretations. No dramatic license'.[1] So claimed one of the press kits for *The Visual Bible*, a word-for-word adaptation of Matthew's Gospel. The filmmakers took that mantra so seriously that periodically they even interrupted Jesus mid-sentence because the text required the narrator to interject with a 'He said'. The premise is misplaced of course: Film is a visual medium, so every costume, prop, facial expression, skin tone,[2] camera angle and choice of lens represents some act of an interpretation, likewise use of sound. Jesus' accent; his emphasis, rhythm and dramatic pauses; not to mention the music, all flow from an artistic vision, a desire to communicate something that the text itself cannot. Indeed, the film's opening words are an invented prologue introducing the narrator as an elderly Matthew (Richard Kiley), the tax collector who 'left everything and became one of his disciples'.

A significant example of this is the film's almost constantly smiling Jesus. Marchiano's 'Jesus in jeans' broke the mould of previous cinematic incarnations and many subsequent adaptations have sought to follow suit.[3] Here Jesus grins, sometimes rather unexpectedly, and rolls in the dust with those he has just healed. Even Jesus' dressing-down of the Pharisees is conveyed with love and regret. After numerous, overly solemn, Sons of God, it's refreshing to see such a bold interpretation, even if eventually it wears a little thin. Almost thirty years later, a solemn-faced Jesus seems unthinkable.

With no cuts to the biblical text, the final product runs to four hours, making it difficult to work through in one sitting. No matter how expert the camera angles, acting and effects, the written text of the Gospel throws up numerous problems when used as a screenplay, not least Matthew's structuring of his gospel around five long sermons. Kiley's invented prologue avoids opening the film with Matthew reciting a lengthy genealogy. Moreover, certain devices are acceptable in literature, but not in film, notably when several characters speak in unison or do not speak at all.

To maintain interest, the filmmakers attempt to invigorate certain scenes. Partway through the Sermon on the Mount Jesus empties a water bucket over Peter's head, amusing the crowd, while demonstrating Jesus' light-hearted side to the audience at home. To some this seems oddly out of place, to others it summarizes something vital about Jesus' personality. To many, Jesus is not the dusty, stern, figure of much religious art, but an inspiring, down-to-earth, leader. The film's subtler moments communicate this best, when Jesus sits with his disciples mending nets, or working shirtless in a field.

At its best, *The Visual Bible* communicates Jesus' ability to change lives. Kiley's Matthew becomes the interpretative lens through which we see Jesus. The old man we meet at the start of the film embodies this, his life irrevocably changed by his encounter. If the nature of the project, and the weakness of the supporting cast makes things a little stilted, the groundbreaking realization of this idea, is embodied at its core in Marchiano's performance. His is a Jesus who cheerfully offers friendship and understanding rather than judgment and damnation – a friend and saviour.

The filmmakers attempted a sequel, a word-for-word adaptation of *Acts* (1994). Ten years later, and following numerous changes at Visual Bible, they produced *The Gospel of John* (2003) this time without Marchiano as the lead.

Notes

1   Cited in Peter T. Chattaway, 'Videos tell story of early church/ Strengths and weaknesses in dramatizing New Testament church', *ChristianWeek* vol.10 no.21, 18 February 1997. Available online: <www.patheos.com/blogs/filmchat/1997/02/ videos-tell-story-of-early-church-strengths-and-weaknesses-in- dramatizing-new-testament-church.html> (accessed 19 Dec. 2021).

2   Given the film was shot in South Africa, it is surprising so few Black actors were used.

3   Marchiano, *In the Footsteps of Jesus* (Eugene, Harvest House, 1997), p. 16.

Al-mohager (*The Emigrant*)

Egypt/France, 1994 – 129 mins
Youssef Chahine

DIRECTOR Youssef Chahine
PRODUCERS Humbert Balsan,
Gabriel Khoury
SCREENPLAY Youssef Chahine,
Rafik El-Sabban, Khaled Youssef
CINEMATOGRAPHY
Ramses Marzouk
EDITOR Rashida Abdel Salam
MUSIC Mohamad Nouh
PRODUCTION COMPANY
MISR International Film
Company/Ognon Pictures
MAIN CAST Khaled El Nabawy,
Mahmoud Hemida, Michel
Piccoli, Hanan Turk, Youssra

Youssef Chahine weathered a storm of protest in his native Egypt for depicting Joseph, an Islamic prophet, despite making numerous changes to the biblical narratives (including the characters' names).[1] Here Joseph becomes Ram, Potiphar is called Amihar, and his wife, Simihit. As with his 1976 *The Return of the Prodigal Son* the film more evokes the biblical story than adapts it. The basic plot is retained and everyday interactions between his characters are expanded to fill in the gaps. Chahine strips the story of its supernatural and mythical elements, and suggests different motives for its characters' actions. Yet these alterations become the film's biggest strength. Shorn of his miraculous ability to receive and interpret dreams, the film is able to

Khaled El Nabaoui as Ram/Joseph in *Al-mohager* (1994).

focus on the person of Joseph far more than other such productions. And ditching the famous coat of many colours distances *Al-mohager* from the campy excesses of 'Joseph and the Technicolor Dreamcoat'.

The end result is that Chahine and his leading man, Khaled El Nabawy, craft a Joseph figure that we actually care about. He still has something of a superiority complex, but is driven by a desire to improve on his life, rather than simply settling for his family's nomadic hand-to-mouth existence. Ram decides to learn how to farm the land beginning his interest in agriculture. The Bible never really explains how Joseph became such a brilliant agricultural strategist, but this idea is arguably the film's biggest concern.

Once sold into slavery in Egypt, Ram's charm,[2] audacity and confidence gain the attention of his otherwise unreachable master. Having repeatedly expressed his desire to learn how to farm, he is eventually given a strip of desert to experiment on. Good coaching, hard work, luck and Ram's cleverness make the endeavour a success. There's still something of a leap, but his progression seems understandable given his love for, and understanding of, farming.

However, having succeeded, he is drawn back towards the city, particularly to Simihit, his master's wife. Simihit is also the high priestess of the local cult and, as her husband is a eunuch, she looks to Ram for fulfilment.[3] Simihit's eyeing of the impossibly handsome Ram is the most obvious of the film's multiple examples of the female gaze.

Much of *The Emigrant*'s success is due to El Nabawy's strong performance as Ram, expertly combining youthful exuberance, drive, fearless confidence and boundless energy. There's a twinkle in his eyes that remains even as he matures, suggesting an explanation (again) for why he treats his brothers the way he does when they arrive at his door begging for food. Wisely, the story is abbreviated at this point, limiting the tricks Ram plays on his brothers before he reveals his identity.

Chahine's sumptuous film owes much to his eye for a good image and Ramses Marzook's spellbinding cinematography. But it's the stunning interiors which impress the most. They feel like authentic spaces where people live and interact, neither overly pristine nor showing signs of age, aided by perfect lighting and composition. There's much that's alien about the world that Chahine takes us to, yet he so ingeniously captures nomadic and civil life in Egypt 3500 years ago, that so much also feels familiar.

Notes

1   Lina Khatib, 'Bab El-Hadid (Cairo Station)', in Gönül Dönmez-Colin (ed.), *The Cinema of North Africa and the Middle East* (London: Wallflower Press, 2007), p. 24.

2   Derek Elley, '*The Emigrant*', *Variety*, 20 November 1994.

Available online: <https://variety.com/1994/film/reviews/the-emigrant-1117909485/> (accessed 19 Dec. 2021).

3   Peter T. Chattaway, 'It's all in the Family: The Patriarchs of Genesis in Film', in Rhonda Burnette-Bletsch (ed.), *The Bible in Motion: A Handbook of the Bible and Its Reception in Film*. vol. 1 (Berlin/Boston: De Gruyter, 2016), p. 61.

Jeremiah (*1998*)
Italy/Germany/USA, 1998 – 92 mins
Harry Winer

DIRECTOR Harry Winer
PRODUCERS Matilde Bernabei,
Lorenzo Minoli
SCREENPLAY Harry Winer
CINEMATOGRAPHY
Raffaele Mertes
EDITOR David A. Simmons
MUSIC Bruce Broughton
PRODUCTION COMPANY
LUBE–Lux–Beta Film
MAIN CAST Klaus Maria
Brandauer, Patrick Dempsey,
Oliver Reed, Vincent Regan

Between 1993 and 2003 Lux Vide released seventeen different films as 'The Bible Collection', running to around 37½ hours.[1] Each film in the series was released as a standalone title, but two entries in particular stand out: *Jesus* (1999) and *Jeremiah* (1998), the only significant treatment of the Bible's longest book. Whilst Jeremiah has more words than any other book of the Bible, most are his legendarily miserable prophecies. Aside from the odd high point or worthy quotation, the book's size, unfamiliar genres and jumbled chronology, make it difficult to appreciate.

Writer/director Harry Winer does an excellent job pulling together the various scraps of narrative scattered throughout the book and moulding them into credible, engaging drama. Whereas some of the series' invented subplots are trite or distracting, here they serve to humanize a character who might otherwise seem remote. Jeremiah's legendary moments of depression require an audience to empathize with what he feels. Hence, the scene where Jeremiah (Patrick Dempsey, pre-*Grey's Anatomy*) and the woman he loves are separated heightens the emotions by interweaving it with his calling. Such hypothetical character motivation only adds to the sense of melancholy that seeps so powerfully through his writings.

Winer's script excels in placing Jeremiah's prophecies in a broader context and linking them to other parts of the Hebrew Bible. By staking out the narrative and pinning Jeremiah's utterances onto that framework, he enables the audience to understand the significance of such earth-shattering events.

There are a few memorable scenes in the film. When the lost book of the law is re-discovered during the reign of Judah's King Josiah, a point-of-view shot from inside the sealed compartment where it had been hidden for centuries almost turns the lost scroll a character in itself, highlighting its story. Lost and neglected for years, now finally liberated. Point-of-view shots re-occur later, as a flashback to Jeremiah's childhood shows him hearing God's call. His mild disgust resurfaces when Jeremiah returns to the temple as an adult, only now he sees with God's eyes as well as his own. Now the point-of-view shots are no longer just Jeremiah's, but God's too. Winer also aligns Jeremiah with Jesus. When Jeremiah ventures down the side streets near the temple he is appalled by market traders selling idols. He flings over the tables in a fashion not only reminiscent of Jesus' action in the temple, but also shot similarly to other cinematic adaptations of the incident. Numerous other subtleties link the portrayal of Jeremiah here with the series' portrayal of Jesus in its 1999 *Jesus* mini-series. Both portray a chaste, handsome lead who appears to be romantically available, yet is out of reach.

Ultimately, Jeremiah annoys numerous leaders with his negative outbursts regarding his people's standing before God. Oliver Reed's General Safan throws Jeremiah in a hole and later drops his prophetic writings strip by strip into a fire. In a harrowing finale, Jeremiah's indifferent King, Mattaniah, witnesses his sons' murder seconds before his own eyes are put out. If the film's winsomely optimistic epilogue falls a little flat, it is only because the images preceding it are genuinely disturbing.

Patrick Dempsey as the title character in *Jeremiah* (1998).

Having brought to life such a dense and difficult literary work, it seems a shame this was Winer's sole contribution to the series and that he has only written one other screenplay in the twenty years since. The Bible Collection had its moments, but it rarely pulled everything together as well as it did here.

Notes

1   Appendix 1 lists all the entries in 'The Bible Collection'.

The Prince of Egypt
USA, 1998 – 99 mins
Brenda Chapman, Steve Hickner and Simon Wells

DIRECTORS Brenda Chapman,
Steve Hickner, Simon Wells
PRODUCERS Penney Finkelman
Cox, Sandra Rabins
SCREENPLAY Philip LaZebnik,
Nicholas Meyer
EDITOR Nick Fletcher
MUSIC Stephen Schwartz,
Hans Zimmer
PRODUCTION COMPANY
Dreamworks Animation
MAIN CAST Sandra Bullock,
Ralph Fiennes, Jeff Goldblum,
Danny Glover, Val Kilmer,
Helen Mirren, Michelle Pfeiffer,
Patrick Stewart

'I didn't want us to tell fairy tales' executive producer Jeffrey Katzenberg once recalled, 'I wanted us to pick an interesting, dramatic, epic ... embracing all the techniques of animation'.[1] Katzenberg left Disney to form DreamWorks with David Geffen and Steven Spielberg and *The Prince of Egypt* delivered a stunning visual labour of love, care and thought, typified by its attention to detail.

Produced at a time when traditional, hand-drawn, animation was still strong, but CGI was beginning to have an impact, the film blends the two techniques to great effect, particularly its incredible backdrops. Richie Chavez's expressionistic mountains and sweeping deserts, and Darek Gogol's towering architecture, make *Prince of Egypt* as gigantic and splendid as sweeping epics *Lawrence of Arabia* (1962) which is referenced alongside *The Ten Commandments* (1956) and *Ben-Hur* (1959).[2] As the Israelites prepare to leave Egypt, the film's catchiest song – 'There Will be Miracles' – reprises. Images flick by revealing the destruction wrought

The seventh plague strikes in *The Prince of Egypt* (1998).

on Egypt's once great kingdom. Each 'scene' lasts only a few seconds, but many are so immense that no live action filmmaker would dare attempt them. Gogol's work is particularly notable, connecting his dominating architecture to the Egyptians' psyche. The Egyptians' all-encompassing self-belief reflected in stone, physically towering over the slaves building it, an expression of their masters' dominance. Both Rameses and his father Seti unknowingly adopt the shapes and poses of the art that surrounds and honours them.

While both brothers are prone to bouts of teenage irresponsibility, Rameses' is weighed down by his worry, self doubt and fear of being a Pharaoh who lets down his ancestors. The bitter irony is that his fear of failure results in the very outcome he is so desperate to avoid. In contrast, Moses' carefree playboy simply never experiences suffering until he humiliates his future wife, notices the effect of his loutish behaviour and feels a sudden pang of guilt. Similarly, his killing of the Egyptian results from him witnessing a suffering with which he is utterly unfamiliar. As he later reflects 'I did not see because I did not wish to see'.

Throughout, the film relies on its visuals to carry its themes and much of the story. When Rameses' son dies, the film becomes monochromatic.[3] From the camera's opening movement (through the mist up to a giant carving of Pharaoh's face) to the montages which accompany the musical numbers, the 'camera' thinks like a real camera. Occasionally part of a shot is left out of focus, or certain objects or characters are placed at the edge of the frame. There are zooms and shifts in the depth of focus all of which make the images feel like they are more real than they actually are.

The film's most celebrated sequence occurs following Moses' discovery that he is a Hebrew saved from the very man he then came to call father. As his world begins to unravel, hieroglyphics on the palace walls come alive in a display of drama, inventiveness and technical mastery. The story hurries from one surface to another, combining an objective account of the events with a subjective expression of Moses' feelings. Suddenly Seti appears at Moses' side, his unconvincing justification accompanied by Hitchcockian strings.

Yet the film's ending feels a little rushed. Moses stands above a huge crowd nursing the stone tablets. Nevertheless, like so many of the shots that have preceded it, it forms an indelibly majestic closing image.

Notes

1   Jeffrey Katzenberg in 'Making of *The Prince of Egypt*' [DVD Commentary]. DreamWorks, 2006.

2   Nicole LaPorte, *The Men Who Would Be King: An Almost Epic Tale of Moguls, Movies, and a Company Called DreamWorks* (Boston/New York: Houghton Mifflin Harcourt, 2010), p. 116.

3   Thomasine Lewis, *The Prince of Egypt: The Movie Scrapbook – An In-Depth Look Behind the Scenes* (London: Puffin, 1998), pp. 32–3.

The Book of Life
France/USA, 1998 – 63 mins
Hal Hartley

DIRECTOR Hal Hartley
PRODUCERS Caroline Benjo,
Thierry Cagianut, Pierre
Chevalier, Matthew Myers,
Carole Scotta
SCREENPLAY Hal Hartley
CINEMATOGRAPHY
Jim Denault
EDITOR Dov Hoenig
PRODUCTION COMPANY
True Fiction Pictures,
Haut et Court
MAIN CAST Martin Donovan,
P. J. Harvey, Miho Nikaido,
Thomas Jay Ryan,
Dave Simonds

'It was the morning of December 31, 1999 when I returned, at last, to judge the living and the dead. Though still … I had my doubts'. So ends Jesus' opening monologue in Hal Hartley's *The Book of Life* (1998). It's a moment that sums up so much about the film: the premise; actor Martin Donovan's deadpan delivery; the sharpness of the script; and it's witty, irreverent, approach to the subject matter.

The Second Coming has been responsible for some dreadful movies, not least both *Left Behind* films (2000 and 2014), often because attempting to portray Revelation's bizarre imagery in a pseudo-literal, yet modern fashion, looks absurd. In contrast, *Book of Life* playfully toys with the imagery. 666 is the locker where Jesus stores The Book of Life, which, it turns out, is just a MacBook computer, albeit an 'ancient' model made in Egypt.

P. J. Harvey and Martin Donovan in *The Book of Life* (1998).

As with most of Hartley's early work, the production is explicitly set in New York to 'ground the film in the familiar and particular'.[1] New York here has a singular role as a specific representative of Earth as a whole. Likewise, the characters' '"flattened" style of line delivery' shifts the focus onto their internal emotions.[2] Jesus, in particular, is uncomfortable with his role in the Apocalypse, and Donovan's voiceover – a regular Hartley trait – intensifies this. Furthermore, both Magdalena (an enthralling P. J. Harvey) and the dishevelled Devil (Thomas J Ryan), deliver monologues in ways which draw attention to the film's artificiality, whilst also making Ryan easier to relate to. Elsewhere Hartley uses slow motion blur, tilt, visual distortion, unusual camera angles and so to give the film a disorientating, other-worldly feel. Dubbed 'a controversial retelling of the Apocalypse' the film's playful visual, comic elements and pastiche of different styles and genres enable more profound questions to be asked.

Sensing Jesus' reservations, God's legal representatives try to pressure him into getting on with judging humanity. The Devil wants The Book of Life to prevent the Apocalypse ('Revelation 12.12, Not my favourite passage.'), whilst tempting a barfly atheist into a Faustian pact with his girlfriend's soul. Hartley often focuses on relationships, particularly on forming alternate 'families'. When the grubbily pragmatic Devil observes that Jesus is 'addicted to human beings', Jesus cannot disagree. The film ends with the two seeing in the new millennium with Magdalena; the couple from the bar; and the former receptionist from God's law firm. Seeing such celebrations twenty years later it seems absurd that when the film was produced, there was genuine fear about the potential consequences of the millennium bug.

These shots cross cut to Jesus' stunning internal monologue from on-board the Staten Island Ferry. Seemingly changed forever by becoming human, his compassion can only see the future possibilities awaiting the human race. 'The possibility of disaster and the possibility of perfection'. The jarring presence of the Twin Towers reminds us of the former, as if intentionally dashing the very hopes the movie dares to imagine. Yet despite all that has happened in the intervening twenty years these possibilities remain. We can only hope we can find the compassion we need.

Notes

1   Sebastian Manley, *The Cinema of Hal Hartley* (London: Bloomsbury, 2013), p. 103.
2   Manley, *Cinema of Hal* Hartley, pp. 7–8.

La Genèse (*Genesis*)
Mali/France, 1999 – 102 mins
Cheick Oumar Sissoko

DIRECTOR
Cheick Oumar Sissoko
PRODUCERS Jacques Atlan,
Chantal Bagilishya,
Ibrahima Touré
SCREENPLAY Jean-Louis
Sagot-Durvaroux
CINEMATOGRAPHY
Lionel Cousin
EDITOR Aïlo Auguste-Judith
MUSIC Michel Risse, Pierre
Sauvageot, Décor Sonore
PRODUCTION COMPANY
Kora Films – Balzan CNPC
MAIN CAST Fatoumata
Diawara, Balla Moussa Keïta,
Salif Keïta, Sotigui Kouyaté

Far from over-familiar Hollywood epics, Cheick Oumar Sissoko's *La Genèse* bristles with fresh insights. Telling the story of Isaac's family from an African perspective – specifically the Bambara-speaking people of Mali – it instinctively understands the nomadic tribal contexts from which those stories derive, but explores fratricidal conflict, genocide and reconciliation by adopting its own African perspective.[1]

The film's non-linear approach and convoluted plot line, replete with flashbacks and stories within stories, improves the narrative flow. Refusing to lionize its protagonists it provides a broad sweep of Jacob's dysfunctional and unstable clan, undermining the Sunday School image of the patriarchs as noble and grandfatherly.

Sissoko's newly arranged narrative opens with a brief shot of Esau. Despite being an incidental figure around the film's margins, Esau's looming presence casts a shadow across the unfolding story. The incident that drives the plot, however, is Dinah's rape by Shechem and her brothers' revenge on the Shechemites (Genesis 34). The Shechemites' tacit approval of Shechem's crime portrays her rape as both a sexual and a political act. His father Hamor's attempt to make amends, results in a wince-inducing mass circumcision. The pain is brought home by grim faces, crude-looking tools, and the men hobbling around post-operation. Judah and Simeon exploit the Shechemites weakness, unleashing their vengeance with a slaughter so disturbingly thorough that only Hamor survives.

The annihilation of Hamor's line is sufficient cause for the *palaver* (reconciliation council) to convene, occupying most of act two. In addition to Dinah's story the tribes hear Tamar's complaint against her father-in-law Judah (Genesis 38).[2] It is this sequence that feels most embedded in Malian culture.[3] Tamar's case is serious, yet its telling is accompanied by bursts of rhythmical music, dance and mocking of Judah. Finally Jacob leaves his tent to tell the story of his parents' betrothal. Both scenes are shown in flashback with images emphasizing the gulf between the original story's culture and our own. Then Esau arrives to wreak his revenge.

La Genèse is beautifully filmed and the astonishing landscapes capture the empty space that perhaps typified the world several thousand years ago. Sissoko uses complementary colours to great effect, contrasting the bright blue of Jacob's family with the orange of Hamor's to highlight the gulf that between their two tribes. Jacob pleads at length with God for Esau's forgiveness so that his family will not be destroyed. No sooner are the words out of his mouth than an angel, in the form of a boy, summons him to an encounter with God. In the film's most visually creative moment, God arrives in a dazzling display of white, speaking with many voices from amongst a crowd of children.

While the film's stark brutality stares unflinchingly at the story's violent elements, its real power lies in its testimony of universal human values: the fear, hate, love, revenge and desire for justice, which

Gabriel Magma Konaté as Judah in *La genèse* (1999).

survive even in today's wealthier economies.[4] These stories maintain their power today because of how they voice those emotions. *La Genèse*'s real strength is not novelty value, but the extra depth and verve it brings to the story's latent emotions, bringing them closer to home even for those of us who inhabit a world distant from Jacob and his tribe.

Notes

1   Lindiwe Dovey, *African Film and Literature: Adapting Violence to the Screen* (New York: Columbia University Press, 2009), pp. 252–74.

2   When Judah prevents Tamar's remarrying, she disguises herself as a prostitute and gets pregnant by him. He fails to pay her and discovering her pregnancy orders her execution, unaware the child is his.

3   Rhonda Burnette-Bletsch, 'Cheick Oumar Sissoko: West African Activist and Storyteller' in Rhonda Burnette-Bletsch (ed.), *The Bible in Motion: A Handbook of the Bible and Its Reception in Film.* vol. 1 (Berlin/Boston: De Gruyter, 2016), p. 708.

4   Olivier Barlet, 'La Genèse', africultures.com, 30 April 1999. Available online: <www.africultures.com/la-genese-5378/> (accessed 19 Dec. 2021).

Jesus
Italy/Germany/USA/France/Spain/Czech Republic/Netherlands/UK, 1999 – 180 mins
Roger Young

DIRECTOR Roger Young
PRODUCERS Russell Kagan,
Heinrich Krauss, Lorenzo Minoli,
Paolo Piria
SCREENPLAY Suzette Couture
CINEMATOGRAPHY
Raffaele Mertes
EDITOR Benjamin A. Weissman
MUSIC Patrick Williams
PRODUCTION COMPANY
LUBE–Lux–Beta Film
MAIN CAST G. W. Bailey,
Jacqueline Bisset, Debra
Messing, Gary Oldman, Jeremy
Sisto, Luca Zingaretti

Roger Young's Jesus mini-series is the best known film in Lux Vide's 'The Bible Collection' and its theological apex.[1] Vide's international funding model is reflected in its combinations of big name Anglo-American actors with an international cast and Moroccan extras. Here, Gary Oldman played a scheming Pontius Pilate who manipulates the Sanhedrin for his own amusement – emphasizing the Romans' political dominance over the Jews. Suzette Couture's screenplay skilfully casts Oldman as a puppet master manipulating the chief priests into handing Jesus over. As a result the film largely avoids antisemitism.

Unsurprisingly, this television mini-series has less to offer visually than some of its cinematic counterparts, though using an aqueduct as a backdrop lends the crucifixion and deposition scenes echoes of Pietro Perugino's triptychs. The pooled international resources enabled this to be the first Bible film to use CGI, during the scenes of Jesus' temptation and his anguish in Gethsemane. CGI enables Satan to switch between male and female forms, make the temple to suddenly appear, and flash forward through the history of

Jeremy Sisto as (Jesus) is baptised in *Jesus* (1999).

Christendom.[2] These sequences raise some of the philosophical concerns that today's audiences have about atrocities Christians carried out in Jesus' name. While this was a bold move by the producers, its execution was overly bombastic and the sequences have aged poorly.

Like Scorsese's *Last Temptation of Christ* over a decade before, the series was shot near Ouarzazate in Morocco and dabbles in some of the same issues, but without the more potentially blasphemous or sexually explicit content. Instead of the angsty esoteric Christ of Scorsese's film, here Jesus (Jeremy Sisto) is relaxed, easy to be around and exudes warmth and compassion, making identification with him far easier.[3] When Joseph dies, suddenly Jesus struggles to handle his pain and grief, making him seem far less remote. Jesus loves Mary of Bethany and was tempted to settle for domesticity, but now realizes he cannot marry her without rejecting God's call. When he is tempted, in both the desert and in Gethsemane, he struggles to overcome doubts about following the path prepared for him.

Young manages to inject his leading character with real dynamism. When Jesus is overtaken by a group of zealots, moments before they attack a group of Romans, he breaks into a sprint in order to try and dissuade them. His teaching is 'interactive',[4] yet he's enough at ease to laugh off the occasional heckle. Rather than fearing him, his disciples treat him as a friend. Young goes to great lengths to show this more playful Jesus enjoying life. He splashes the disciples with water, swings children around as he walks, and not only dances, but encourages his disciples to do likewise.

The first few instances of this more jovial Jesus are like a breath of fresh air, but eventually this ends up becoming a little distracting. There are moments when we see Jesus' anger and passion, but overall his abundant warmth, fun and charisma seem to come at the expense of substance, drive and authority. Sisto's Jesus lacks gravitas and ultimately it is unclear what exactly Jesus stands for and why he dies. The result is a Jesus for the twenty-first century who leaves us wanting more, though it's hard to say whether that is because we are charmed by him or because the film never really delivers on its early potential.

Notes

1 Appendix 1 lists all the entries in 'The Bible Collection'.
2 Adele Reinhartz, *Jesus of Hollywood. Oxford* (New York: Oxford University Press, 2007), pp. 190–3.
3 W. Barnes Tatum, *Jesus at the Movies* (California: Polebridge Press, [1997] 2013), p. 232.
4 Peter Malone, *Screen Jesus: Portrayals of Christ in Television and Film* (Lanham/Toronto/Plymouth, UK: Scarecrow Press, 2012), pp. 140–1.

The Miracle Maker
Russia/UK, 2000 – 90 mins
Stanislav Sokolov and Derek W. Hayes

DIRECTORS Stanislav Sokolov,
Derek W. Hayes
PRODUCER Naomi Jones
SCREENPLAY Murray Watts
EDITORS Robert Francis,
William Oswald, John Richards
MUSIC Anne Dudley
PRODUCTION COMPANY
S4C, Christmas Films
MAIN CAST Rebecca Callard,
Julie Christie, Ralph Fiennes,
Richard E. Grant, Ian Holm,
William Hurt, Miranda Richardson

Too many have written off *The Miracle Maker* as children's film made using puppets and cartoons, failing to spot its artistry and the weight and complexity with which It approaches the subject. Ironically few live-action films have surpassed its historical credibility or its balance between Jesus' humanity and his divinity.

We meet the film's Semitic-looking Jesus working on a construction site, a more historically plausible interpretation of the word *tektōn* than 'carpenter'.[1] From the start he exudes warmth around people. He is relaxed and frequently smiles, employing gentle humour in his teaching. Yet these touches never compromise the sense that he is someone significant. Perhaps not using an actor makes this easier, but Ralph Fiennes strikes the perfect tone and the northern accent he adopts hints at Jesus' Galilean origins.

A sick girl, Tamar, is struck by Jesus' strength and compassion when he prevents a man from striking Mary Magdalene,[2] parrying his blow. When Tamar dies, her father bids Jesus come. The scene's dramatic use of

Jesus and Tamar in *The Miracle Maker* (2000).

chiaroscuro lighting dissipates as he restores her life. However, this high point of Jesus' ministry is immediately followed by news that Herod has killed John the Baptist, Jesus' cousin and forerunner. The joy of the miracle contrasts bitterly with his grief at his loss and his fear of his future.

The film was a joint project between Russian animators Christmas Films and Wales' Cartwn Cymru. Having enjoyed success with half-hour adaptations of Shakespeare and the Hebrew Bible,[3] they turned to the New Testament. Christmas Films crafted the scenes using traditional Russian stop-motion techniques while Cartwn Cymru created the two-dimensional scenes. Switches to two-dimensional animation here typically indicate different psychological states: flashbacks, parables and the more supernatural aspects of the Gospels.[4] Their approach allows the film to be more emotional and expressionistic at these more imagery-rich moments of the story. The two-dimensional animation is bold and creative. It gives the film a real edge, challenging the audience's expectations, involving them in the story constantly to prevent them becoming passive, and assisting them in internalizing the story.

Murray Watts's outstanding script sets the story against its Jewish and Roman background, exhibiting theological and historical density without ever being cumbersome. An opening note locates the story in 'Sepphoris ... Year 90 of the Roman occupation' disorientating the viewer and re-contextualizing the story as one of a conquered people. Later, Pilate and one of his centurions discuss a revolt they have just quashed. From a Roman perspective Jesus' execution was nothing out of the ordinary. Watts primarily sticks to Luke's Gospel, but draws on resurrection accounts from all four Gospels. Given its short runtime *The Miracle Maker* shows proportionally more post-resurrection episodes than almost any other film about Jesus. For those seeking an adaptation which is faithful to the Gospels, *The Miracle Maker* does a remarkable job of covering the story and crafting a compelling portrayal of Jesus within its 88 minutes.

Indeed it's an exceptional film. Not only is it practically the only animated Jesus film to be theatrically released, but for a film made using stop-motion it's surprisingly moving. The impressive voice cast never disappoint, and its inventive and creative style is superbly executed.

Notes

1   Mark Goodacre, [podcast] 'NT Pod 18: Was Jesus a Carpenter?', *NTPod*, 1 November 2009. Available online: <https://podacre.blogspot.com/2009/11/nt-pod-18-was-jesus-carpenter.html> (accessed 19 Dec. 2021).

2   Adele Reinhartz, *Jesus of Hollywood. Oxford* (New York: Oxford University Press, 2007), pp. 134–5.

3   See Appendix 1 for a list of the nine 30-minute episodes of *Testament*.

4   Peter T. Chattaway, 'Come and See: How Movies Encourage Us to Look at (and with) Jesus', in S. Brent Plate (ed.), *Re-viewing 'The Passion': Mel Gibson's Film and its Critics* (New York: Palgrave MacMillan, 2004), pp. 127–8.

The Real Old Testament
USA, 2003 – 81 mins
Curtis Hannum and Paul Hannum

DIRECTORS
Curtis Hannum, Paul Hannum
SCREENPLAY
Material improvised by the cast
CINEMATOGRAPHY
David Avallone, K.D. Gulko,
Paul F. Perry, Shelli Ryan
EDITOR Steve Hamilton
MUSIC Jon Kull
PRODUCTION COMPANY
PCH Films
MAIN CAST Kate Connor,
Tony Estese, Paul Hannum,
Curtis Hannum, Sam Lloyd,
Laura Meshelle

Shot on an ultra-low budget with improvised dialogue,[1] Curtis and Paul Hannum's *The Real Old Testament* covers the opening thirty or so chapters of the book of Genesis in the style of MTV's pioneering 1990s reality TV show, *The Real World* (1992 onwards). In addition to editing, producing and directing the film the brothers also played the roles of 'God' and 'Snake'.

More importantly, the Hannums were able to assemble a talented cast who could milk the material for all it was worth. The film's most established star was Sam Lloyd (*Scrubs*) as Abraham. It's testimony to

Director Curtis Hannum playing the role of God in *The Real Old Testament* (2003).

the rest of the cast, however, that they match his performance, with Kate Connor's Sarai/Sarah and Laura Meshelle's turn as one of Lot's daughters particularly standing out. But it's Curtis Hannum's own performance which is the most memorable as a somewhat petulant and fickle God. 'I think he's so much happier with Eve than just with the full set of ribs' God reflects in a voiceover, unaware that a shiny sock-puppet snake is about to spoil his creation. The film is divided into segments, interspersed with 'confessional interviews',[2] so it's not long before Cain and Abel, Abraham and Sarah, Lot's family and Jacob and Rachel join proceedings.

In fact, there's very little in the final film which is not directly from the book of Genesis, and whilst it's a fairly scathing portrayal, much of its irreverence derives from the decision to adapt the text in the style of *The Real World*. This is not a film which shows God, or any of its characters, any deference. Yet like *Monty Python's Life of Brian*, it has fans within the church, as well as outside it. *The Real Old Testament* is certainly irreverent, but any offence is tempered by its considered use of the biblical text. Indeed often it is precisely its faithfulness to the text that provides the humour. When it shows Abraham trying to pass his wife off as his sister, or Rachel swapping her chance to sleep with her husband for some mandrake plants, these are actual biblical tales that more pious efforts typically exclude.

In so doing, *The Real Old Testament* sheds new light on often overly familiar texts. De-familiarizing the various stories in Genesis, the film allows them to be seen in a new way. Shooting the Hebrew Bible in such a penetrating modern style, exposes the strangeness of much of what occurred in these characters' lives, cutting through centuries of religious gloss to the very core of the stories.

Yet while a comedy film can be moving, challenging or pioneering, ultimately it has to be funny. Thankfully, the biggest strength of *The Real Old Testament* is that it greatly exceeds that primary goal. Packed with great lines and subtle performances, it is eminently quotable, and only gets funnier on repeated viewings. Whether it is Lot summarizing Sodom as 'you either love it or you hate it', Cain extolling the pleasant virtues of Nod, or Lloyd's Abraham reacting to God's ideas about mass-circumcision, the film rarely, if ever, misses its mark.

Notes

1   Scott Foundas, '*The Real Old Testament*', *Variety*, 25 February 2003. Available online: <https://variety.com/2003/film/reviews/the-real-old-testament-1200543114/> (accessed 19 Dec. 2021).

2   Rhonda Burnette-Bletsch 'God at the Movies', in Rhonda Burnette-Bletsch (ed.), *The Bible in Motion: A Handbook of the Bible and Its Reception in Film*. vol. 1 (Berlin/Boston: De Gruyter, 2016), p. 313.

The Visual Bible: The Gospel of John
Canada/UK, 2003 – 180 mins
Philip Saville

DIRECTOR Philip Saville
PRODUCERS Chris Chrisafis,
Garth H. Drabinsky
SCREENPLAY John Goldsmith
CINEMATOGRAPHY
Miroslaw Baszak
EDITORS Michel Arcand,
Ron Wisman Jr.
MUSIC Jeff Danna
PRODUCTION COMPANY
The Book of John, Inc.,
The Gospel of John, Ltd.
MAIN CAST Stuart Bunce,
Henry Ian Cusick, Daniel Kash,
Christopher Plummer

Released during the build-up of anticipation prior to Mel Gibson's *The Passion of the Christ* the Visual Bible released a very different Jesus film. As with previous releases of *Matthew* (1993) and *Acts* (1994), which found a niche market amongst evangelical Christians, *The Gospel of John* was a word-for-word adaptation of John's entire text.

John is a difficult book to adapt, full of eloquent yet lengthy speeches. While Jesus' seven signs keep the action flowing during the opening eleven chapters, much of the second half is taken up by a long piece of oratory, ahead of Jesus' arrest, death and resurrection. The film livens up proceedings moderately by changing camera angles periodically and locations whenever appropriate, for example, relocating outside partway through Jesus' post-Last Supper monologue.[1] Later DVD releases made significant cuts, reducing its original three-hour runtime to around 120 minutes.

The Visual Bible: The Gospel of John (2003).

In contrast to Gibson's inattention to potential antisemitism with *The Passion of the Christ*, producer Garth Drabinsky and director Philip Saville employed an advisory board featuring Jewish scholars.[2] Opening titles explain the Jewishness of Jesus, the dominance of the Romans and explain how the Gospel was written during 'unprecedented polemic and antagonism' between Christians and some Jews. The Good News Bible was used, partly due to its more sympathetic translation.[3] It's strange, then, that the film visually 'black-hats' Jesus' opponents.

The then unknown Henry Ian Cusick was chosen for the role of Jesus, though his subsequent role in *Lost* (2004) distracts many nowadays. While his half-Scottish, half-Peruvian features are hardly Middle Eastern, his appearance is more appropriate than his blond/blue-eyed predecessors. Cusick delivers a compelling, convincing and challenging portrayal of John's hero which Variety observed 'expresses an energy, eloquence and force of personality that captivate and thoroughly convince'.[4] Cusick's restless, yet compassionate, Jesus paces with purposes as he delivers his articulate speeches. The smile on his face belies the intensity in his eyes and the fire in his belly.

Saville's relaxed interpretation occasionally contradicts the text with its images and has Mary Magdalene attend the Last Supper. Jesus' trial and death reject standard iconography. Once beaten and mocked Jesus' nobility, dignity and poise disappear. He stumbles before Pilate and heads to Golgotha with the cross slung over his shoulder. No crowd of onlookers line his route to the cross. Implementing archaeological discoveries, Jesus' legs are nailed, awkwardly, one either side of the cross.

The other important part is Christopher Plummer's narration. Plummer's 'rich', mellow voice delivers some additional gravitas.[5] Plummer is cleverly linked to Stuart Bunce's role as 'the other disciple', suggesting he is the author/narrator without directly correlating them. The relation between the two is particularly memorable in the final scene where, following Jesus' final resurrection appearance, Jesus, Peter and the other disciple stroll along the beach. On Jesus' final words, 'If I want him to live until I come, what is that to you?', he and Peter file past the camera leaving Bunce alone mid-frame. The footage freezes, the image turns sepia and melts into a sketch while the soundtrack's moving primary motif swells poignantly. The sequence expertly conveys a sense of these actions passing into history and hinting at his followers' future beyond the story's end.

John is an unusual film. As the series' title suggests, it works better as a visual illustration of the biblical text than as a movie to watch in a single sitting. Yet it's an interesting adaptation of the text, illuminating the original for those who give it the opportunity.

Notes

1   Jeffrey L. Staley and Richard Walsh, *Jesus, the Gospels, and the Cinematic Imagination: A Handbook to Jesus on DVD* (Louisville/London: Westminster John Knox Press, 2007), p. 146.

2   Mark Goodacre, 'The Power of *The* Passion: Reacting and Over-reacting to Gibson's Artistic Vision', in Kathleen E. Corley and Robert L. Webb (eds.), *Jesus and Mel Gibson's 'The Passion of the Christ': The Film, The Gospels and the Claims of History*, (London: Continuum, 2004), pp. 35–6.

3   E.g. replacing 'the Jews' with 'the Jewish authorities'.

4   Todd McCarthy, 'The Gospel of John', *Variety* 18 September 2003. Retrieved from: <http://web.archive.org/web/20031001102926/http://www.demossnewspond.com/john/presskit/varietyreview.htm>.

5   Jo-Ann A. Brant, 'Camera as Character in Philip Saville's *The Gospel of* John', in David Shepherd (ed.), *Images of the Word: Hollywood's Bible and Beyond* (Atlanta: Society of Biblical Literature, 2008), p. 150.

The Passion of the Christ
USA, 2004 – 127 mins
Mel Gibson

DIRECTOR Mel Gibson
PRODUCERS Bruce Davey,
Mel Gibson, Stephen McEveety,
Enzo Sisti
SCREENPLAY Benedict Fitzgerald,
Mel Gibson
CINEMATOGRAPHY
Caleb Deschanel
EDITORS Steve Mirkovich,
John Wright
MUSIC John Debney
PRODUCTION COMPANY
Icon Film Ltd.
MAIN CAST Monica Bellucci,
Jim Caviezel, Rosalinda
Celentano, Hristo Jivkov, Maia
Morgenstern, Mattia Sbragia

Almost more than any other film, Mel Gibson's *Passion of the Christ* is surrounded by contradictions. It's an almost unbearably violent film about love; a foreign-language film that's more popular with audiences than critics; the reviving of a dead genre that became a box-office smash; a film beloved by horror fans and church-goers alike. Its traditionalist Catholic theology was embraced by hardcore evangelicals, yet while it preaches tolerance it stands accused of antisemitism. A spiritual meditation, financed entirely by an action-movie star.

Gibson portrayed himself as a warrior in the culture wars, leveraging support into a successful grass-roots marketing campaign. When studios, not unsurprisingly, rejected his vision of an ultra-violent Jesus film based on the antisemitic visions of an eighteenth-century nun (and shot in two dead languages), he made

Jesus on the Via Dolorosa in *The Passion of the Christ* (2004).

supporting his film a mark of religious faithfulness. Then there were the reports interpreted as signs of God's approval: on-set miracles and conversions; claims of the 'Holy Ghost directing traffic';[1] the rumoured papal summary 'it is as it was'; and Gibson's insistence the film would be 'like travelling back in time and watching the events unfold exactly as they occurred'.[2]

The claims of realism quickly fall away in light of Satan's physical presence, the morphing of the faces of Jewish children, and a grotesquely deformed demon-baby. Realism, it transpired, was more a synonym for 'violence', to almost anti-realistic levels. Roger Ebert called it 'the most violent film I have ever seen' though he accepted the legitimacy of its singular vision.[3] Jesus' flagellation, brutalization and crucifixion were undeniably violent: given he died far sooner than was typical, it may have been unusually so.[4] As an artistic choice, a visceral film for those wishing to contemplate the horrendous nature of Christ's death has some validity.

The charge of antisemitism is more problematic. Gibson significantly distorts the Gospels' depiction of Judas, Caiaphas and the Jewish crowds, ignores historical likelihood and invents its own troubling elements. Most Jews in Jerusalem during Passover were unmoved by Jesus. None are shown. Judas is tormented by demonic-children wearing skull caps. Caiaphas is fat, tackily dressed, and surrounded by shadows and sycophants. In contrast, Pilate (who Luke, Josephus and Philo describe as vicious) is portrayed as a clean-cut, noble, deep-in-thought philosopher who speaks in calm measured tones.[5] There's no historical justification for these depictions. How different the film could have been if they were reversed. Further, the Gospels give no indication of the size of the crowd that lobbies for Barabbas's freedom (Mark 15.6–8), but the enormous baying mob here is extreme.

When Gibson was confronted with these issues, he went on the offensive, rather than seeking to understand and unfortunately these problems detract from the film's undoubted strengths. Between the violence there are glimpses of who Jesus was before his torture and execution. He rescues Mary Magdalene, rides into Jerusalem, shares the Last Supper with friends and chats with his mother. Jim Caviezel's performance as Jesus is impressive and deeply affecting. As the violence against Jesus begins to reach its climax, we see the film's intended message come to the fore through these point-of-view flashbacks. On seeing Golgotha Jesus recalls teaching 'Love your enemies' and later 'Love one another'. Gibson intensifies these flashbacks stressing Jesus' death was not purposeless, but about his love for humanity.

Rumours of a sequel to *The Passion* have persisted ever since its initial release. If Gibson does decide to revisit the subject, it is to be hoped that he has learnt from the problems of this film and is able to create something which testifies more to Christianity's strengths than the prejudices of its past.

Notes

1   Kamon Simpson, 'Mel Gibson brings movie to city's church leaders', *The Gazette* (Colorado Springs), 27 June 2003. Retrieved from: <http://web.archive.org/web/20040216002331/http://www.gazette.com/popupNews.php?id=408774>

2   'Mel Gibson's Great Passion', *Zenit* 6 March 2003. Available online: <https://zenit.org/2003/03/06/mel-gibson-s-great-passion-2/> (accessed 19 Dec. 2021).

3   Roger Ebert, 'The Passion of the Christ', *rogerebert.com* 24 February 2004. Available online: <www.rogerebert.com/reviews/the-passion-of-the-christ-2004> (accessed 19 Dec. 2021).

4   Mark Goodacre, 'The Power of *The* Passion: Reacting and Over-reacting to Gibson's Artistic Vision', in Kathleen E. Corley and Robert L. Webb (eds.), *Jesus and Mel Gibson's 'The Passion of the Christ': The Film, The Gospels and the Claims of History*, (London: Continuum, 2004), pp. 35–6.

5   Luke 13.1. Philo and Josephus were non-biblical authors from the time, see Philo's *Gaium* 302 and Josephus' *Antiquities* 18.85–87.

Shanti Sandesham (*Message of Peace*)
India, 2004 – 140 mins
P. Chandrasekhar Reddy

DIRECTOR
P. Chandrasekhar Reddy
PRODUCER Sakamuri
Mallikarjuna Rao
SCREENPLAY
Tripuraneni Maharadi
CINEMATOGRAPHY
Meka Ramakrishna
EDITOR Adirala Ravi Teja
MUSIC Sri Swamiji
PRODUCTION COMPANY
Padmalaya Studios
MAIN CAST Krishna
Ghattamaneni, Suman,
Vinod Kumar

Shanti Sandesham, filmed in Hydrabad in southern India's Telugu-speaking region, is an interesting example of the ways ideas flow back and forth between East and West. While Christianity in India goes back to long before the colonial era and subsequently has developed its own distinct identity, it retains an association with empire. *Shanti Sandesham*, like the earlier *Karunamayudu* (1978), was produced by western mission organizations working in tandem with Indian film producers and remains a mixture of these two cultures.

Created in Bollywood-esque style,[1] director P. Chandrasekhar Reddy's film is structured around five song-and-dance numbers. As is typical for Indian musicals the sound is pre-recorded by a playback singer, giving each song a hermetically sealed feeling. Deliberately drawing attention to its artificiality takes the viewer out of the moment and highlights particular emotions. *Shanti* should be judged not as 'a realistic, western-type film with a linear narrative but a film that conforms to a different set of aesthetic imperatives'.[2] The songs chart the story's key emotional highs and lows, firstly as Jesus begins transforming lives through his miracles and then accompanying Salome's dance and John the Baptist's resulting beheading. Even Jesus (Krishna Ghattamaneni) sings when he draws children to himself, including those of the pharisees. A fourth number celebrates Lazarus returning from the dead at the pinnacle of Jesus' ministry.

The mournful final song, 'Rakshakuda' (Protector), accompanies the most striking part of the film as Jesus trudges to Golgotha. Lasting eight minutes, the sequence pauses only briefly for Jesus to speak. Editing speed increases dramatically and the compositions become far more varied, featuring God shots, close-ups and shots from Jesus' point of view. The fast cutting and a dizzying array of angles disorientates, heightening the emotions. Jesus' image becomes fragmented and more subjective, as if there is no single authoritative interpretation of what is happening, perhaps reflecting India's diverse religious perspectives.

One of the most noticeable elements of the film is its bright colour palette, contrasting with the muted colours of recent Hollywood biblical films. Purples, oranges, yellows and greens are all prominent. Many men wear checked /plaid garments with brightly-coloured headscarves. These vivid colours differ from the traditional colours of western Christian iconography, shifting its aesthetics towards its own culture. Similarly, the Last Supper scene reproduces Leonardo's famous composition, but reworks the colour scheme with greens and reds, replacing solid blocks of colour with checks.

Shanti also references several USA-made Jesus films, notably the roving, interactive Sermon on the Mount from *Kings of Kings* (1961) and the feeding of the 5000 from *Jesus* (1979). Perhaps unsurprisingly, *Shanti* mirrors the scene where Jesus invites Peter to walk on water from *Karunamayudu*, using similar blue filters, day-for-night lighting and shot composition. Influences from Indian mythologicals are similarly apparent, notably the portrayal of Satan whose bearded face, thick hair, black robes, and exaggerated gestures are without parallel among western Jesus films.

Krishna Ghattamaneni in *Shanti Sandesham* (2004).

Having renounced Satan's temptation to adopt worldly values, Jesus qualifies for the fourth and final *ashrama* (stage) of Hindu life, *sannyasa*. His quest for truth certifies him as a *sadhu* (holy man). It's significant, then, that Reddy addresses the caste system and social inclusion. Bakker describes how 'the Jewish leaders are pictured as the leaders of a caste' who charge Jesus for his lack of respect for the caste system, and for mixing with *dalits* (untouchables).[3] Likewise the Samaritan women spreading Jesus' message is significant because the disciples call her people 'untouchables'. This is typical of *Shanti*'s concern with the importance of women to Jesus, highlighted again on the road to Golgotha and his resurrection. Women are also prominent at his ascension which ends with Jesus surrounded by stars and galaxies. No western Jesus film would even consider such a shot, which only underlines the benefits such a different cultural perspective can bring.

Notes

1   Officially Bollywood films are shot in or around Mumbai.
2   K. Moti Gokulsing and Wimal Dissanayake, *Indian Popular Cinema: A Narrative of Cultural Change* (Stoke on Trent, UK: Trentham Books, 2004), p. 31.
3   Freek Bakker, 'Shanti Sandesham, a New Jesus Film Produced in India: Indian Christology in Pictures'. *Exchange*, vol. 36, 2007, p. 61.

Color of the Cross
USA, 2006 – 89 mins
Jean Claude LaMarre

DIRECTOR Jean-Claude LaMarre
PRODUCERS Horacio
Blackwood, Ken Halsband,
Jessie L. Levostre,
Cecil L. Murray
SCREENPLAY Jean Claude
LaMarre, Jean Claude Nelson,
James Troesh
CINEMATOGRAPHY
Paul Mayne
EDITOR Darlene Haussmann
MUSIC Flexx,
Jean-Claude LaMarre
PRODUCTION COMPANY
Grubb Productions
MAIN CAST Adam Green,
Jesse Holland, Johann John
Jean, Jean-Claude LaMarre

2006 was the year two films featured Black actors playing Jesus. *Jezile* (Son of Man) gained critical acclaim, but *The Color of the Cross*, written, produced and directed by Jean Claude LaMarre, is the more radical film. Whereas *Jezile* asks 'What if Jesus had come into a modern African context?' *Color of the Cross* boldly asserts that Jesus *was* Black.

LaMarre, who also plays Jesus, revitalizes the ancient tradition of depicting Jesus as Black. For at least a millennium Ethiopian Bible illustrations, Russian icons and European 'Black Madonna' statues have portrayed an African-looking Jesus. The twentieth century saw theologians Professor James Cone and Bishop Albert Cleage side with Malcolm X's claim 'Christ was a Black man'.

This is not recontextualization. Jesus (here called Yoshua) and his family are Black, but most of the Jewish characters in the film, including some disciples, are olive-skinned or white. The film's website cited Revelation 1's description of Jesus' hair as 'woolly'.[1] The presence of Moses' 'Cushite' wife (Numbers 12.1) demonstrates other races were assimilated as Israelites, and clearly their descendants would have been Black.

Naturally many of Yoshua's opponents are racially motivated, but racism is not the only factor in his death. Were it so, the story would lose its ultimate significance and become just another terrible story about white lynching. LaMarre shockingly heightens comparisons with the modern world by omitting Jesus' trials, as if Yoshua is executed without one. One moment he is taken into custody, the next he appears on the verge of death, after secret beatings while under arrest. It is no coincidence Jesus is tied to the cross with rope, rather than nailed to it. Meanwhile, Nicodemus and Joseph of Arimathea's intellectual dithering jabs at white liberal inaction today.

In addition to its emphasis on Jesus' Black identity, the film captures some of the story's Jewish context. There are Jewish prayers spoken in Hebrew, and the Romans frequently spit out the word 'Jew' at their subjects. There are frequent references to the Torah, rabbis and seders, including intercutting the Last Supper with footage of others sharing a Passover meal. Yoshua's youngest brother even asks the traditional question from Passover Seder 'What's so special about tonight?' This extended sequence is typical of the film's emphasis on community. Unfortunately sometimes the accents of some Jewish characters veer into stereotype and removing Jesus' trials minimizes the Romans' role in Jesus' death.

As the film draws to a close, two moments in particular stand out. One where Yoshua washes his disciples' feet which strips the moment of its usual poise and dignity. The other occurs when Yoshua prays in Gethsemane. The camera gets extra-close to Jesus' face and LaMarre portrays such fear and desperation that it makes for deeply uncomfortable viewing, evoking images from other films depicting Black men facing violent, racially-motivated deaths.

Jean Claude LaMarre's Jesus in *Color of the Cross* (2006).

Occasionally the film is let down by overly-earnest acting or clunky dialogue, but that is only to be expected from a film shot on such a low budget. Moreover, such weaknesses seem almost secondary for a film which is of critical importance, not only for those of African diaspora but a vital reminder to all that much still has to be done in our time to overcome prejudice and racism.

Notes

1   'Facts', *colorofthecross.com*, March 2006. Retrieved from <http://web.archive.org/web/20060505104220/http://www.colorofthecross.com/faqs.html>.

Jezile (*Son of Man*)
South Africa, 2006 – 91 mins
Mark Dornford-May

DIRECTOR Mark Dornford-May
PRODUCERS Camilla Driver,
Brigid Olen
SCREENPLAY Andiswa Kedama,
Pauline Malefane,
Mark Dornford-May
CINEMATOGRAPHY
Giulio Biccari
EDITORS Ronelle Loots,
Anne Sopel
MUSIC Charles Hazlewood,
Pauline Malefane, Sibulele Mjali
PRODUCTION COMPANY
Spier Films
MAIN CAST Noluthando
Boqwana, Andile Kosi, Pauline
Malefane, Andries Mbali

Mark Dornford-May's *Jezile* relocates the Jesus story in a modern, African township. Were Jesus to come to earth today, many argue this is the kind of place in which he would be found, criticizing the politics and corruption that leaves millions living in shacks. Pilate maintains power by manipulating local gangland leaders Caiaphas and Annas into controlling their people while his troops pose as peacekeepers from a neighbouring country.

Jezile (Andile Kosi), is almost the polar opposite of the image of the blond European in a white bathrobe. A shaven-headed Black African dressed in jeans and a checked shirt who blends strength, compassion, and an easy going nature, with a compelling and passionate personality, a 'Steve Biko Christ figure'.[1]

The modern setting heightens the reality. Herod's slaughter of the infants is brought uncomfortably close to home, creating fear and tension even though Jezile's survival is assured. The disciples feature peaceful men and women alongside freedom fighters who are challenged to lay down their weapons as well as their lives. *Jezile's* creativity and initiative embody the biblical narratives while also tearing through pious and kitsch tradition. There are references to classic European Christian art – notably a pietà referencing Michaelangelo and a shot of Jesus as a baby, again seated on his mother's knee – however it also fashions its own memorable imagery such as angels depicted as young boys wearing feathers, particularly as they rise up a hill in a final ascension-like finale.

Dornford-May uses various touches to reinvigorate the story, blending naturalistic, intimate footage, with scenes shot in the style of news footage and miracles filmed as if shot with a camcorder. Such methods reflect the way Jesus' activity was recorded and preserved for a wider audience. As well as filming Jezile's miracles, his other actions start to be recorded and celebrated in murals on the township walls, re-telling the stories about him to a wider audience, in language they can understand. His popularity grows, and thus he begins to be perceived as a threat to those in power.

Despite a degree of Afro-pessimism,[2] the film's handling of Jesus' passion tells the story in a manner that fits its modern context – a radically political end to a very politically charged version of the Jesus story. Just as during apartheid families began displaying the corpses of their murdered relatives, so after Jezile's death in custody his mother puts his body on public display.[3] The film's starkest deviation from the text is a radical political comparison.

Whilst the film has little doubt about Jezile's divinity – showing several miracles – its biggest concern is this political aspect of Jesus' brief time on earth. Jezile's key statement 'this is my world/land' is both theological *and* political. Just as proclaiming Jesus is Lord/King implied Caesar was not, so 'this is my land' is conceivably reclaiming 'stolen indigenous land'.[4] Such radical, political statements lie at the heart of *Son of Man*. Setting his story in such a politically charged context is a salient reminder of Jesus' critique of power.

Jezile's preaching in the townships attracts the authorities' attention in *Jezile* (2006).

Notes

1   Katleho K. Mokoena, 'Steve Biko Christ figure: A Black Theological Christology in the *Son of Man* film', HTS Teologiese Studies/ Theological Studies 73(3), 2017, a4667. Available online: <https://hts.org.za/index.php/hts/article/view/4667/10365> (19 December 2021).

2   Despite traces of white colonialism being eradicated, violent unrest continues, 'the dream of the … "rainbow nation" in tatters' – West, Gerald O. (2016) *The Stolen Bible: From Tool of Imperialism to African Icon*, Boston: Brill. p. 427.

3   Reinhold Zwick, '*Son of Man* (*Jezile*)', in Adele Reinhartz (ed.), *Bible and Cinema: Fifty Key Films* (London/New York: Routledge, 2013), p. 245.

4   Mokoena, 'Steve Biko Christ figure', p. 7.

The Nativity Story
USA, 2006 – 97 mins
Catherine Hardwicke

DIRECTOR Catherine Hardwicke
PRODUCERS Marty Bowen,
Wyck Godfrey
SCREENPLAY Mike Rich
CINEMATOGRAPHY
Elliot Davis
EDITORS Robert K. Lambert,
Stuart Levy
MUSIC Mychael Danna
PRODUCTION COMPANY
New Line Productions
MAIN CAST Hiam Abbass,
Shohreh Aghdashloo, Ciarán
Hinds, Keisha Castle-Hughes,
Oscar Isaac

In less than twelve months *The Nativity Story* went from being an idea in screenwriter Mike Rich's head, to premiering at the Vatican. Emboldened by the surprise success of *The Passion of the Christ*, New Line wanted their film released before the buzz had dissipated. Given the abundance of Christmas films, and the story's centrality to western culture, it seems hard to believe that only one English language, feature film about the Nativity story has reached cinemas since 1914, although the subject has proved popular outside Hollywood.[1]

While the title suggests a mythic retelling aimed at the family, director Catherine Hardwicke came to the project having enjoyed success with two realist films about teenagers from lower-income backgrounds. Consequently *Nativity Story* is somewhat uneven. The early scenes exhibit Hardwicke's typically gritty realism but the film morphs into a road movie as Mary and Joseph get acquainted and begin to appreciate each another. Then when the holy couple reaches Bethlehem, any remaining realism is supplanted by 'Christmas-magic' culminating with star beams shining through a hole in the stable roof bathing the new family in its light.

Keisha Castle-Hughes as Mary in *The Nativity Story* (2006).

The best moments occur in Nazareth when Hardwicke's grittier style is to the fore. Her experience as a production designer enables the film to brilliantly capture a first century Galilee whose peasant inhabitants survive barely a whisker above poverty and destitution.[2] Hardwicke's camera weaves between the crumbling dwellings, immersed in the dirt of peasant life. It's a world where people sell on their small surpluses to neighbours, and where both adults and children are constantly working at one small task or another. Unanticipated tax collections or failed harvests meant catastrophe. The fields are not swaying with golden, post-agricultural revolution grain, but straggly plants struggling to poke their heads above the mud. It's easy to see how this world might incubate a revolutionist dream, something underlined by the failed, crucified zealots that are encountered merely as a feature of everyday life.

For Mary, the filmmakers chose Keisha Castle-Hughes who, at sixteen, already had an Oscar nomination and who became pregnant during filming.[3] Ciarin Hinds adds menace as King Herod, but the performance which most impresses belongs to, the then unknown, Oscar Isaac, making Joseph the most interesting and compelling character. In one of the film's best scenes, he dreams about stoning Mary only to be brought to his senses by an angel.

Sadly, the writing often fails to live up to the promise of this wordless scene. It's often forced, awkward, clunky or banal. At times the narrative flow is sacrificed for unnecessary factoids, or weak humour. The use of Middle Eastern accents only highlights the script's deficiencies. The magi – used ineptly for comic effect – are the weakest aspect of the film only serving to give the film the kind of Christmassy schmaltz that the opening moments worked so hard to eradicate.

Yet overall, the good just about edges out the bad. The opening scenes wonderfully flesh out the scant details in the Gospels, and the middle section brings us closer to Mary and Joseph than any previous cinematic attempt. Even the Hallmark-esque finale is effective enough to ensure that, for many, watching this film has become part of their Christmas tradition.

Notes

1   Matthew Page, 'The Nativity Re-Born: Genre and the Birth and Childhood of Jesus', in Wickham Clayton (ed.), *The Bible Onscreen in the New Millennium: New Heart and New Spirit* (Manchester: Manchester University Press, 2020), pp. 102–121.

2   John Dominic Crossan, *The Historical Jesus: The Life of a Mediterranean Jewish Peasant* (New York: Harper Collins, 1992), pp. 45–6.

3   Catherine O'Brien, *The Celluloid Madonna: From Scripture to Screen* (New York: Columbia University Press, 2011), p. 6.

Mesih (*Jesus, the Spirit of God*)
Iran, 2007 – 83 mins
Nader Talebzadeh

DIRECTOR Nader Talebzadeh
SCREENPLAY Nader Talebzadeh
EDITOR Mahdi Mokhtari
PRODUCTION COMPANY
Shabakeh-ye Avval-e Seda
Va Sima-ye Iran
MAIN CAST
Ahmad Soleimani-Nia

Nader Talebzadeh's *Mesih* or *Jesus, the Spirit of God* (2007) was produced alongside an 800-minute television version and combines Qu'ranic material about Isa (Jesus) with the Gospel of Barnabas.[1] While the Sunni form of Islam bans portraying prophets, discouraging even the depiction of humans and animals, Shia Islam is less restrictive. In recent years Iran (where ninety percent are Shia) has seen several films released about characters who feature in both the Bible and the Qur'an, including Shahriar Bahrani's *Saint Mary* (2000) and *Kingdom of Solomon* (2010).

Talebzadeh cast Iranian army veteran Ahmad Soleimani-Nia as Isa. Soleimani-Nia's long, blond, curly hair runs counter both to expectations about an Islamic Jesus, and to the traditions of western Christian art. Neither the canonical gospels, the Qu'ran nor Barnabas's Gospel describe Jesus' appearance, but the Hadith (Sahih Bukhari 3438) describes Isa as having 'curly hair and a reddish complexion'. Soleimani-Nia's distinctive looks make him a striking figure, giving him an air of one at home in this world, yet nevertheless distinct from it.

Jesus speaks to his disciples among olives groves in *Mesih* (2007). Courtesy Nader Talebzadeh.

While *a* Gospel of Barnabas was alluded to in the sixth century (and some claim earlier), it is unclear if this is the same text which (re-) emerged in the seventeenth century. It contains much of Matthew, Mark, Luke and John, as well as its own material, but aligns more with Islamic theology, expressly clarifying that Jesus is not divine. Whilst the Qur'an denies Isa died, both Barnabas and Talebzadeh's adaptation show Judas being transformed to look like Isa, and dying in his place while Isa is transported to Heaven.[2] Talebzadeh voiced his desire to 'open the door for dialogue',[3] so includes an abridged 'Christian narrative' of Isa's death before a lengthier presentation of Barnabas' version. While films with multiple endings, like *Wayne's World* (1992), have proliferated recently, it is an unusual, yet ecumenical, approach for a religious film.

Mesih features other elements absent from most Jesus films including Caiaphas bowing before Isa and worshipping him; the Roman Senate pronouncing that Isa is neither God nor his son; and Isa's insistence that the Messiah should be a descendant of Ishmael.

When Isa saves a woman accused of adultery, he creates a mirror in the sand, horrifying her accusers by reflecting back their own sin. Like *Last Temptation of Christ*, Paul, (here' Sha-oul'), murders the recently raised Lazarus, beginning a campaign of terror against Isa's followers. Barnabas himself is included amongst the twelve disciples and is shown writing down events as they happen.

Aside from the script, Talebzadeh frequently adopts slightly below eye-level camera positions, not nearly so deferential as most low shots, but enough to suggest Isa's superiority is not about a certain context or a particular moment, but more integral to who he is. The subtlety of the position reinforces that Isa is special compared to those around him, but only to a degree. He's not a god, just a prophet. While questioning Jesus' identity is hardly unusual among Bible films, what makes *Mesih* so interesting is the way its respectful questioning of Jesus' identity arises from the filmmaker's belief in a different monotheistic faith.

Notes

1   The Qu'ranic material about Jesus features in smaller sections across fifteen *surahs*.

2   Peter Malone, *Screen Jesus: Portrayals of Christ in Television and Film* (Lanham/Toronto/Plymouth, UK: Scarecrow Press, 2012), p. 294.

3   'Islamic film offers Muslim view of Jesus', *ABC*, 16 January 2008. Available online: <https://www.abc.net.au/news/2008–01-16/islamic-film-offers-muslim-view-of-jesus/1013840> (accessed 19 Dec. 2021).

The Passion
UK, 2008 – 180 mins
Michael Offer

DIRECTOR Michael Offer
PRODUCERS Zakaria Alaoui,
Miara Martell,
Nigel Stafford-Clark
SCREENPLAY Frank Deasy
CINEMATOGRAPHY
Tony Miller
EDITOR Paul Knight
MUSIC Debbie Wiseman
PRODUCTION COMPANY
BBC, HBO Inc.
MAIN CAST Paloma Baeza,
Ben Daniels, Tom Ellis, Stephen
Graham, John Lynch, Joseph
Mawle, James Nesbitt, Paul
Nicholls, Penelope Wilton

Over fifty years after Jesus first appeared on the BBC in 1956's *Jesus of Nazareth*, a four-part miniseries was broadcast in the run up to Easter. The pre-release publicity for *The Passion* stressed the importance of telling the story in context.[1] In addition to the usual focus on Jesus and his scruffy bunch of disciples, it spends considerable screen time developing the characters of Caiaphas, the Jewish high priest, and Roman governor Pontius Pilate presenting the story from these three different perspectives.

In contrast to many Jesus films, Caiaphas (Ben Daniels) is not the nasty villain in the big hat, but a family man, handed an almost impossible job at the most difficult time of the year. Caught between the most powerful empire on earth and his own oppressed, angry and, consequently, volatile people, he has to keep the peace to prevent Rome from flattening Judea once more. His concern at Jesus apparently declaring himself Messiah is understandable. For him, 'Jesus isn't a bad man'; he's just misguided enough to provoke a Roman clampdown.

For his part, Pilate (played by James Nesbitt) has come to Jerusalem to police the Passover, desperately hoping it will pass without incident so he can return home to Caesarea. Keen to avoid trouble, he quickly stamps out any sort of disturbance. Nesbitt's petulant performance adds steel to Pilate's character by using his 'natural Ulster accent',[2] recalling the region's recent history of religious and political turmoil.

Introducing this 'historical time frame' early on enables the action to flow more freely as the series develops.[3] Frank Deasy's script cleverly picks out little details from the Gospels and uses them not only to explain the drama, but also to create it. Furthermore, Deasy breathes new life into some of Jesus' best known soundbites. *The Passion* rephrases classic lines, enabling us to hear them again as if for the first time. They sound like words someone might actually say, rather than pronouncements from a holy book.

This is helped by Joseph Mawle's fantastic performance as Jesus. Underneath his relaxed appearance lies a steely determination as he delivers his religious and social critiques with a glint in his eye. Moreover, it's a very physical performance from Mawle, who fills the screen and grabs our attention in every scene he features in. The supporting roles are strong too. Stephen Graham is excellent, as ever, as Barabbas, and Paul Nicholls' Judas – forced to choose between his two father figures, Caiaphas and Jesus – evinces great sympathy.

From a visual point of view, the external scenes, shot in Ouarzazete in Morocco are particularly striking. The ramshackle, narrow streets of Jerusalem and the scruffy costumes of Jesus and his followers, emphasize the poverty of most of the people, stressing the gulf between them and the elite. The occasional red Roman cloak or Black priestly turban punctuates the variety of light browns which dominate the colour scheme.

The ending grapples with the unusual accounts at the end of the Gospels in a way that, like the rest of the programme, left both believers and unbelievers feeling fairly treated, while giving those in the middle plenty to think about. While some criticised its lack of 'frisson',[4] overall its high production values and strong performances elevate a remarkable script which strives to get the history right as well as the language. *The Passion* manages to inform, educate and entertain in a way which is visually, dramatically and historically satisfying.

Joseph Mawle in *The Passion* (2008).

Notes

1   Mark Goodacre, '*The Passion* and its historical context', BBC website, February 2008. Retrieved from : <http://web.archive.org/web/20080305021702/http://www.bbc.co.uk/religion/programmes/thepassion/articles/>.

2   Peter Malone, *Screen Jesus: Portrayals of Christ in Television and Film* (Lanham/Toronto/Plymouth, UK: Scarecrow Press, 2012), p. 175.

3   Catherine O'Brien, *The Celluloid Madonna: From Scripture to Screen* (New York: Columbia University Press, 2011), p. 41.

4   Giles Fraser, 'Thou shalt not offend anyone: BBC's Jesus is nice but dull', *The Guardian*, 1 March 2008. Available online: <www.theguardian.com/media/2008/mar/01/bbc.religion1> (accessed 19 Dec. 2021).

El cant dels ocells (*Birdsong*)
Spain, 2008 – 93 mins
Albert Serra

DIRECTOR Albert Serra
PRODUCERS Lluís Miñarro,
Montse Triola
SCREENPLAY Albert Serra
CINEMATOGRAPHY
Jimmy Gimferrer, Neus Ollé
EDITOR Àngel Martín
PRODUCTION COMPANY
Caprici
MAIN CAST Lluís Serrat
Batlle, Lluís Carbó, Lluís Serrat,
Montse Triola

Birdsong from Catalan director Albert Serra adapts the same material as *The Nativity Story* (2006), but is otherwise poles apart. Just as Pasolini's *Il vangelo secondo Matteo* opposed mid-century biblical epics such as *King of Kings* (1961), so *Birdsong* functions as an antidote to *The Nativity Story*'s excesses. Instead of lavish sets, the action occurs outside on deserted landscapes, featuring only six cast members. There are no moral victories, or analogies between past and the future, indeed the line between the two is blurred.

Serra's 'anti-epic' style is typical of his 'cinema of gentle observation and slow demeanour, in which eccentric characters incarnated by non-professional actors bring new dimensions to well-known fictional and religious archetypes'.[1] His 2006 version of Don Quixote *Honor de Cavelleria* was equally sparse, and *Història de la meva mort* (*Story of my Death, 2013*) similarly drains the stories of Cassanova and Dracula of their melodramatic excesses. Such films 'create images that seem to resist … the "excess image" dominating screens in the contemporary world' opting instead 'for simplicity and restraint'.[2]

El cant dels ocells (2008).

Instead of putting the film in context and recounting all the events surrounding Jesus' birth, Serra reduces their story to the magi's wanderings across deserts, plains and mountains, dwarfing them against these vast backdrops. The extended shots of these 'solitary wanderings undermine narrative momentum, inviting the viewer to contemplate … the empty landscape he traverses'.[3]

The result of the Serra's long static takes, beautiful compositions and minimal soundtrack is not unlike viewing a series of paintings in a gallery. Serra treats his audience to incredible image after incredible image, somehow investing each with great meaning. The starkly beautiful black and white photography, the ordinary-looking actors and the stripped-down feel are all very reminiscent of Pasolini's masterpiece. It even features an angelic figure, portrayed by a dark-haired young woman, wearing a plain white smock. Serra humanizes the kings to an even greater degree than Pasolini. They bicker over which way to go, each trying to nudge the others into making a decision as if to escape blame if the plan fails. They hide from the rain, pause their quest to go swimming and even seem to get lost at one point.

So low key is the film's aesthetic that the story's most iconic moment almost passes unnoticed. When the kings finally find Jesus there is no crowd of curious onlookers. The holy family are on their own; their visitors are without an entourage. Birdsong's low-key encounter between earthly kings and divine royalty arrives without the spectacle that typically accompanies such moments, in line with Serra's desire to capture 'the tradition of Dreyer, Rossellini [and] Pasolini'.[4] Serra produces 'a moment of pure reverence … when the three men finally prostrate themselves before the mother and child'.[5] This understated moment is the culmination of the slow gradual build-up which preceded it.

While Serra injects humour by portraying three men with a reputation for wisdom, acting like ordinary people, he resists revealing too much about who these men are, refusing to strip-away their mystery. Birdsong is a slow contemplative film whose strength is that, on the surface, nothing really happens.

Notes

1   Maria M. Delgado , 'Introduction', in M. M. Delgado and R. W. Fiddian (eds.), Spanish Cinema 1973–2000: Auteurism, Politics, Landscape and Memory (Manchester: Manchester University Press, 2013), p. 12.

2   Javier Moral, 'Behind the Enigma Construct: A Certain Trend in Spanish Cinema', in Duncan Wheeler, Fernando Canet (eds.), (Re)viewing Creative, Critical and Commercial Practices in Contemporary Spanish Cinema (Bristol: Intellect Books, 2014), p. 96.

3   Tiago De Luca, 'Realism of the Senses: A Tendency in Contemporary World Cinema', in Lúcia Nagib, Chris Perriam, Rajinder Dudrah (eds.), Theorizing World Cinema (London: I.B Tauris, 2012), p. 194.

4   Darren Hughes, 'Albert Serra Interviewed on El cant dels ocells (Birdsong)', Senses of Cinema April 2009. Available online: <http://sensesofcinema.com/2009/conversations-on-film/albert-serra-interview/> (accessed 19 Dec. 2021).

5   Catherine O'Brien, The Celluloid Madonna: From Scripture to Screen (New York: Columbia University Press, 2011), pp. 109–110.

Oversold
USA, 2008 – 32 mins
Paul Morrell

DIRECTOR Paul Morrell
PRODUCERS Beth Ann Bard,
David C. Cowan, Paul Morrell,
Josh Sullivan
SCREENPLAY David C. Cowan,
Paul Morrell, Luke Price
CINEMATOGRAPHY
Royce Allen Dudley
EDITOR Paul Morrell
MUSIC Jimmy Jernigan
PRODUCTION COMPANY
Supergubs. Inc.
MAIN CAST Grant Henderson,
Crissy Outlaw, Tracey Ann-Marie
Nelson, Stephen Zimpel

Hosea is a notoriously difficult text. To some, the ultimate redemptive love story, to others, pornographic propaganda which shields abusive manipulation behind a patriarchal worldview.[1] God orders Hosea to marry Gomer, who he perceives as promiscuous, and when she has children he gives them prophetically meaningful names.[2] When she leaves him for another, he subsequently takes her back.

Oversold, a low-budget short, adapts the text into a multi-layered modernisation covering not only the story of Hosea and Gomer, but also Jesus' message of redemption. On the surface it's seemingly an unlikely sounding tale of a Pastor, Joshua, who travels to Vegas and falls in love with a stripper called Sophi (unaware of her profession). Sensing God's approval he marries her and brings her back home, but her abusive boyfriend/manager, Ethan, forces her to return to her former life by threatening Josh. Josh sells everything to redeem Sophi's debt to Ethan and brings her home again.

Director Paul Morrell wrote *Oversold* with best friend Dave Cowan, a real-life pastor who appears on camera at strategic points to comment on the events being portrayed. Josh is played by Stephen Zimpel, but it's Crissy Outlaw's portrayal of Sophi which is the more notable. There are similarities between *Oversold* and Outlaw's personal journey from a survivor of sexual abuse who ended up acting in pornographic movies to discovering Christianity. Understandably, there's an incredible vulnerability and fragility to Outlaw's performance. The real-life story of her conversion and the love she felt which enabled her to leave the sex industry, permeate the film, its raw emotions generating a moving, emotionally affecting atmosphere.

In addition to the parallels between the Hosea/Jesus/Joshua storylines,[3] the film also relies on visual symbolism. Ethan appears as a Satan figure, at one point dressed in red looking down across the city while declaring 'I own this town', evoking Satan during Jesus' temptation. The first time we see Ethan he is wearing a shirt with a cross sewn onto the back, a fake cross with no concept of grace. In a later scene Sophi accidentally cuts herself ending up with blood on her hands. This may represent a popular Christian metaphor about being washed in Jesus' blood, or highlighting how humanity has blood is on its hands, but it also evokes the possibility of self-harm or suicide and her desperate mental state.

In places the dialogue is a little clunky, but that is most noticeable at the points in the story where this is what might be expected in real life. In contrast to the witty banter between couples in many romantic films conversations in real life often are a little awkward.

Whilst Josh and perhaps the filmmakers are a little guilty of white-knightism, the way the church community behind *Oversold* welcomed Outlaw (in contrast to their fictional counterparts), intensifies the film's poignancy, demonstrating that escaping our past is not just something that happens in the movies. Three other church-based adaptations of Hosea and Gomer's story have been produced since Morrell's film, *Amazing* Love (2012), *Hosea* (2019) and *Redeeming Love* (2022).

Crissy Outlaw as Sophi and Stephen Zimpel as Josh in *Oversold* (2008). (Courtesy of David Cowan)

Notes

1   Cheryl Exum, *Plotted, Shot, and Painted: Cultural Representations of Biblical Women* (Sheffield: Sheffield Phoenix Press, 2012), pp. 105–131.

2   The precise meaning of the Hebrew word used here is unclear. It could denote 'temple prostitute', or simply 'promiscuous woman'.

3   These are three variations on the same root name heightening the parallels between them.

Year One
USA, 2009 – 97 mins
Harold Ramis

DIRECTOR Harold Ramis
PRODUCERS Judd Apatow,
Clayton Townsend
SCREENPLAY Lee Eisenberg,
Gene Stupnitsky, Harold Ramis
CINEMATOGRAPHY
Alar Kivilo
EDITORS Craig Herring,
Steve Welch
MUSIC Theodore Shapiro
PRODUCTION COMPANY
Columbia Pictures Industries Inc.
MAIN CAST Hank Azaria,
Jack Black, Michael Cera,
David Cross, Oliver Platt,
Juno Temple, Olivia Wilde,
Paul Rudd

Reflecting the gross-out humour so typical of the 2000s and particularly producer Judd Apatow's partial-ly-improvised comedic style, *Year One* pulled together the 'Frat-Pack' group of actors who were dominating Hollywood comedies at the time. Jack Black and Michael Cerra took the lead roles of Zed and Oh, two cavemen who are booted out of their tribe and stumble into Genesis-era Canaan. Paul Rudd, Hank Azaria, Juno Temple and Olivia Wilde co-star.

The first half of the film turns into a historical road movie, where they meet characters from Genesis (Cain and Abel, Adam and Eve, Abraham and Isaac). Zed and Oh reject Adam's family, (including his murderous son), a circumcision-obsessed Abraham, and the deity that both families follow. But as their adventures unfold they discover their own tribe has been enslaved and taken to Sodom. Consequently, the second part of the movie becomes Zed and Oh's quest to free the women they love, Maya and Eema, from Sodom in the hope their love will be returned.

Unfazed by the subject matter, writer/director Harold Ramis sets about his task in predictably scatological fashion. There are characters eating excrement, strange things happening at orgies and numerous jokes about sex. The *Carry On* films appear to have had some bearing on the film, including Ramis' loose approach to history, in contrast to more meticulous parodies like *Life of Brian*, the benchmark for any historical/religious comedy. There are certain similarities, however: both films mine humour from relocating contemporary attitudes to the ancient world; neither film has the Bible as the primary focus of the story; both challenge the idea of unquestioned religious authority. Ramis's Jewish background meant he was keen to challenge the 'notion of chosenness',[1] and urge 'people to take personal responsibility, no matter what they believe God is or isn't'.[2] Yet whereas *Life of Brian* maintains the laughs even while making its point, *Year One* temporarily puts the comedy on hold to bring in a crescendo-ing orchestra. It's a minor mis-step.

At times any concept of god seems to be disregarded. Yet ultimately Zed prays and eventually what he prays for happens, opening up a range of interpretations from divine approval of Zed's new message, through to merely fortunate timing. Either way, it's notable that Zed's message relies on such coincidence to reach a wider audience.

Year One finds plenty of original material, even from a subject that has been used many times before and amidst all the sex and fart jokes there are more serious ideas at play. Whilst not as amusing as *Life of Brian* or even *The Real Old Testament*, it's notable that even the gross-out comedy sub-genre includes a biblical adaptation.

Notes

1   Elizabeth Oppriecht (2009) 'Harold Ramis Interview: A
    Lifetime of Achievements With a Chicago Look at *Year One*',
    Hollywood Chicago, June 19. Available online: <https://www.
    hollywoodchicago.com/news/8007/harold-ramis-interview-a-
    lifetime-of-achievements-with-a-chicago-look-at-year-one>
    (accessed 19 Dec. 2021).

2   Doug Ganley, '*Year One* polishes forbidden fruit in comedic
    poke at the Bible', *CNN*, 18 June 2009.
    Available online: <https://edition.cnn.com/2009/SHOWBIZ/
    Movies/06/18/year.one.cast/index.html> (accessed 19 Dec.
    2021).

Io sono con te (*Let it Be*)[1]
Italy, 2010 – 100 mins
Guido Chiesa

DIRECTOR Guido Chiesa
PRODUCER Antonio Tacchia
SCREENPLAY Guido Chiesa,
Filippo Kalomenidis,
Nicoletta Micheli
CINEMATOGRAPHY
Gherardo Gossi
EDITORS Luca Gasparini,
Alberto Masi
MUSIC Nicola Tescari
PRODUCTION COMPANY
Colorado Film Production
MAIN CAST Mustapha Benstiti,
Ahmed Hafiane, Nadia Khlifi,
Rabeb Srairi

Giudo Giudo Chiesa's radical *Io sono con te* portrays Mary, Jesus' mother, as a proto-feminist challenging the patriarchal society around her. To maximize the effect, Chiesa retains the most famous moments in her life, from the annunciation to losing Jesus at the temple, but reinterprets them from a feminist angle, challenging patriarchal religion. Fifteen-year-old Nadia Khlifi excellently portrays Mary's strength, determination, and vision contrasted against the violence and patriarchal structures surrounding her.

Chiesa's beautifully photographed film spurns several of the traditional elements of biblical epics. The costumes, props and the size of the cast all differ significantly. Nearly all the cast, including Khlifi, are Tunisian born and the characters speak in Arabic. 'In a country where the Catholic Church is still quite powerful, a Mary who has North African features and speaks Arabic has potential subversive implications'.[2]

Nazareth is typified by *mezuzah* on the door posts, attendance at the synagogue and religious discussion about the law. The fifteen-year age gap between Khlifi and Mustapha Benstiti's Joseph is initially disturbing. Their arranged marriage never becomes a romance. He is supportive but this is her story, not theirs. The women wear long, brightly-coloured, striped woollen *kaftan*-type garments. The men wear *tallit*s. The blending of ancient, modern, Jewish and Islamic dress and traditions puts the story in an unfamiliar context, one different from both the past (as typically presented in biblical films) and the present.

This somewhat orientalist mixing of costumes and traditions enables Chiesa to argue against circumcision, which he called '*violenza contro un innocente*' (violence against an innocent), and to show the practice behind '*mascheramento tipico delle religioni*' (its typical religious mask).[3] In one scene, Mary is appalled by a baby being circumcised. The scene consists of a fast montage with multiple short shots spliced together like the famous sequences in *Un Chien Andalou* (1929) and *Psycho* (1960). The film draws on the heritage of these films to reflect Mary's horror. Consequently, Mary refuses to have Jesus circumcised removing a key marker of Jesus' Jewish identity. While this pre-figures the way Jesus' followers would move away from the practice some Jewish groups and film critics expressed concerns about the film reducing Judaism to a '*fenomeno primitivo/arcaico violentissimo e retrogrado*' (primitive/archaic violent and retrograde phenomenon) compared to Mary's modern view.[4]

Mary's feminist, non-violent views mark her out as distinctly different from the world she inhabits. She is clear-eyed and unafraid in pursuing what she believes is right, refusing to partake in political violence, be it against Roman soldiers strong-arming the local populace, or against Jewish rebels seeking revenge. Religious violence and animal sacrifice repeatedly circles her. Even the annunciation occurs while she is milking goats and later she witnesses animals being slaughtered in the temple. Significantly, both Mary and (later) Jesus quote Hosea's words 'I desire mercy not sacrifice.' The two of them are appalled at their community's ostracizing a man designated unclean and forced to live outside of the village.

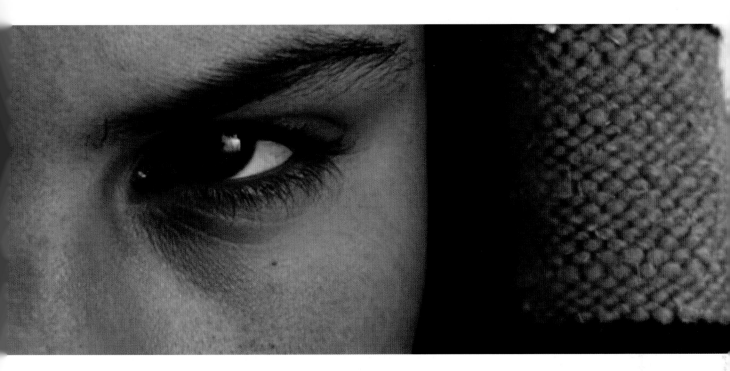

Nadia Khlifi's feminist Mary in *Io sono con te* (2010).

By highlighting the differences and anachronisms between past and present, Chiesa provides a powerful invective against practices which he wishes confined to the past. It's an emotive reminder of how different the past was from today though not without its problems.

Notes

1 Released with the translated title *I Am With You* in some regions.
2 Cosetta Gaudenzi, 'Guido Chiesa and Postmodern *Impegno*', in Giancarlo Lombardi, Christian Uva (eds.), *Italian Political Cinema: Public Life, Imaginary, and Identity in Contemporary Italian Film*, (Bern: Peter Lang, 2016), p. 170.
3 Guido Chiesa, '*Io sono con te*: Genesi di un film', *guidochiesa. net* 2011. p. 14. Available online: <http://guidochiesa.net/media/opera/nicoletta-micheli-e-guido-chiesa/io-so/Genesi%20di%20un%20film.pdf> (accessed 19 Dec. 2021).
4 Film critic Maurizio G. De Bonis in Jewish publication Kolòt.it. 'Continua la riscrittura della Storia da parte cattolica attraverso il cinema', 17 November 2010. Available online: <www.kolot.it/2010/11/17/continua-la-storia-da-parte-cattolica-attraverso-il-cinema/> (accessed 19 Dec. 2021).

Su re (The King)
Italy, 2012 – 76 mins
Giovanni Columbu

DIRECTOR Giovanni Columbu
PRODUCER Giovanni Columbu
SCREENPLAY Giovanni Columbu,
Michele Columbu
CINEMATOGRAPHY
Francisco Della Chiesa, Emilio
Della Chiesa, Massimo Foletti,
Uliano Lucas
PRODUCTION COMPANY
Luches Film
MAIN CAST Fiorenzo Mattu,
Pietrina Mennea, Tonino
Murgia, Paolo Pillonca

Giovanni Columbu shot his version of the passion on the island of Sardinia with hand-held cameras, putting the island's stark and dramatic scenery to great effect. The result is a Jesus film that looks quite unlike any before it. It's a dark, grimy film, brought out by greying filters and gritty filmstock. The largely non-professional cast wear their own rough clothes for costumes. The epitome of Columbu's approach is his choice of Fiorenzu Mattu to play Jesus. Unlike almost all screen Christs, Mattu is neither lean nor handsome. In Columbu's 2001 *Arcipelaghi* he played a hitman, a role more in keeping with his looks, which Lloyd Baugh describes as 'stocky' and 'brutish' with a 'round bulldog face' and 'bulging eyes'.[1]

Columbu very much follows in Pasolini's footsteps, the handheld camera, grainy footage, rugged landscape, artful compositions, even down to occasional choices of headwear. Like Pasolini he dwells on close-ups of real, unadorned faces – often those of non-professional actors – even while the person speaking is off screen. However, the film utilizes a non-linear narrative, featuring only events from Jesus' passion. This is not simply the use of flashes backwards or forwards, but a more jumbled and disorientating approach, akin to *Pulp Fiction* (1992), transforming a familiar story into something unsettling and unpredictable. The crucifixion features early on, only to jump back to snippets of Jesus' trial. The film often revisits the same scene from different angles with subtle variations, jumping back, then further back, then forwards again.

These moments do not go out of their way to stress the specific changes between individual gospels. Instead they highlight how the Gospels have different perspectives, drawn from various written and oral sources, accompanied by their own interpretations and theology. In each the sands have shifted slightly, not to reveal a radically altered and contradictory new version of events, but just another landscape on which the events can unfold. *Su Re* isn't a pedantic exposé: it simply 'respects and explores [the] differences' inherent In the Gospels' kaleidoscopic visions of Jesus.[2]

Similarly, just as the Gospels were drawn, in part, from the collective memory of Jesus' early followers, so the flashbacks here carry a sense of accessing shared earlier memories. The sense of disorientation is also heightened by the way the different scenes segue into one another. It's not always clear when one scene ends and a new one begins. It's an invitation to look at Jesus' last hours again, in a different light; to experience them as if we were present. Consequently, *Su Re* avoids pushing one particular idea about Jesus identity – much is left to the viewer's interpretation.

However, one thing about Jesus is clear: he is not in control of the unfolding events. He never addresses the authorities persecuting him with certainty and confidence, nor does he defiantly drag himself up in the middle of his scourging. Jesus is a victim. Shorn of his previous ministry or any future glory we behold the man: forsaken, confused, scared and alone. The film's opening words from Isaiah's Suffering Servant (Isaiah 53) echo throughout.[3] Like him, Columbu's Jesus becomes an outsider, an unbeautiful victim, deserted and discarded in an abandoned corner of the dominant Roman Empire.

The unbeautiful Jesus of *Su re* (2012).

Notes

1   Lloyd Baugh, 'A Revolutionary Passion Film: Giovanni Columbu's Su Re (The King)', in Richard J. Walsh (ed.), *The T&T Clark Companion to the Bible and Film*, (London: Bloomsbury T&T Clark, 2018), p. 347.

2   Lloyd Baugh, 'Three Revolutionary Gospel Films: By the People, with the People, and for the People', in Richard J. Walsh (ed.), *The T&T Clark Handbook of Jesus and Film*, (London: Bloomsbury T&T Clark, 2021), p. 146.

3   Baugh, 'Revolutionary Passion', pp. 347–8.

The Bible
USA, 2013 – 440 mins
Crispin Reece, Tony Mitchell and Christopher Spencer

DIRECTORS Tony Mitchell,
Crispin Reece,
Christopher Spencer
PRODUCERS Mark Burnett,
Roma Downey
SCREENPLAY Colin Swash,
Nic Young, Alexander Marengo,
Christopher Spencer, Richard
Bedser, Adam Rosenthal
MUSIC Lorne Balfe,
Hans Zimmer
PRODUCTION COMPANY
Lightworkers Media and Hearst
Productions Inc.
MAIN CAST Roma Downey,
William Houston, Diogo
Morgado, Con O'Neill,
Mohamen Mehdi Ouazanni,
David Rintoul

Evangelical Christian couple Roma Downey and Mark Burnett have become the largest producers of onscreen Bible-related content outside of Brazil, with productions such as the recent version of *Ben-Hur* (2016), Netflix's *Messiah* (2020) and another adaptation of Hosea, *Redeeming Love* (2022). But it was The History Channel's *The Bible* which got them started following their decision to invest their own money into producing it, seemingly regarding 'its promulgation as something of a mission'.[1]

Condensing the 'entire' Bible into ten, 45-minute episodes, the series covered the Hebrew Bible in the first five episodes and the New Testament in the final five.[2] Despite its extended running time, tales from the Hebrew Bible rush by, while more incidental elements are repeatedly over-blown or over-emphasized. Episode 1 deftly covers the stories of the creation, fall, flood and the patriarchs with tremendous efficiency, only to devote a considerable proportion of its forty minutes to armour-clad angels slow-motion-hacking their way

An armour-clad angel delivers a message to Samson's (unnamed) mother in *The Bible* (2013).

through the streets of Sodom. Similarly, the final episode shows Paul (pre-conversion) smashing up houses and torturing Christians, but finds time for neither the Council of Jerusalem, nor Paul's decades on the road.

Such unevenness is typical of Downey and Burnett's approach which attempts to reflect modern sensibilities and make the Bible more entertaining in order to reach a wider audience.[3] 'This program is an adaptation of Bible Stories that changed our world' the opening credits announce, as if justifying *The Bible*'s place on our screens. They continue 'It endeavours to stay true to the spirit of the book', perhaps a pre-emptive strike against complaints it meanders from the text. The History Channel lends the production a veneer of intellectual credibility, whilst highlighting the need for artistic licence also signals a desire for a mainstream audience. As much as this hints at the filmmakers' priorities, it also reveals much about the opposing and entrenched views about the Bible's place in American culture.

However, claiming 'to stay true to the spirit of the book' implies the existence of a single viewpoint from which the Bible is written, rather than it being an anthology of many, very different, books. The 'spirit' of Ecclesiastes, say, is not necessarily the same as the spirit of Acts, Leviticus or Revelation. In this respect the production's visual style is unduly coherent. Throughout the series the same grimy filters are used on the cameras, and the same grungy approach is taken with costume design (barring exemplary dentistry). Scenes nearly always last for two to three minutes. Shot duration is typically short, the camera work is often dramatic and showy, and Hans Zimmer's central soundtrack motif pounds away repeatedly. While these features could be seen as strengths, it highlights the decision to present these stories as part of the same, over-arching, narrative.

Naturally, the narrative, climaxes with Jesus' story. Jesus performs a few miracles, utters the odd wise saying and is nice to the marginalized and disempowered, but both his life and his death seem stripped of any real meaning. Yet following the series' relative success, much of the footage from the life of Jesus was re-mixed and released in cinemas as *Son of God* (2014), without ever appearing to find anything worthwhile to say about him.

The production values are generally solid. The sets, costumes, hair/make-up, props and lighting all acheive a high standard. Occasionally the CGI effects impress, though too often they are bombastic and distracting. Moreover, the poor writing and incoherent narrative detracts from the series' strengths. A spin-off series, *A.D. Kingdom and Empire*[4] followed based on the Book of Acts, Eventually it shook off these weaknesses and produced a show that was dramatically and historically satisfying. It was cancelled, leaving the apostles forever adrift in Acts 12.

Notes

1   J. Cheryl Exum, 'Samson and Delilah in Film' in Rhonda Burnette-Bletsch (ed.), *The Bible in Motion: A Handbook of the Bible and Its Reception in Film*. vol. 1 (Berlin/Boston: De Gruyter, 2016), p. 94.

2   The series is sometimes divided into five, double-length episodes instead.

3   A commendable example of this is the actors' diverse backgrounds.

4   Also known as *A.D. The Bible Continues*.

Noah
USA, 2014 – 138 mins
Darren Aronofsky

DIRECTOR Darren Aronofsky
PRODUCERS Scott Franklin,
Arnon Milchan, Mary Parent
SCREENPLAY Darren Aronofsky,
Ari Handel
CINEMATOGRAPHY
Matthew Libatique
EDITOR Andrew Weisblum
MUSIC Clint Mansell
PRODUCTION COMPANY
Paramount Pictures and
Regency Entertainment
MAIN CAST Jennifer Connelly,
Russell Crowe, Anthony
Hopkins, Emma Watson,
Ray Winstone

As with many films about the great flood, Darren Aronofsky's *Noah* (2014) takes a creative approach. Whilst an atheist, Aronofsky's Jewish background is clearly influential. The mythical style he applies to the material is a reminder that the story was known to many cultures beyond the Israelites and he revels in the text's strangeness. *Noah* was twenty years in the making after a school project caught Aronofsky's attention. The result feels like a cross between *Lord of the Rings* Trilogy (2001–03), *Waterworld* (1995) and *Mad Max* (1979). *Noah* isn't so much an adaptation, as a film using Genesis as a 'mood board' whose bizarre, uneven, style is part of its appeal.[1]

Superficially, it's a biblical epic and certain scenes rank amongst the genre's best. The minutes leading to the ark's launch are magnificent. Noah (Russell Crowe) rescues his son from Cain's descendants and climbs aboard. Meanwhile the 'watchers' protect the ark from on-rushing hordes, culminating in their angelic souls spectacularly beaming up to heaven as waters from the deep break forth. Clint Mansell's score accentuates the tension superbly. It almost feels like *The Ten Commandments'* parting of the Red Sea. But this sequence is far from what DeMille would ever produce. The 'watchers' are angels (the 'Nephilim' of Genesis 6) who literally fell to earth and found its surface stuck to their bodies. The resulting 'rock monsters' evoke Ray Harryhausen's special effects.

The movie's other breathtaking sequence occurs shortly after the ark's launch. As Noah retells the creation story, Aronofsky illustrates it with a time-lapse/stop-motion style montage depicting creation as an evolutionary act. The sequence ends at the Tree of Life (referencing Aronofsky's 2006 *The Fountain*) with a glowing snakeskin wrapped around Noah's arm like *tefillin* straps. Add in the lunar-esque Icelandic landscape; an odd cameo as Methuselah from Anthony Hopkins; and Noah's nightmares alternating between blood underfoot and torrents overhead, and it's easy to see why some dismiss the film's unevenness. Such pastiche hints at the divergent sources behind the Genesis story. Aronofsky creates a context which explores the questions the text raises, and those its characters might have faced.

Once onboard, the film morphs into a dark psychological drama, as Noah feels pulled towards taking The Creator's work to its grimly 'logical' conclusion.[2] Aronofsky's often dwells 'on the idea that purity or perfection is impossible, and that the pursuit of these things is self-destructive',[3] and *Noah* unpacks similar themes. Ironically, many described the film's antihero as a homicidal maniac, overlooking the vast number The Creator drowns. Aronofsky's Noah is not a psychopath who *wants* to kill his granddaughter – indeed ultimately he cannot – he just believes that is The Creator's desire. Noah's readiness to follow such horrific commands places him alongside Abraham.

The resulting emotional devastation only adds to the flood's physical destruction. Aronofsky repeatedly frames Crowe like the famous final shot from *The Searchers* (1956), outside the civilized family's dwelling. The film's epilogue finds Noah alone, drunk, on the beach wracked with 'survivor's guilt'.[4] Can he ever return to

Noah numbing his survivor's guilt with alcohol in *Noah* (2014).

his family after almost committing such a horrific act? Has saving his grandchild doomed the planet to destruction?

Three years later Aronofsky's *mother!* (2017) would suggest fresh acts of creation are doomed to fail; that The Creator will endlessly destroy, and misguidedly restart, his world. But here, the despair has not yet overcome. Noah's partial rehabilitation leaves the film on a more hopeful note. The film's warning of environmental apocalypse ends offering a fig leaf of possibility, urging us to act before it's too late.

Notes

1   John Wilson on *Front Row*, BBC Radio 4, 31 March 2014. Available online: <www.bbc.co.uk/sounds/play/b03z9gn0> (accessed 19 Dec. 2021).
2   Noah calls God 'The Creator' throughout.
3   Peter T. Chattaway, 'Flood Theology', *Books and Culture* Vol 20 No.3, May/June 2014. Available online: <www.booksandculture.com/articles/2014/mayjun/flood-theology.html?paging=off> (accessed 19 Dec. 2021).
4   Darren Aronofsky Interviewed by Ryan Gilbey, 'Just Say Noah', *The Guardian*, 27 April 2007. Available online: <www.theguardian.com/film/2007/apr/27/1> (accessed 19 Dec. 2021).

The Savior
Palestine/Jordan/Bulgaria, 2014 – 131 mins
Robert Savo

DIRECTOR Robert Savo
PRODUCERS John Dorr, Azza Hourani, Rula Nasser, Henia Savo, David Varod
SCREENPLAY Philip Dorr
CINEMATOGRAPHY Emil Topuzov
EDITORS Ruslan Grudev, Alexander Tsvetkov
MUSIC Talal Abu-Alragheb
PRODUCTION COMPANY Geolink Resource Consultants LLC
MAIN CAST Yussuf Abu-Warda, Mohammad Bakri, Abeer Issa, Zohir Al Nobani

Not only was Robert Savo's *The Savior* recorded in Arabic, it is probably the first film to feature an actor from Israel (Shredy Jabarin) playing Jesus.[1] Jabarin manages to be provocative without losing his compassion, and to add gravitas without becoming dull, stodgy or overly severe. He smiles occasionally but always feels like someone with bigger, more pressing issues on his mind.

The filmmakers steer away from many of the scenes that appear in most of the other Jesus biopics. So there's no Sermon on the Mount or woman accused of adultery, for example. Instead there's the exorcism in the local synagogue (Mark 1), the healing of the widow of Nain's son (Luke 7) and the 'mini-apocalypse' of Mark 13. Indeed the film crams a considerable amount of Jesus' ministry into the first hour before he and his disciples arrive in Judea. Savo's economical scene selection combined with the decision to avoid over-elaboration means *The Savior* tends to jump from one scene to the next without making connections, not unlike the Gospels, which leaves the film a little light on drama and character development. Individually, each scene offers a reasonably credible portrayal, but what motivates the characters is often obscured. That said, the film adroitly contrasts Jesus' humility in washing his disciples' feet with their arguments as to who among them is greatest.

At times the film has a bracing bluntness, such as Jesus' wince-inducing circumcision, or the sight of John the Baptist's head rolling across the floor of his cell. The wailing sound of the Widow of Nain and her friends as they mourn her son's death feels like real grief, rather than the set-up for a miracle and the beatings Jesus takes from the soldiers seem credible rather than foretold.

Despite limitations of budget there is some enjoyable camerawork: the lighting when a man seeking healing is lowered through the roof; and the moment Jesus and the disciples emerge over the hill overlooking Jerusalem. Occasionally there's striking use of colour and camera filters, and while the soundtrack is not necessarily original, it certainly contributes to the distinctive atmosphere. Unfortunately, the special effects are rather mixed. The effect used with the widow of Nain's son is simple, but clever, and more importantly, effective, whereas the temptation in the desert tries hard to impress but fails to deliver.

Aside from the uneven effects, there are a few other mis-steps. The jarring and rather sporadic use of Luke as narrator, may demonstrate the lengths to which he went just to prepare his ink, but it adds little, and the film is generally better without him. Even more problematic is the recycling of antisemitic tropes. In Gethsemane, Judas's face turns briefly into the devil's.[2] Shortly afterwards black-clad, odd-eyed priests conspire to have Jesus' executed while Pilate sheds a tear.

Overall, however, Savo's film has a good sense of restraint and most of it works well because he understands the restraints and brings out the best given his limitations. Many of the actors are not very experienced, so Savo leans heavily on Jabarin. And after years of seeing western productions *The Savior* gives a sense of place, time and sensibility which captures the first century Palestinian context where these stories occurred, in a way that few, other films about Jesus have managed.

Chiascuro lighting in *The Savior* (2014).

Notes

1   Peter T. Chattaway, 'Filmmakers Move Away From White Jesus', *The Federalist*, 27 March 2015. Available online: <https://thefederalist.com/2015/03/27/filmmakers-move-away-from-white-jesus/> (accessed 19 Dec. 2021).

2   William Nicholls, *Christian Antisemitism: A History of Hate* (New York: Rowman & Littlefield, [1993] 2004), pp. 140–41.

Exodus: Gods and Kings
UK/Spain/USA, 2014 – 144 mins
Ridley Scott

DIRECTOR Ridley Scott
PRODUCER Peter Chernin
SCREENPLAY Jeffrey Caine,
Bill Collage, Adam Cooper,
Steven Zaillian
CINEMATOGRAPHY
Dariusz Wolski
EDITOR Billy Rich
MUSIC Alberto Iglesias
PRODUCTION COMPANY
Twentieth Century Fox Film
Corporation
MAIN CAST Christian Bale,
Joel Edgerton, Ben Kingsley,
Aaron Paul, John Turturro,
Sigourney Weaver

Given its big-budget and epic scale, it's tempting to think of Ridley Scott's *Exodus: God's and Kings* as a remake of *The Ten Commandments* (1956) for the 3D age, but in many ways it's more of a live action remake of *The Prince of Egypt* (1998). Both films explore the theme of brotherhood, underlined by Scott's dedication of the film to his late brother. Whilst *The Ten Commandments* also dwells on the rivalry between Ramses and Moses, there the two are hostile from the start with Ramses' jealousy-fuelled disdain clashing with Moses' impassive morality.

Here however, the bromance-turned-sour theme rests on solid performances from Christian Bale (Moses) and his 'cousin' Ramses (Joel Edgerton). Early on Ramses' father Seti (John Turturro) expresses his qualms about Ramses' faults, but when Seti dies just as discoveries about Moses' past are resurfacing, Ramses swoops to secure his throne.

Bale's portrayal of Moses as a combative fighter-general turned terrorist is one of the best aspects of the film. Bale's more muscular performance bring the film into new territory, particularly as Scott draws out the sense of dread and paranoia about the 'threat' of a slave uprising due to Edgerton's nuanced, and not unsympathetic, turn as Ramses. However, Scott squanders his wealth of acting talent, Sigourney Weaver, Aaron Paul, John Turturro and Ben Kingsley (who played the lead in 1996's *Moses*) have little more than cameos. Scott's justification was his need to gain sufficient finance, the same excuse he used to respond to criticism that 'nearly every major role in the movie is played by a white actor'.[1] Nevertheless, 11-year old Isaac Andrews impresses as Malak, a divine messenger/God-figure whose inconsistency and occasional petulance reflects the occasional note in Exodus.[2]

Scott's scepticism results in ambiguity rather than a credible debunking indeed the film's internal logic undoes many of the scientific theories it advances. Moses' head injury immediately before his first encounter with God opens the possibility that he was suffering from some kind of hallucination. Yet Moses' rational, anti-religious scepticism suggests that he, of all people, would question whether his concussion caused to his vision. Likewise Scott explores the theory that the plagues were a chain reaction,[3] but puts it on the lips of Ewen Bremner's professional sceptic, portrayed as a comically incompetent charlatan, rather proto-scientist, ahead of his time. Scott's reason for the water turning to blood is a plague of crocodiles attacking a fishing boat, before turning on each other, neither causing sufficient pollution to trigger a domino effect, nor explaining the crocodiles' unusual behaviour. Later the Red Sea parts because of a tsunami which eventually hits both Moses and Ramses with full force, yet somehow both survive. Scott is caught between forwarding rational alternative explanations and presenting a spectacular biblical action movie. Perversely explaining away such phenomena when literary criticism generates far simpler explanations suggests Scott wants to have his cake whilst his audiences eat it.

Christian Bale and John Turturro in *Exodus: Gods and Kings* (2014).

Yet it is at least as palatable as many blockbuster historical epics. The pacing and tension are good throughout, and the detailed sets, costumes and CGI make for an imposing spectacle. Whilst not on a par with Scott's *Gladiator* (2000) these elements, Bale and Egerton's performances, and its sympathy for those on both sides, elevate it above some of Scott's other historical adaptations.

Notes

1   Joel Baden and Candida Moss, 'Does the new 'Exodus' movie whitewash the Bible?', *CNN* Entertainment, 11 December 2014. Available online: <https://edition.cnn.com/2014/12/10/showbiz/exodus-whitewash-bible/index.html> (accessed 19 Dec. 2021).

2   For example, Exodus 4.24–26, where having just commissioned Moses, God then attempts to kill him.

3   Anne Raver, 'Biblical Plagues: A Novel Theory', *New York Times*, 4 April 1996. Available online: <www.nytimes.com/1996/04/04/garden/biblical-plagues-a-novel-theory.html> (accessed 19 Dec. 2021).

The Red Tent
USA, 2014 – 176 mins
Roger Young

DIRECTOR Roger Young
PRODUCERS Elizabeth Chandler,
Peter McAleese
SCREENPLAY Elizabeth
Chandler, Anne Meredith,
Anita Diamant
CINEMATOGRAPHY
Michael Snyman
EDITORS Arthur Tarnowski,
Sylvain Lebel
MUSIC Laurent Eyquem
PRODUCTION COMPANY
Sony Pictures Television Inc.
MAIN CAST Morena Baccarin,
Minnie Driver, Rebecca Ferguson,
Iain Glen, Debra Winger

The Red Tent moves Jacob, Joseph and his brothers to the sidelines to focus on the women of Jacob's clan – Rebecca, Leah, Rachel, Bilhah, Zilpah, Tamar and Dinah – on whom so much rests, yet who receive so little credit, and looks at Genesis from their point of view. At the centre of the story is Dinah, not here a victim of rape but a self-determining woman who falls in love with a tribal prince (Shechem) and decides of her own volition to sleep with him.[1]

If *La Genèse* (1998) is a bleakly pessimistic take on Dinah's story then *The Red Tent* is a naïvely optimistic one, presenting a world where one-sided patriarchy is substantially beneficial for the women who inhabit it. Shechem seeks Dinah's consent, Laban's daughters decide between them to both marry Jacob,[2] who in turn treats his female sex slaves with the same anachronistically-high level of respect he shows for his wives. I'm

Leah (Minnie Driver) and Rachel (Morena Baccarin, background) in *The Red Tent* (2014).

not sure it satisfies feminists any more than biblical traditionalists, but it's intriguing to watch such a perspective played out. Is the accusation of rape a cover up for Dinah's unapproved love, or does the film minimize a rare example of the voice of an oppressed woman coming briefly to prominence?

Dinah and the other women voice their displeasure at Laban's treatment of his wife, but for all the film's female empowerment, it's Jacob's action returning to the land of his father that drives the plot on into the second and third acts. Dinah's romantic involvement may be the spark that propels the violence between Israel and the inhabitants of Shechem, but its Jacob's decision to move and develop closer ties with Hamor that set the wheels in motion.

When the massacre of the Shechemites arrives, it's vicious and very bloody. Up to this point everything about the production is typical of Young's work on *The Bible Collection*.[3] It's filmed in Morocco and the skies, sets, costumes, indeed everything about its look and feel mirrors the earlier series. Yet the massacre is jarringly out of sync with anything from that earlier work. The discrepancy could be seen as a weakness, but here Levi and Simon/Simeon's violence should shock us: It's a barbaric act of horrific violence and an unprecedented tear in the social fabric. Reparation had been made (so it was thought) and a treaty had been agreed. Simeon

and Levi's actions leave Jacob reeling in disbelief and fearing for his tribe's future. Young jolts the viewer out of the previously homely narrative of twee mutual sisterhood and into the horrors of violent and unrestrained patriarchy.

Despite his horror at the events Jacob still struggles to appreciate the weaknesses inherent in the whole woman-as-property system. Jacob attempts to put some of the blame for his son's actions on what he calls Shechem and Dinah's 'sin'. 'There was no sin' Dinah fires back, 'we were married...Your sons have slaughtered righteous men'. The rift between father and daughter is so great that Dinah flees into the arms of her mother-in-law and the two move to Egypt, allowing the film to continue to interweave its fictional exploration with the more established story of Joseph in Egypt.

Young's project creates an alternative story within and around the text of Genesis. Certainly that makes this an interesting experiment which throws fresh light on one of the more overlooked parts of the Bible and offers a good deal of food for thought. Objections when it was originally broadcast were muted, perhaps because the original story is hardly beloved amongst the faithful. Perhaps somewhat appropriately, *The Red Tent* nurtured measured discussion rather than creating unnecessary conflict.

Notes

1   Rhonda Burnette-Bletsch, 'Mediating Dinah's Story in Film', in Susanne Scholz (ed.), *The Oxford Handbook of Feminist Approaches to the Hebrew Bible* (New York: Oxford University Press, 2020), p. 362.

2   Peter T. Chattaway, 'It's all in the Family: The Patriarchs of Genesis in Film', in Rhonda Burnette-Bletsch (ed.), *The Bible in Motion: A Handbook of the Bible and Its Reception in Film*. vol. 1 (Berlin/Boston: De Gruyter, 2016), p. 58.

3   A full list of films from *The Bible Collection* can be found in Appendix 1.

Os Dez Mandamentos: O Filme (*The Ten Commandments: The Movie*)

Brazil, 2016 –120 mins[1]

Alexandre Avancini

DIRECTOR Alexandre Avancini
PRODUCER Leandro Santa Rita
SCREENPLAY Joaquim Assis, Emílio Boechat, Maria Claudia Oliveira, Paula Richard, Altenir Silva
CINEMATOGRAPHY Ricardo Fujii
EDITOR Paulo Henrique Faria
MUSIC Daniel Figueiredo
PRODUCTION COMPANY Paris Filmes
MAIN CAST Giselle Itié, Sergio Marone, Camila Rodrigues, Guilherme Winter

Telenovelas, extremely long television series which can run for hundreds episodes have long been a popular form in Brazil and the 2010s saw a wave of biblical telenovelas sweep the nation's screens. Rede Record's Moses series, *Os Dez Manadmentos* (2015–16), proved so popular – peaking with 144 million viewers [2] – that footage was edited down to create a cinematic version. *Os Dez Manadmentos: O Filme* sold 11 million tickets,[3] ending 2016 at the top of the rankings, outstripping even Hollywood productions like, *Captain America: Civil War*.

References abound to 1956's *The Ten Commandments* and *Exodus: God's and Kings* (2014) and at one point Moses unrolls a scroll bearing hieroglyphics that might have been peeled off the sets from *Prince of Egypt*. However, the film takes different aesthetic choices to Hollywood cinema, such as its frequent use of slow-motion, time-lapse and montage (often in combination), likewise, its colour scheme and fixed, even,

Horror imagery as water turns to blood in *Os Dez Mandamentos: O Filme* (2016).

soap-opera-style lighting. There's also a reliance on melodrama. When Moses re-enters Pharaoh's throne room after years in exile, a goblet drops to the floor in slow-motion.

There are also numerous montage sequences, presumably resulting from abridging such a volume of material. Occasionally, one senses an entire episode (such as Moses' victory over the Amalekites) has been reduced to a ninety-second montage. A fleeting shot of a maid listening through a keyhole suggests her broader narrative was omitted. Given how telenovelas expand on their characters' back-stories, in places *Mandamentos'* characterization seems flat. Similarly, the deterioration in Moses and Ramesses relationship must have been left on the cutting-room floor. When Moses first returns, he is moved by Pharaoh and his family's welcome – 'It was really hard to see the happiness and love they showed me'. Yet Moses' disconnection with palace life is apparent in the stark contrast between the pristine and luxurious Egyptian costumes and his shabby robes.

The film's second half features more effects and (poorly blended) CGI, beginning with the plagues. The first, water turning to blood, provide the film's two most arresting images which draw on horror imagery. Firstly, Pharaoh's wife emerges during an underwater swim covered in blood. Moments later her husband holds his bloodied hands before him in horrified disbelief. The infestations of frogs, lice, flies and locusts feel particularly repulsive. Then the Angel of Death, shown as streaks of bright white light, arrives with terrible inevitability. Occasionally someone exhibits fleeting defiance before the situation inevitability reaches its grim conclusion.

Unlike previous Moses movies which attempted to rationalize the plagues and other supernatural events, *Mandamentos* intensifies them. The grand exodus scenes show millions departing. The pillars of cloud and fire are strikingly, but literally, rendered. When Moses' sister walks on the bed of the Red Sea she exclaims 'It's dry'. Moses is shown not only writing Genesis but predicting what the remainder of Exodus will say. The film is robustly and unapologetically Pentecostal in its approach with a strong emphasis on Christianity, miracles and prosperity. This tendency is personified in the idealized and sexualized portrayal of Moses, played by the smouldering Guilherme Winter, who sprints about urging his people across the Red Sea, with shouts of 'Vamos!'

Perhaps the most disconcerting part of the film occurs towards the end. Footage of Moses' supporters killing those who worshipped the golden calf is interspersed with that of Joshua telling his soldiers 'Now is the time to conquer what is ours!' His words echo those of Rede's owner Edir Macedo, the billionaire leader of Brazil's biggest church network who allegorizes Brazilian evangelicals as the Israelites claiming 'Moses' mission was to … guide them to possession of their own kingdom'.[4] Given the political rise of right-wing evangelicalism in Brazilian politics, such validation of Moses and Joshua's violence and its dehumanization of the Egyptians/non-evangelicals is somewhat troubling.

Notes

1   Theatrical release, 120 minutes. DVD version, discussed here, 78 minutes.
2   Mariane Zendron and Tiago Dias 'Com ajuda de fiéis, filme *Os Dez Mandamentos* já vendeu 150 mil ingressos', *UOL* 1 January 2016. Retrieved from: <http://web.archive.org/web/20190125205957/https://cinema.uol.com.br/noticias/redacao/2016/01/05/com-ajuda-de-fieis-filme-os-dez-mandamentos-ja-vendeu-150-mil-ingressos.htm>.

3   'Ranking de filmes 2016 (por público)' *Database Brasil*. Available online: <www.filmeb.com.br/database2/html/Menu_Database_Ano.php?getmenu_ano=2016> (accessed 19 Dec. 2021).
4   Cited and translated in Alexander Zaitchik and Christopher Lord, 'How a Demon-Slaying Pentecostal Billionaire is Ushering in a Post-Catholic Brazil', *The New Republic*, 7 February 2019. Available online: <https://newrepublic.com/article/153083/demon-slaying-pentecostal-billionaire-ushering-post-catholic-brazil> (accessed 19 Dec. 2021).

Risen
USA, 2016 – 103 mins
Kevin Reynolds

DIRECTOR Kevin Reynolds
PRODUCERS Patrick Aiello,
Mickey Liddell, Pete Shilaimon
SCREENPLAY Paul Aiello
CINEMATOGRAPHY
Lorenzo Senatore
EDITOR Steve Mirkovich
MUSIC Roque Baños
PRODUCTION COMPANY
Fifty Days Productions I.I.C.
MAIN CAST Cliff Curtis,
Tom Felton, Joseph Fiennes,
Peter Firth

While the biblical epic supplanted film noir as the leading genre in the 1950s, more recently a handful of epics have sought to combine the two genres with Roman-Christian-detective films such as *The Inquiry* (1987), its remake nineteen years later, *The Final Inquiry* (2006), and *Risen* (2016) which follows a sceptical Roman tribune investigating Jesus' death.[1]

The film opens with Joseph Fiennes' tribune Clavius stumbling into a desert tavern, soon explaining the events of the last few weeks to the inn-keeper. The action jumps back to Clavius' men quashing a Jewish rebellion. Just a few hours after Barabbas' infamous release he's already back fighting Romans. Pontius Pilate, however, is more preoccupied with the man who took his place and orders Clavius to ensure that he dies.

So when rumours begin to circulate that Jesus has come back to life, Clavius is instructed to investigate. The chief priests are determined to cover things up and Pilate demurs to their increasingly pernickety requests. But Clavius can neither find the body to disprove the growing rumours, nor track down the disciples. Even when he finds an inanely grinning Bartholomew, he cannot get any sense out of him and decides he's an idiot. The film oddly misfires like this several times. Jesus' burial cloth is shown to bear the same image as the Turin Shroud. Even the Catholic audience at *Risen's* Rome première groaned at that.[2]

A more troubling problem is the film's recycling of various antisemitic stereotypes, particularly Pilate's description of the Jewish crowd as a 'lathered mob' and their jeering at Jesus' death. Caiaphas' repeated trips back to Pilate to suppress the truth about the resurrection characterize him as paranoid, sly, dishonest and irritating.

Despite its post-9/11 parallels,[3] *Risen* has its bright spots. Filmed in Malta and Spain the striking 'jagged' landscapes and architecture provide a great backdrop to the story.[4] Director Kevin Reynolds, (*Robin Hood: Prince of Thieves*) introduces some interesting cinematic touches, notably riffing on *The Searchers* (1956) as Clavius hovers in a doorway unsure whether to remain an untamed outsider or join the new community inside. The score's occasionally unsettling strings express the inherent strangeness of the post-resurrection stories, and the gradual change in Clavius' clothing reflects his transformation within. Furthermore, while the time Jesus spends on the screen is relatively brief, it's a decent performance by Cliff Curtis, though Greydanus finds him 'less compelling than the figure built up *in absentia* in the first half'.[5]

Predictably Clavius eventually catches up with 'the truth', but even so, the filmmakers make one unexpected decision that significantly changes the nature and direction of the story. While it's interesting to see a film dwell in the time between the crucifixion and the ascension, sparsely treated in most Jesus films, the direction the film chooses to go requires too much of a leap of faith. Ultimately, it's clear why Clavius believes in his story, but difficult to swallow for those who do not already believe it.

Joseph Fiennes as Clavius in *Risen* (2016).

Notes

1   'CSI Jerusalem' quipped *The Guardian*'s Jordan Hoffman. '*Risen* review – biblical CSI: Jerusalem loses faith in its premise', 19th February 2016. Available online: <www.theguardian.com/film/2016/feb/19/risen-review-joseph-fiennes-jesus-crucifixion> (accessed 19 Dec. 2021).

2   Personally witnessed by the author.

3   Fernando Gabriel Pagnoni Berns and Emiliano Aguilar, 'The Biblical-Trial Film: Social Contexts in L'Inchiesta and *Risen*' in Wickham Clayton (ed.), *The Bible Onscreen in the New Millennium: New Heart and New Spirit* (Manchester: Manchester University Press, 2020), pp. 230–46.

4   Peter T. Chattaway, 'Review: *Risen* (dir. Kevin Reynolds, 2016), *FilmChat*, 20 February 2016. Available online: <www.patheos.com/blogs/filmchat/2016/02/review-risen-dir-kevin-reynolds-2016.html> (accessed 19 Dec. 2021).

5   Steven D. Greydanus, ' Through Other Eyes: Point of View and Defamiliarization in Jesus Films', in Richard Walsh (ed.), *The T&T Clark Handbook to Jesus on Film* (London: Bloomsbury, 2021), p. 85.

Get Some Money (2017)
Kenya, 2017 – 113 mins
Biko Nyongesa

DIRECTOR Biko Nyongesa
PRODUCERS Wangui Ngunjiri, Winnie Njoki
SCREENPLAY Biko Nyongesa
CINEMATOGRAPHY Victor Ombogo
EDITOR Odhiambo Akwa
MUSIC Chris Adwar, Jublak, Otiende Noah, Carlisto Ochieng
PRODUCTION COMPANY Legit Films, OFL Group
MAIN CAST Naomi Mburu, Dennis Mwangi Dyb, Collins Ochieng, Stichy Stich

Shot in 15 days at Kenya Marble Quarries,[1] forty miles south of Nairobi, *Get Some Money* is a Jesus film quite unlike any other. Not only is it an African film, made for Africans by Africans, but it's also performed in Sheng, a rapidly evolving hybrid slang combining English, Swahili and other languages popular in Kenya. The distinctive locations, sets, costumes and props give the film a timeless feel. The contemporary freshness of a youth-orientated street language like Sheng, combines with touches of the ancient world and more recent times.

The Kenyan aesthetics of the film percolate through its atmosphere, enhancing this new perspective, particularly the starkly beautiful landscapes and Kamba soundtrack. Much of the film consists of scenes which appear lit by candles and oil lamps. The dialogue and its delivery, particularly the chat amongst minor characters all contribute to its unique flavour.

Stichy Stich as 'Tichia' (Jesus) in *Get Some Money* (2017). (Courtesy L. Biko Nyongesa)

The film began as a seven-minute short raising awareness about suicide. Realizing 'the Judas story is universal',[2] writer and director L. Biko Nyongesa decided it was an ideal vehicle to address the issue. The short's success led Nyongesa to create a feature-length treatment along similar lines. Though an ensemble film, Judas (Collins Ochieng) remains its most developed character. Portrayals of Judas have become more sympathetic as cinema has matured. After scores of movies where his actions are driven by a single issue, here his tragic decision derives from numerous complex factors. Judas has had suicidal thoughts even before the film begins. In his (unrequited) obsession for Magda he buys increasingly extravagant gifts to woo her. Eventually he abuses his position as group treasurer, using to their funds to buy presents for her, rather than paying the groups' taxes. In public, he behaves normally, unlike someone struggling with depression, which only makes Ochieng's portrayal more realistic. Just as he is hitting rock bottom he hears the Romans are offering a bounty for Tichia (the film's name for Jesus). His problems, compounded by his guilt over Tichia's death and Petero's torture, result in him taking his own life only metres away from his mother.

What is more surprising about the film, however, is the way it combines its serious subject with light touch comedy and its thoroughly desacralized portrayal its characters, including Jesus. The use of Sheng, the young age of Tichia and his gang, and their behaviour, combine to place the viewer on the outside of the movement. The disciples bicker, fool around, fart and do drugs. It's clear that the older figures in the story – fellow villagers as well as authorities – are concerned. Tichia struggles to lead this unruly bunch and the film strips him of the aura of authority that typically comes with the role. Jesus is not mocked, and his costume and dreadlocked hair mark him as special, but no-one affords him prior status.

Indeed, most of what we learn about Tichia and his disciples comes indirectly, via reports of villagers, concerned parents and the leaders of more established gangs such as Kayafa, Pilato and the ultimate boss/Caesar figure, Kisari. There's little to shape our opinion about Tichia, meanwhile rumours swirl about him and his followers. The script tweaks certain gospel incidents. Villagers worry how Jesus driving demons into pigs will damage pork prices, or that the woman he saved from stoning will continue 'destroying' families. What emerges is an outsider's perspective, one primarily informed by the kinds of people who called Jesus a 'glutton and a drinker' (Matt 11.19).

Though the film avoids making Judas into an idealized figure, no longer is he simply 'the man who betrayed the Son of God', he's merely a follower who finds betrayal is his best option. He's a sympathetic, complex, yet normal character with strengths and weaknesses. Meanwhile, *Get Some Money* gets behind hallowed Gospel portraits to show a Jesus whose identity remains unclear and contested.

Notes

1   Shirley Genga, '*Get Some Money*: Tale of Jesus Being Betrayed in Sheng', *The Standard*, 21 February 2017, though Genga mistakenly calls the quarry 'Kenya Mining Quarries'. Available online: <www.standardmedia.co.ke/entertainment/nainotepad/2001230192/get-some-money-tale-of-jesus-being-betrayed-in-sheng> (accessed 19 Dec. 2021).

2   L. Biko Nyongesa interviewed on ' Film Speak: One on one with a Netflix Actor and Film Director', *Kenya Citizen TV* 6 January 2017. Available online: <www.youtube.com/watch?v=FevKzWJ_p_c> (accessed 19 Dec. 2021).

Mary Magdalene
UK/Australia/USA, 2018 – 120 mins
Garth Davis

DIRECTOR Garth Davis
PRODUCERS Iain Canning,
Emile Sherman, Liz Watts
SCREENPLAY Helen Edmundson,
Philippa Goslett
CINEMATOGRAPHY
Greig Fraser
EDITORS Alexandre de
Franceschi, Melanie Oliver
MUSIC Hildur Guðnadóttir,
Jóhann Jóhannsson
PRODUCTION COMPANY
Water Productions Ltd,
Sprint Films Holdings
Pty Limited
MAIN CAST Chiwetel Ejiofor,
Rooney Mara, Joaquin Phoenix,
Tahar Rahim

Mary Magdalene brings a feminist, contemporary sensibility to the Jesus story, providing a more meditative feel via its combination of mesmerizing visuals and gentle pacing. While the film is not the first to tell the story from Magdalene's perspective, it's a worthy attempt to 'reclaim a dismissed figure' and liberate her from the church's labelling of her as a prostitute, and dramatists' portrayal of her as Jesus' love interest.[1]

Director Garth Davis focuses intently on Rooney Mara's features and her 'gaze' as he shapes Mary into a far more compelling figure than the man she follows.[2] Helen Edmundson and Philippa Goslett's script picks up in Magdala, where Mary lives with her family. Faced with the prospect of an unwanted marriage she heads to the village synagogue to pray,[3] upsetting its religious officials and her relatives. The two groups of men decide to drown the demons out of her and are then at a loss about what to do when she is traumatized by the experience. Eventually her brother summons 'The Healer'.

Jesus turns up, and peers into Mary's soul, soothing her and healing her bruised spirit. She flees her over-bearing and abusive family and follows him. Jesus welcomes her presence, not least because she seems to intuitively understand both him and his message better than his male disciples. The disciples talk of war and revolution; she asks 'what it feels like to be one with God'. She helps him realize how he is making it hard for

Rooney Mara in *Mary Magdalene* (2018).

women to join him, encouraging him to preach in the areas of town where the women gather, explaining how 'The women are too afraid to be baptized with the men'.

Joaquin Phoenix's Jesus seems less well developed than Mary. He gets several good lines, but brought together they amount to very little. Mary may intuitively understand his vision but it's not because he has told her. Whilst his sensitivity and spirituality appeal, he lacks passion and drive. The passion in the film comes from Mary, all the time skilfully avoiding being castigated as pushy. She's an advocate for change, love and inclusivity – it's no coincidence that it is perhaps the first Jesus film to treat Judas compassionately even after Jesus' crucifixion.

Edmundson and Goslett's script never forgets it's about Mary, not Jesus, elaborating on minor elements in the Gospels to enrich its theme while respecting the source material. Scenes often show the moment itself, liberated from the Gospels' narrative framing. Jesus raises a man from the dead, but is it Lazarus or the widow's son? When Mary and Peter (Chiwetel Ejiofor) travel alone to spread the message, there's no build-up showing Jesus sending them out in pairs. We simply join them on the road as they go, her mercy clashing with his pragmatism. Ejiofor's Peter, Mary's chief critic amongst the disciples, channels Carl Anderson's charisma, bristling scowls, and assured self-confidence from *Jesus Christ, Superstar* (1973). He too thinks Mary has misled his scruffy, laid-back, master.

Naturally the narrative ends up in Jerusalem, but the script skilfully handles the material, honouring the significance of Jesus' trials without losing its balance or focus on Mary. Despite the disciples' rejection of Mary's vision, the closing titles summarize past wrongs while offering hope for the future.

Whilst the film's feminist credentials are a little over-praised, it's Mary who comes out as the bold, flawless, creative and original visionary in contrast to Phoenix's Jesus who is a weak leader and misguided dreamer. Hildur Guðnadóttir and Jóhann Jóhannsson's haunting score, Davis' lingering shots of ruggedly beautiful landscapes and its unhurried rhythm give viewers plenty of time to contemplate the film's more compassionate vision.

Notes

1   Wickham Clayton, *The Bible Onscreen in the New Millennium: New Heart and New Spirit* (Manchester: Manchester University Press, 2020), p. 11.

2   Michelle Fletcher, 'Seeing Differently with *Mary Magdalene*', in Richard Walsh (ed.) *The T&T Clark Handbook of Jesus and Film*, (London: Bloomsbury, 2021), pp. 55–65.

3   Peter T. Chattaway, 'Obscure Elements in Jesus Films', in Richard Walsh (ed.) *The T&T Clark Handbook of Jesus and Film*, (London: Bloomsbury, 2021), p. 23.

Paul, Apostle of Christ
USA, 2018 – 103 mins
Andrew Hyatt

DIRECTOR Andrew Hyatt
PRODUCER David Zelon
SCREENPLAY Terence Berden
CINEMATOGRAPHY
Gerardo Madrazo
EDITOR Scott Richter
MUSIC Jan A. P. Kaczmarek
PRODUCTION COMPANY
Tarsus LLC
MAIN CAST Jim Caviezel,
James Faulkner, John Lynch,
Olivier Martinez,
Joanne Whalley

Despite the film's title, *Paul, Apostle of the Christ* is as much about Priscilla, Aquila and the ordinary Christians of Rome as it is about the superstar apostle. As the closing dedication confirms, this is a film about those persecuted for their faith.

Paul is set in 67 A.D. with Nero's persecutions wreaking havoc amongst the Christian community. Paul is in prison while Priscilla, Aquila and their community are in hiding, trying to decide if they should stick it out in Rome, or flee for pastures new. An accomplished, but grim, opening shot tracks Luke as he arrives in Rome and is immediately confronted with the sight of his fellow Christians being burned alive to light the city. Luke dodges the Roman soldiers long enough to arrive safely at Priscilla and Aquila's house and spends much of the rest of the film going between there and Paul's cell.

Whilst Paul seems resigned to his fate others are less certain about their future path. When one of their number is killed, some Christians want Roman blood in revenge. The officer overseeing Paul's imprisonment finds his orders distasteful, but not to the extent he will risk his life to defy his emperor. His wife blames his ambiguity about religion for his daughter's illness, yet when the illness starts to threaten the child's life, she soon urges him to do whatever it takes to save her.

James Faulkner's grizzled Paul in *Paul, Apostle of Christ* (2018).

Despite several TV series about Paul, films about him are rare.[1] There are brief roles in Roman-Christian epics such as *Quo Vadis* (1951) but *Paul, Apostle of Christ* was the first feature-length treatment of Paul's life released in cinemas.[2] It's unusual, then, that the film focuses on the small part of Paul's life which we only know about from later, contradictory, traditions rather than the wealth of biblical material that originates from his thirty years of ministry.[3]

This is largely by design. *Paul* is quite unlike the traditional Roman-Christian epic. Rather than spectacle, grandeur, huge crowd scenes, life-changing miracles, a swelling soundtrack and exciting battles,[4] *Paul* is a more sombre and mature affair. It's deliberately heavy on ideas and dialogue. Thankfully the cast is generally strong, particularly James Faulkner in the title role, though Joanne Whalley and John Lynch as Priscilla and Aquila also impress. The sets and costumes hold their own.

Of course, part of the pleasure of watching a Paul adaptation is noting the quotations the screenwriters have worked into the script. Here the balance is good between the biblical and the fictional and Faulkner does a great job delivering Paul's famous words. However, the problem is, that with Paul more or less confined to his cell, Faulkner is not left much else to do, such that insight into his character and personality is lower than might be expected.

Yet for a faith-based film, such reliance on dialogue is a sign of maturity. The film never feels like it is trying to grab everyone's attention so it can swoop in for a sermon. Indeed its meandering pace and use of dialogue make for a far more satisfying experience. Furthermore, director Andrew Hyatt introduces various interesting and impressive shots. There's the odd misstep – the jailer's daughter's sudden recovery is a little too saccharin, for example – but overall it's an interesting look at the persecution Jesus' early followers faced and a timely reminder of the early church's non-violent response.

Notes

1   Richard Walsh, 'Paul and the Early Church in Film', in Rhonda Burnette-Bletsch (ed.), *The Bible in Motion: A Handbook of the Bible and Its Reception in Film*. vol.2, (Berlin: De Gruyter, 2016), pp. 497–515.

2   Peter T. Chattaway, 'Review: *Paul, Apostle of Christ* (dir. Andrew Hyatt, 2018)', *FilmChat*, 21 March 2018. Available online: <www.patheos.com/blogs/filmchat/2018/03/review-paul-apostle-of-christ-dir-andrew-hyatt-2018.html> (accessed 19 Dec. 2021).

3   Richard Walsh, 'Ready for His Closeup? Pasolini's *San Paolo* and *Paul, Apostle of Christ* (2018)', *Journal of the Bible and its Reception* Vol.6 (1), 24 April 2019 (Boston: De Gruyter), pp. 5–7.

4   Bruce Babington and Peter William Evans, *Biblical Epics: Sacred Narrative in the Hollywood Cinema* (Manchester: Manchester University Press, 1993), pp. 64–5.

Seder-Masochism
USA, 2018 – 78 mins
Nina Paley

DIRECTOR Nina Paley
PRODUCERS Nina Paley,
Producer X
SCREENPLAY Nina Paley
EDITOR Nina Paley
MUSIC Greg Sextro
MAIN CAST Hiram Paley,
Nina Paley

Nina Paley's *Seder-Masochism* is a satirical exploration of the Exodus story whose charmingly-quirky, and often hilarious, animation masks a biting critique of Moses and patriarchal religion in general. Yet Paley carries a genuine affection for her Jewish roots and the Passover traditions she has inherited. Indeed only two spoken sources punctuate the near-perfect soundtrack: Barry Gray presiding over the 'Moishe Oysher Seder' (1955) (illustrated by animated sections of Vicente Juan Masip's 'Last Supper' with Jesus likewise officiating); and a conversation Paley recorded with her terminally-ill father Hiriam the year before his death in 2012.

It is the pathos of the latter recording which supplies the film's beating heart. The relaxed, intimate, chit-chat back through family history, and indeed their own. Him, cast as the pyramid from the dollar bill, made-up with a long, flowing (literally), white beard, to look like God, complete with crown. Her, as a cute, black sacrificial goat, precariously perched on top of her pyre.[1] They discuss the Passovers he spent as a boy and his subsequent loss of faith. Indeed Paley's own misgivings about parts of text not only reflect her father's own ('the Exodus … was happy and sad'), but even those of her great uncle, who objected to celebrating 'the killing of the firstborn Egyptians'. Portraying her father as God, and the obvious tenderness between them, deftly offsets the seriousness of her critique of patriarchal monotheism such that it never feels bitter or disrespectful.

Having opened with a goddess/Mother Earth inspired retelling of creation, the film jumps to the calling of Moses accompanied, naturally, by a slice of *Singin' in the Rain*'s 'Moses Supposes'. Jesus/Barry Gray introduces the four goblets of wine around which the Passover Seder and the majority of the film is structured. Moses, complete with bushy eyebrows and head shaped like his tablets of stone, heads to Egypt to tackle Pharaoh. However first he passes through 35,000 years of grooving female fertility figures from 'Venus' of Hohle Fels through to Kilpeck church's sheela-na-gig.

The animation is bold, playful and simple, with more than a nod to the famous hieroglyphics scene in *The Prince of Egypt* (1998). Moses confronts Pharaoh to the sound of Louis Armstrong's version of 'Let My People Go'. When he refuses, the plagues ensue, including the death of the firstborn. The angel of death incorporates both Death from Bergman's *Seventh Seal* (1957) and No Face from Miyazaki's 2001 *Spirited Away*, while the Israelites march jauntily out of Egypt accompanied by The New Seekers' 'Free to Be … You and Me' and a dazzling pillar of fire.

Paley's feelings over her religious heritage come most to the fore when Moses ascends a phallus-shaped Mount Sinai and returns to smash all traces of the once widespread goddess-worship. The sequence ends with real life footage of Isis raiders smashing similar artefacts in modern day Syria. Moses and Aaron (with a head shaped like the Star of David) install the beautifully rendered tabernacle and sacrificial systems with apparent glee. The closing numbers lament in various ways that the goddess worship was ousted by male-dominated monotheism, culminating in a mercilessly poignant parody of Andy Willams's 'This Land is Mine'.

Nina Paley's humourously animated *Seder-Masochism* (2018).

While the film's rhythm is a little off in the final 20 minutes and its veneration of ancient fertility rites is, somewhat over-sentimental,[2] this is nevertheless a powerful, fascinating, witty piece of stunningly-rendered animation dealing with complex issues of inheritance and belief. It's a deeply personal and heart-felt film whose affectionately comical medium masks a deep-seated confrontation with the past and the faith of our forefathers.

Notes

1   Ben Croll, 'Annecy: *Seder-Masochism* Director Nina Paley: "I Have No Idea How This Movie Will Go Into the World"', *Variety*, 10 June 2018. Available online: <https://variety.com/2018/film/festivals/annecy-seder-masochism-nina-paley-1202839427/> (accessed 19 Dec. 2021).

2   Peter T. Chattaway, 'VIFF capsule reviews: *Seder-Masochism*', *FilmChat*, 24 September 2018. Available online: <www.patheos.com/blogs/filmchat/2018/09/viff-capsule-reviews-seder-masochism-the-lost-city-of-the-monkey-god-bergman-a-year-in-a-life.html> (accessed 19 Dec. 2021).

Assassin 33 A.D. (2020) [1]

USA, 2020 – 109 mins

Jim Carroll

DIRECTOR Jim Carroll

PRODUCERS Beth Jasper, Brad Keller, Joey Stewart

SCREENPLAY Jim Carroll

CINEMATOGRAPHY Ron Gonzalez

MUSIC Chris George

MAIN CAST Donny Boaz, Ilsa Levine, Heidi Montag, Morgan Roberts

PRODUCTION COMPANY 2018 Timed Out Productions

After heated protests about *Life of Brian* (1979), *Last Temptation of Christ* (1988) and *Jerry Springer: The Opera* (2005), the most sacrilegious Jesus film of all time turns out not to be one made by sceptics searching for a quick buck, but conservative Christians. *Assassin 33 A.D.* is well-intended Christertainment so jaw-droppingly idiosyncratic, it's hard to stop thinking about it afterwards. After all, when else did a movie have the sheer audacity to send terrorists back in time to assassinate Jesus?

The 'Christian movie' elements are heavy from the off. Brandt (Donny Boaz) is relocating his family to start his new job as Head of Security when a juggernaut ploughs into their car killing his wife and children. In his grief, Brandt's glowers at the sky, and growls 'I am not your guy anymore'. The next scene introduces two new characters in a university lecture hall – an increasingly popular location for Christian movies – socially-awkward (though not in a loveable way) Ram Goldstein and fellow scientist Amy Lee. The two are competing for highly-paid jobs at the same mysterious tech company as Brandt and both are chosen to work on a project developing a matter transfer device.

Just three months later and the team have completed the teleporting machine, and modified it to also travel through time. Ram and Amy's employers reveal themselves as Islamic terrorists who decide to go back in time to 'eliminate Jesus before the resurrection', thus 'dismantling Christianity' and 'correcting the greatest deception of all time'. Before anyone can stop to ask how putting a bullet in Jesus' brain will prevent rumours spreading about his resurrection, Brandt and his SWAT team are dispatched to Gethsemane with machine guns and body armour.

A complex mess of tangled timelines, alternative realities, eccentric theology and convenient plot devices follows. *Assassin 33 A.D.*'s unusual combination of genres (sci-fi and biblical epic) enable it to manoeuvre out of any narratorial tight-spot with either pseudo-scientific babble ('time doesn't change instantaneously, it has to re-write itself') or theological cliché (someone actually utters 'God works in mysterious ways' at one point). Scientists and SWAT team jump back and forth between past and present resulting in multiple different Jesus timelines. On top of suspect science, theology and general implausibility, the filmmaker's attempts at diversity only result in racial stereotyping. Simon, an African-American, tells his colleagues to 'be cool' and is portrayed as lazy, while Felix, a Latino, invokes various Hispanic stereotypes.[2] All of the Muslim characters are Islamic terrorists.

Paradoxically, *Assassin 33A.D.* is 'both thoroughly sincere in its obvious love for Jesus, and also the most blasphemous thing ever made by filmmakers'.[3] Moments where Simon and Jesus discuss *The Passion of the Christ* (2004) and trade lines from *The Terminator* (1984) jar with its themes of terrorism, salvation and determinism. Minor players in the Gospels have their places filled by time travellers. Occasionally interesting ideas crop up, but somehow every one is fumbled.

Simon becomes part of the Jesus story in *Assassin 33 A.D.* (2020).

Any attempt to fix its problems would only strip the film of its curious appeal, indeed it seems destined to become a cult classic. Only Trump's America could conceive such a film, a 'faith-based' story whose greatest villain is a naturalized citizen who escaped terrorism as a child, and where a peaceful, unarmed, Middle-Eastern, protester gets shot in the head at point-blank range by a white man in body armour. Its god would rather go to extraordinary lengths to reverse a crisis of faith, than prevent a simple accident. Having toured the festival circuit for years seeking a distributor it was eventually released amidst the Covid-19 pandemic. Somehow, that could not be more fitting.

Notes

1   For a time this film was known as *Resurrection Time Conspiracy* and *Black Easter Resurrection*. It was re-released in 2021 as *Black Easter*.

2   Charles Ramírez Berg, 'Hispanic Stereotyping', in Richard Delgado, Jean Stefancic (eds.), *The Latino/a Condition: A Critical Reader*, Second Edition (New York: New York University Press, 2011), pp. 183–88.

3   Laura Robinson (@LauraRbnsn), 'The movie is honestly charming', *Twitter* 28 April 2020. Available online: <https://twitter.com/LauraRbnsn/status/1254949214666317825> (accessed 19 Dec. 2021).

Lamentations of Judas
Netherlands/France, 2020 – 98 mins
Boris Gerrets

DIRECTOR Boris Gerrets
PRODUCERS Boudewijn Koole,
Iris Lammertsma, Eric Velthuis
SCREENPLAY Boris Gerrets
CINEMATOGRAPHY
Nic Hofmeyr
EDITOR Boris Gerrets
MUSIC Sibisi Thuthuka
MAIN CAST Verónica Carols,
Jonas Luvango, Rafael Siata
Temba, Former soldiers of
32 Battalion
PRODUCTION COMPANY
Witfilm/KV Films/Les Filmes
d'Ici/EO

Just as the first film of these hundred blurred the distinction between documentary and drama, so too does the last, albeit in markedly different fashion. *Lamentations of Judas*, directed by Dutchman Boris Gerrets, is a documentary about the notorious '32 Battalion' – Black Angolan soldiers who fought on the South African side in both the Namibian War of Independence and the related Angolan Civil War – but it also selects these former combatants to act out several scenes from Jesus' life.

The film is a collage of four distinctly different types of material. An opening montage of archive footage explains the background to the war and these soldiers' subsequent role in suppressing anti-apartheid uprisings in South-African townships. The remainder is split between interviews with some of the soldiers themselves; landscapes of their decaying town of Pomfret and its surrounding geography, accompanied by poetic reflections; and a dramatic reconstruction of Jesus' life, performed by some of those interviewed. Jesus rides past the crumbling architecture of Pomfret as a crowd wave palm branches. The blind see. A woman pours out her expensive oil to anoint Jesus' feet. These conventional episodes of the Gospels are transformed into something powerful yet intangible.

The link between Judas' betrayal and the way these men supposedly turned away from their countrymen is suggested by the film's title, but their reminiscences often switch to the role of the soldiers who arrested Jesus. What choice did they have and how should they be judged? The interplay between these segments reflects a 'therapeutic process' the men undertook.[2] There are no easy answers, just a sense of melancholy that permeates through the entire film.

Over the years many films have sought to understand Judas and his motivation, yet *Lamentations* generates fresh options. By getting behind his character in very a different fashion, it uncovers possibilities that might otherwise have escaped. Yet just as the film helps us look at Judas in a new way, it also demonstrates the Bible's power to illuminate lives today. When the men of the 32 Battalion – nicknamed the 'Terrible ones' – tell their stories it begins to emerge that they are victims of circumstance, in many cases forced into fighting against their fellow citizens. Likewise, towards the end of the film Judas and Jesus talk alone. 'Out of the twelve disciples, I am the only one you chose, master.' As with the residents of Pomfret, he is just one man following a path he neither wants nor can turn away from. With Judas the tragedy is that, like others who take their own lives, the feeling of being trapped and the feeling of despair block out other possibilities.

Yet Gerrets's film offers other faint notes of hope. For him, the camera can 'unlock a space of imagining and becoming'.[3] It's most apparent here in both the beautiful natural light casting shadows across the dry savannah and it's re-appropriation of 'traditional Christian' imagery with a more southern African feel. The costumes are neither those of today's Angola or Namibia, nor of Europe's Christian art, but the projected image an imagined past. An African Jesus bursting into the midst of a past colonial canvas offering fresh hope.

Lamentations of Judas (2020), a Borris Gerrets film. (Courtesy of Alexandra Sophia Handal)

Gerrets died shortly after filming completed. He leaves behind a wonderful film; deeply emotional and profoundly affecting. Almost imperceptibly it volunteers redemption and forgiveness, not as simple, painless words, but as a heart-wrenching grasp into the darkness, daring to hope the possibility of coming to terms with our pasts somehow still remains.

Notes

1   For a time this film was known as *Resurrection Time Conspiracy* and *Black Easter Resurrection*.
2   Melanie Page interviewed in '*Lamentations of Judas*', *Bible Films Podcast*, 22 August 2020. Available online: <https://jesusfilms.podbean.com/e/lamentations-of-judas-2020/> (accessed 19 Dec. 2021).
3   Boris Gerrets, 'Director's Note', *Witfilm* 2020. Available online: <http://lamentationsofjudas.com/film.html> (accessed 19 Dec. 2021).

Appendix 1: Bible Film and Television Series

In addition to standalone films, the following six series of short films or television programmes sought to cover multiple stories from the Bible by devoting each episode to a different narrative. Episodes are listed in order of the biblical stories which they cover.

The Living Bible Series (1952–58)

Edward Dew: US

Old Testament Scriptures (14-episode series, 1958); covering
'Abraham – Man of Faith' (1958)
'Jacob – Bearer of the Promise' (1958)
'Joseph – The Young Man' (1958)
'Joseph – Ruler of Egypt' (1958)
'Moses – Called by God' (1958)
'Moses – Leader of God's People' (1958)
'Joshua – The Conqueror' (1958)
'Gideon – the Liberator' (1958)
'Ruth – a Faithful Woman' (1958)
'Samuel – A Dedicated Man' (1958)
'David – A Young Hero' (1958)
'David – A King of Israel' (1958)
'Solomon – A Man of Wisdom' (1958)
'Elijah – A Fearless Prophet' (1958)
Living Bible [Jesus] (26-episode series, 1952)
Book of Acts (10-episode series, 1957)

The Greatest Heroes of the Bible (1978–9)

James L. Conway: US
'Noah and the Deluge' (Two parts)
'The Tower of Babel'
'Abraham's Sacrifice'
'Sodom and Gomorrah'
'Jacob's Challenge'
'Joseph and his Brothers'
'The Story of Moses' (Two parts)
'The Story of the Ten Commandments'
'Joshua and the Battle of Jericho'

'Samson and Delilah'
'David and Goliath'
'Judgement of Solomon'
'The Story of Esther'
'Daniel and Nebuchadnezzar'
'Daniel in the Lions' Den'

Tezuka Osamu no Kyûyaku Seisho Monogatari (*In the Beginning*, 1993)

Osamu Tezuka and Osamu Dezaki: Japan/Italy
'Tiandì chuangzao' (The Creation)
'Kain to Aberu' (Cain and Abel)
'Noa no hakobune' (The Story of Noah)
'Baberu no to' (The Tower of Babel)
'Chichi Aburahamu' (Abraham, the Forefather)
'Sodomu to Gomora' (Sodom and Gomorrah)
'Isaku to ishumaeru' (Isaac and Ishmael)
'Aburahamu, Isaku o sasageru' (Isaac's Destiny)
'Yakobu ichizoku no saikai' (Jacob's Children)
'Yosefu no yume uranai' (Joseph's Triumph)
'Mose no tanjo' (Moses, the Egyptian)
'Sabaku no hi' (The Fire in the Desert)
'Mose to farao' (Moses and the Pharaoh)
'Ejiputo dasshutsu' (The Exodus)
'Jukkai' (Laws Carved in Stone)
'Isuraeru no uragiri' (Israel's Treachery)
'Yakusoku no chi' (New Alliance)
'Eriko' (Jericho)
'Hajimete no o sauru' (One King for Israel)
'Sauru no haiboku' (King Saul)
'Dabide-o' (King David)
'Soromon no okoku' (King Solomon)
'Dai ni ju san-wa babironhoshu' (The Exile of Israel)
'Dorei kara no kaiho' (Release from Bondage)
'Sabaku no yogensha-tachi' (Prophets in the Desert)
'Iesu no tanjo' (The Birth of Jesus)

The Bible Collection (1993 – 2002)

Directors as stated: Italy, Germany, USA.

Genesis: Creation and Flood (Ermanno Olmi, 1994)

Abraham (Joseph Sargent, 1993)

Jacob (Peter Hall, 1994)

Joseph (Roger Young, 1995)

Moses (Roger Young,1995)

Samson and Delilah (Nicolas Roeg, 1996)

David (Robert Markowitz, 1997)

Solomon (Roger Young, 1997)

Jeremiah (Harry Winer, 1998)

Esther (Raffaele Mertes, 1998)

Jesus (Roger Young, 1999)

Close to Jesus: Joseph of Nazareth (Raffaele Mertes, 2000)

Close to Jesus: Mary Magdalene (Raffaele Mertes and Elisabetta Marchetti, 2000)

Close to Jesus: Thomas (Raffaele Mertes, 2001)

Close to Jesus: Judas (Raffaele Mertes, 2001)

St. Paul (Roger Young, 2000)

The Apocalypse (Raffaele Mertes, 2000)

Testament: The Bible in Animation (1996)

Directors as stated: Russia and Wales

Creation and Flood (Yuri Kulakov)

Abraham (Nataliya Dabizha)

Joseph (Aida Zyablikova)

Moses (Gary Hurst)

Ruth (Derek Hayes)

David and Saul (Gary Hurst)

Elijah (Derek Hayes)

Jonah (Valeriy Ugarov)

Daniel (Lyudmila Koshkina)

The Bible Miniseries (2013)

Crispin Reece, Tony Mitchell and Christopher Spencer: US.

'Beginnings' – [Genesis]

'Exodus' – [Moses]

'Homeland' – [Joshua and Samson]

'Kingdom' – [Saul, David and Solomon]

'Survival' – [Jeremiah, Daniel, Ezra]

'Hope' – [Nativity, Jesus' Ministry]

'Mission' – [Jesus' ministry]

'Betrayal' – [Jesus' ministry]

'Passion' – [Jesus' ministry]

'Courage' – [Jesus' Resurrection, Acts & Revelation]

A spin off series, *A.D. The Bible Continues* (also known as *A.D. Kingdom and Empire*) was broadcast in 2015 and covered the first twelve chapters of the Book of Acts.

Appendix 2: The 100 Films in Biblical Order

Due to certain films covering a wider range of material than others, the films in each section are listed in order of release date. Consult individual entries for details about the stories covered.

Genesis (Primeval Era)

La Sacra Bibbia (1920), Noah's Ark (1928), The Green Pastures (1936), The Bible: In the Beginning... (1966), The Real Old Testament (2003), The Bible (2013), Noah (2014).

Genesis (Ancestral Era)

Sodom und Gomorrha (1922), Lot in Sodom (1933), The Green Pastures (1936), The Bible: In the Beginning... (1966), Al-mohager (1994), La Genèse (1999), The Real Old Testament (2003), Year One (2009), The Bible (2013), The Red Tent (2014).

Exodus to Deuteronomy

L'Exode (1910), The Ten Commandments (1923), The Green Pastures (1936), The Ten Commandments (1956), Moses und Aron (1975), The Prince of Egypt (1998), The Bible (2013), Exodus: Gods and Kings (2014), Os Dez Mandamentos: O Filme (2016), Seder-Masochism (2018).

Joshua, Judges and Ruth

 Jaël et Sisera (1911), Jephthah's Daughter: A Biblical Tragedy (1909), Samson and Delilah (1949), The Story of Ruth (1960), I grandi condottieri (1965), Samson dan Delilah (1987), The Bible (2013).

Books of the Kingdoms (Samuel and Kings)

David and Bathsheba (1951), Sins of Jezebel (1953), Solomon and Sheba (1959), King David (1985), The Bible (2013).

Esther

Esther and the King (1960), Esther (1986).

Prophetic Books

Martyrs Chrétiens (1905), The Green Pastures (1936), Jeremiah (1998), Oversold (2008), The Bible (2013).

Deuterocanonical Books (Apocrypha)

Judith of Bethulia (1914), Il vecchio testamento (1962).

Gospels (Nativity only)

Star of Bethlehem (1956), Cammina cammina (1983), Je vous salue, Marie (1985), The Nativity Story (2006), El cant dels ocells (2008), Io sono con te (2010).

Gospels

La Vie et la passion de Jésus-Christ (1898), La Vie du Christ (1906), Vie et Passion de Notre Seigneur Jésus-Christ (1907), From the Manger to the Cross (1912), Intolerance (1916), Blade af Satans bog (1920), Der Galiläer (1921), Salomé (1922), Ben-Hur: A Tale of the Christ (1925), The King of Kings (1927), Golgotha (1935), The Last Days of Pompeii (1935), Jesús de Nazareth (1942), The Robe (1953), The Prodigal (1955), Celui qui doit mourir (1957), Ben-Hur (1959), King of Kings (1961), Barabbas (1961), Il vangelo secondo Matteo (1964), The Greatest Story Ever Told (1965), La Voie lactée (1969), Son of Man (1969), Jesús, nuestro Señor (1971), Jesus Christ Superstar (1973), Godspell (1973), Il messia (1975), The Passover Plot (1976), Jesus of Nazareth (1977), Karunamayudu (1978), Jesus (1979), Monty Python's Life of Brian (1979), The Last Temptation of Christ (1988), Jésus de Montréal (1989), The Garden (1990), The Visual Bible: Matthew (1993), Jesus (1999), The Miracle Maker (2000), The Visual Bible: The Gospel of John (2003), The Passion of the Christ (2004), Shanti Sandesham (2004), Color of the Cross (2006), Jezile (2006), Mesih (2007), The Passion (2008), Su re (2012), The Bible (2013), The Savior (2014), Risen (2016), Get Some Money (2017), Mary Magdalene (2018), Assassin 33 A.D. (2020), Lamentations of Judas (2020).

Acts

Quo Vadis (1951), Les Actes des apôtres (1969), The Bible (2013), Paul, Apostle of Christ (2018).

Revelation

The Book of Life (1998), The Bible (2013).

Further Reading

Atkinson, Barry, *Heroes Never Die: The Italian Peplum Phenomenon 1950–1967*, (London: Midnight Marquee, 2018).

Babington, Bruce and Peter William Evans, *Biblical Epics: Sacred Narrative in the Hollywood Cinema* (Manchester: Manchester University Press, 1993).

Baugh, Lloyd, *Imaging the Divine: Jesus and Christ Figures in Film* (Franklin, Wisconsin: Sheed & Ward, 1997).

Burnette-Bletsch, Rhonda (ed.), The Bible in Motion: A Handbook of the Bible and Its Reception in Film (2 vols) (Berlin/Boston: De Gruyter, 2016).

Campbell, Richard C. and Michael R. Pitts, *The Bible on Film: A Checklist, 1897–1980* (Metuchen, NJ, and London: Scarecrow Press, 1981).

Clayton, Wickham (ed.), *The Bible Onscreen in the New Millennium: New Heart and New Spirit* (Manchester: Manchester University Press, 2020).

Dumont, Hervé, *L'antiquité au cinema: Vérités, légendes et manipulations*. (Paris: Nouveau Monde Editions, 2009) Available online: <www.hervedumont.ch/page.php?id=fr10&idv=1#> (accessed 19 Dec. 2021).

Elley, Derek, *The Epic Film: Myth and History* (London: Routledge & Kegan Paul, 1984); 2nd edn, Abingdon and New York: Routledge, 2014).

Exum, Cheryl, *Plotted, Shot, and Painted: Cultural Representations of Biblical Women* (Sheffield: Sheffield Academic Press, 1996); 2nd rev. edn, (Sheffield: Sheffield Phoenix Press, 2012).

Forshey, Gerald E., *American Religious and Biblical Spectaculars* (Westport, CT: Praeger, 1992).

Fraser, George MacDonald, *The Hollywood History of the World* (New York: Beech Tree Books, 1988); rev. updated edn, (London: The Harvill Press, 1996).

Grace, Pamela, *The Religious Film: Christianity and the Hagiopic* (Chichester: John Wiley and Sons Ltd, 2009).

Hebron, Carol, Judas Iscariot: Damned or Redeemed – A Critical Examination of the Portrayal of Judas in Jesus Films (1902–2014) (London: Bloomsbury T&T Clark, 2016).

Kinnard, Roy and Tim Davis, *Divine Images: A History of Jesus on the Screen* (New York: Citadel–Carol Publishing Group, 1992).

Kreitzer, Larry J., The New Testament in Fiction and Film: On Reversing the Hermeneutical Flow (Melksham, Wilts.: Sheffield University Press, 1993).

Kreitzer, Larry J., The Old Testament in Fiction and Film: On Reversing the Hermeneutical Flow (Melksham, Wilts.: Sheffield University Press, 1994).

Langkau, Thomas, Filmstar Jesus Christus: Die neuesten Jesus-Filme als Herausforderung für Theologie und Religionspädagogik (Berlin: LIT Verlag, 2007).

Leitch, Thomas (ed.), Film Adaptation and its Discontents: From 'Gone With the Wind' to 'The Passion of the Christ' (Baltimore: The John Hopkins University Press, 2007).

Lindsay, Richard A., *Hollywood Biblical Epics: Camp Spectacle and Queer Style from the Silent Era to the Modern Day* (Santa Barbara, California/Denver, Colorado: Praeger, 2015).

Llewellyn-Jones, Lloyd, *Designs of the Past: How Hollywood Created the Ancient World* (Edinburgh: Edinburgh University Press, 2018).

Malone, Peter, *Screen Jesus: Portrayals of Christ in Television and Film* (Lanham/Toronto/Plymouth, UK: Scarecrow Press, 2012).

Meyer, Stephen C., *Epic Sound: Music in Postwar Hollywood Biblical Films* (Indianapolis: Indiana University Press, 2015).

O'Brien, Catherine, *The Celluloid Madonna: From Scripture to Screen* (New York: Columbia University Press, 2011).

Reinhartz, Adele, 'Jesus in Film: Hollywood Perspectives on the Jewishness of Jesus', *Journal of Religion and* Film vol. 2 no. 2 (1998). Available online at: <https://digitalcommons.unomaha.edu/cgi/viewcontent.cgi?article=1853&context=jrf> (accessed 19 Dec. 2021).

Reinhartz, Adele, *Jesus of Hollywood*. (Oxford /New York: Oxford University Press, 2007).

Reinhartz, Adele, *Bible and Cinema: An Introduction* (Abingdon: Routledge, 2013).

Richards, Jeffrey, *Hollywood's Ancient Worlds* (London: Continuum UK, 2008).

Sanders, Julie, Adaptation and Appropriation: The New Critical Idiom (Abingdon/New York: Routledge, 2006); 2nd rev. edn, (Abingdon / New York: Routledge, 2016).

Shepherd, David J., The Bible on Silent Film: Spectacle, Story and Scripture in the Early Cinema (Cambridge: Cambridge University Press, 2013).

Shepherd, David J. (ed.), The Silents of Jesus in the Cinema (1897–1927) (New York/London: Routledge, 2016).

Sobchack, Vivian, '"Surge and Splendour": A Phenomology of the Hollywood Historical Epic', in Barry Keith Grant (ed.), Film Genre Reader II (Austin TX: University of Texas Press, 1995), pp. 280–307.

Solomon, Jon, The Ancient World in the Cinema (New York: A.S. Barnes, 1978); rev. & expanded edn, (London/New Haven: Yale University Press, 2001).

Staley, Jeffrey L. and Richard Walsh, Jesus, the Gospels, and the Cinematic Imagination: A Handbook to Jesus on DVD (Louisville/London: Westminster John Knox Press, 2007); rev. edn published as Jesus, the Gospels, and Cinematic Imagination: Introducing Jesus Movies, Christ Films, and the Messiah in Motion, (London/New York: Bloomsbury, 2021).

Stern, Richard C., Clayton N. Jefford and Guerric Debona, Savior on the Silver Screen (New York/Mahwah NJ: Paulist Press, 1999).

Tatum, W.Barnes, Jesus at the Movies: A Guide to the First Hundred Years (California: Polebridge Press, 1997); rev. & expanded, (2004); 3rd edn, (2013).

Thomson, David, The New Biographical Dictionary of Film 4th edn, (London: Little, Brown, 2002); 6th edn, (London: Abacus, 2014); originally published as A Biographical Dictionary of Cinema (Secker & Warburg: London, 1975).

Turner, Katie, Costuming Christ: Re-dressing First-Century 'Jews' and 'Christians' in Passion Dramas (London: Bloomsbury 2022).

von Tunzelmann, Alex, Reel History: The World According to the Movies (London: Atlantic Books, 2015).

Walsh, Richard, Reading the Gospels in the Dark: Portrayals of Jesus in Film (London and New York: Trinity Press International, 2003).

Walsh, Richard (ed.), The T&T Clark Companion to the Bible and Film (London: Bloomsbury, 2018).

Walsh, Richard (ed.), The T&T Clark Handbook to Jesus on Film (London: Bloomsbury, 2021).

Wood, Michael, America in the Movies, or Santa Maria, It Had Slipped My Mind (New York: Basic Books, 1975); rev. edn (New York: Columbia University Press, 1989).

Wyke, Maria, Projecting the Past: Ancient Rome, Cinema and History (London/New York: Routledge, 1997); Rpt, (2013).

Online Sources

Chattaway, Peter T., FilmChat with Peter Chattaway. Available online: <www.patheos.com/blogs/filmchat/> (accessed 19 Dec. 2021).

Goodacre, Mark, Celluloid Jesus: The Christ Film Web Pages. Available online: <https://sites.duke.edu/jesusfilms/> (accessed 19 Dec. 2021).

Page, Matthew, Bible Films Blog. Available online: <https://biblefilms.blogspot.com> (accessed 19 Dec. 2021).

Verreth, Herbert, De Oudheid in Film. Filmografie. Available online: <https://bib.kuleuven.be/artes/films-in-de-oudheid/oudheid-in-film-filmografie-2014.pdf> (accessed 19 Dec. 2021).

Index

Film titles are in *italics* and are typically listed by their original language with definite and indefinite articles following the main body of title. **Bold** numbers signify main entry for a film. For key incidents in the lives of Jesus and Moses see sub-entries under 'Jesus' and 'Moses'.

List of Illustrations

While considerable effort has been made to correctly identify the copyright holders, this has not been possible in all cases. We apologise for any apparent negligence, and any omissions or corrections brought to our attention will be remedied in any future editions.

Les Actes des apôtres, RAI/ORTF/TVE Studio Hamburg; *Assassin 33 A.D.*, Timed Out Productions; *Barabbas*, Dino De Laurentiis Cinematografica/Columbia Pictures Corporation/© Turner Entertainment Company; *Ben-Hur*, © Loew's Incorporated/Metro-Goldwyn-Mayer/ © Turner Entertainment Company; *Ben-Hur: A Tale of the Christ*, © Metro-Goldwyn-Mayer; *La bibbia*, © Dino De Laurentiis Cinematografica S.p.A.; *The Bible*, LightWorkers Media; *Blade af Satans bog*, Nordisk Film; *The Book of Life*, Reel FX Animation Studios/20th Century Fox Animation; *Camminacammina*, Raiuno/Scenario Film/ZDF (Photo by Mondadori via Getty Images); *Celui qui doit mourir*, Indusfilm/Prima Film/Cinétel/Filmsonor/Da Ma Produzione; *Color of the Cross*, BlackChristianMovies.com/Nu-lite Entertainment; *David and Bathsheba*, © Twentieth Century-Fox Film Corporation; *Os Dez Mandamentos: O Filme*, Casablanca/Rede Record; *Esther*, Agav Films/Österreichischer Rundfunk-Fernsehen/IKON/United Studios/Channel Four; *Esther and the King*, Galatea Film; *L'Exode*, Gaumont; *Exodus: Gods and Kings*, © Twentieth Century-Fox Film Corporation/Producciones Ramses A.I.E./TSG Entertainment LLC; *From the Manger to the Cross*, Kalem Company; *The Garden*, Basilisk (Photo Liam Daniel, courtesy & © Basilisk Communications); *La Genèse*, Kora-Film/Balanzan/CNPC Mali/Cinéma Public Films; *Gesù* (1999), Lux Vide S.p.A./LUBE/ Five Mile River Films/KirchMedia; *Get Some Money*, © Crow Motion Africa/Legit Films; *Godspell*, Columbia Pictures Corporation; *Golgotha*, Ichtys Film; *I grandi condottieri*, San Pablo Films (Photo by FilmPublicityArchive/United Archives via Getty Images); *The Greatest Story Ever Told*, George Stevens Productions/United Artists; *The Green Pastures*, Warner Bros.; *Intolerance: Love's Struggle Throughout the Ages*, Wark Producing Corporation/Majestic Motion Picture Company; *Io sono con te*, Colorado Film Production/Magda Film; *Jaël et Sisera*, Pathé Frères; *Je vous salue, Marie*, © JLG Films; *Jephthah's Daughter: A Biblical Tragedy*, Vitagraph Co. of America/BFI National Archive; *Jeremiah*, Lux Vide; *Jesus* (1979), Genesis Project/Campus Crusade; *Jesus* (1999), RAI Fiction/MTM Enterprises/CBS; *Jesus Christ Superstar*, Universal Pictures; *Jésus de Montréal*, Max Film Productions/ Gérard Mital Productions; *Jesús de Nazareth* (1942), Pereda Films; *Jesus of Nazareth* (1977), ITC/RAI; *Jesús, nuestro Señor*, Panorama Films/Producciones Zacarías S.A.; *Jezile*, © Spier Films; *Judith of Bethulia*, Biograph Company; *Karunamayudu*, Radha Chitra; *King David*, Paramount Pictures Corporation; *King of Kings*, © Metro-Goldwyn-Mayer/Samuel Bronston Productions, Inc.; *King of Kings, The* (1927), Pathé Exchange; *Lamentations of Judas*, KV Films/Les Films d'ici/Witfilm; *The Last Days of Pompeii*, © RKO Radio Pictures; *The Last Temptation of Christ*, Universal Pictures Company/Cineplex Odeon Films; *Lot in Sodom*, Webber Watson/Wilder, Wood, O'Brien; *Martyrs Chrétiens*, Pathé Frères; *Mary Magdalene*, © Water Productions Limited/Spirit Film Holdings Pty Limited; *Il messia*, Orizzonte 2000/Procinex; *The Miracle Maker*, © SAF/Christmas Films; *Al-mohager*, Misr International Films; *Monty Python's Life of Brian*, Python (Monty) Pictures/HandMade Films; *Moses und Aron*, Filmproduktion Janus/ARD/Janus Film und Fernsehen/Nouvelles Éditions de Films/ORTF/RAI/Österreichischer Rundfunk-Fernsehen/Taurus Film/NEF Diffusion/Straub-Huillet; The Nativity Story, © New Line Productions, Inc.; *Noah*, © Paramount Pictures Corporation; *Noah's Ark*, Warner Bros.; *Oversold*, Elevation Church/sumoJACK; *The Passion*, BBC/Deep Indigo Productions/HBO Films; *The Passion of the Christ*, © Icon Distribution, Inc.; *Paul Apostle of Christ*, © Tarsus LLC; *The Passover Plot*, Atlas Film/Coast Industries/Golan-Globus Productions; *The Prince of Egypt*, © DreamWorks SKG; *The Prodigal*, © Loew's Incorporated; *Quo Vadis*, © Loew's Incorporated; *The Red Tent*, Kasbah Films/Sony Pictures Television; *Risen*, © 50 Días Producciones A.I.E.; *The Robe*, © Twentieth Century-Fox Film Corporation; *La Sacra Bibbia*, Appia Nuova/Vay-Film/Nordisk Film; *Salomé*, © Nazimova Productions; *Samson and Delilah*, © Paramount Pictures; *The Savior*, Grace Productions/The Imaginarium; *Seder-Masochism*, Courtesy of Nina Paley; *Sins of Jezebel*, Lippert Productions; *Solomon and Sheba*, Theme Pictures; *Son of Man*, BBC; *The Star of Bethlehem*, Primrose Productions; *The Story of Ruth*, Samuel G. Engel Productions/Twentieth Century-Fox Film Corporation; *Su re*, Luches Film; *The Ten Commandments* (1923), © Famous Players-Lasky Corporation; *The Ten Commandments* (1956), Paramount Pictures; *Il vangelo secondo Matteo*, Arco Film/Lux Compagnie Cinématographique de France; *Il vecchio testamento*, Cineproduzioni Associate/Comptoir Français du Film Production; *Vie et passion de notre seigneur Jésus Christ*, Pathé; *La Vie et la passion de Jésus-Christ*, Lumière; *La Vie du Christ*, Gaumont; *The Visual Bible: Matthew*, Visual Bible/Visual International; *The Visual Bible: The Gospel of John*, Gospel of John Ltd/Toronto Film Studios/Visual Bible International/Visual Bible; *La Voie lactée*, © Greenwich Film Production; *Year One*, © Columbia Pictures Industries, Inc.